P. Le Page Renouf

Lectures on the Origin and Growth of Religion

As illustrated by the religion of ancient Egypt

P. Le Page Renouf

Lectures on the Origin and Growth of Religion
As illustrated by the religion of ancient Egypt

ISBN/EAN: 9783337323240

Printed in Europe, USA, Canada, Australia, Japan

Cover: Foto ©Lupo / pixelio.de

More available books at **www.hansebooks.com**

THE HIBBERT LECTURES, 1879.

LECTURES

ON THE

ORIGIN AND GROWTH OF RELIGION

AS ILLUSTRATED BY THE

RELIGION OF ANCIENT EGYPT.

DELIVERED IN MAY AND JUNE, 1879.

BY

P. LE PAGE RENOUF.

SECOND EDITION.

WILLIAMS AND NORGATE,
14, HENRIETTA STREET, COVENT GARDEN, LONDON;
AND 20, SOUTH FREDERICK STREET, EDINBURGH.

1884.

To my dear Wife,

IN GRATEFUL AND AFFECTIONATE REMEMBRANCE

OF OUR JOURNEY THROUGH THE LAND

WHOSE ANCIENT RELIGION

IS HERE VERY IMPERFECTLY DESCRIBED.

PREFACE TO THE SECOND EDITION.

THE only alterations which have been made in the text of these Lectures are corrections of a few errata and of the transcriptions of a couple of Egyptian words. Other corrections will be found in the notes. My general views remain unchanged, but the continued study of Egyptian texts has led me to the solution of an important problem arising out of the conclusions arrived at in the Lectures.

"The Egyptian mythology, as far as I can see," it is said, p. 250, "dealt only with those phenomena of nature which are conspicuously the result of fixed law, such as the rising and setting of the sun, moon and stars."

This is most strictly true if spoken of the *gods* of Egypt. Every one of these gods represents a fixed and unalterable Law. It is in consequence of the unvaried succession of physical phenomena that a god is said to be *neb maāt*, an expression literally translated by "lord of law," but really signifying "conspicuous by fixed rule." And it may be held as certain that every explanation of an Egyptian god or goddess which does not satisfy this canon is utterly erroneous.

But Egyptian mythology was not confined to the persons of gods. There are mythological personages who are never spoken of as gods. Mythological *personification* does not necessarily imply deification. Nor does mythology deal with persons only. There are mythological trees as well as reptiles and other animal forms.

For the results of an inquiry into these "residual phenomena," and also respecting some points upon which I spoke hesitatingly in these Lectures, I must refer to a paper on "Egyptian Mythology, particularly with reference to Mist and Cloud," which I read on the 7th March, 1882, before the Society of Biblical Archæology, and has been published in the Society's Transactions of the present year.

The following extracts relate to the identification of gods:

"I do not think I was wrong in identifying Nephthys with the Sunset, and Isis, Hathor, Neith, and other goddesses, with the Dawn. But M. Naville was also right in his conjecture that Nephthys might represent the morning, and Isis the evening, twilight. There were, in fact, according to Egyptian ideas, two Dawns, and a word which means Dawn also means Sunset. In the vignettes of the 17th chapter of the Book of the Dead, the goddesses Isis and Nephthys twice appear together, once on the Eastern and once on the Western direction of the bark of the Sun-god. Again, Isis is said to give birth to the sun-god Horus, and Nephthys to nurse him. This is, of course, on the eastern horizon. Yet both Isis and Nephthys are called 'goddesses of the West.' According to one of the glosses of the 17th chapter, Isis and Nephthys are the two feathers on the head of the ithyphallic god Ames, who (we are told in the same place) is no other than Horus, the avenger of his father. In the more recent texts, the hieroglyphic sign representing the rising sun between Isis and Nephthys, is ideographic of the word *tuau*, morning. When they are associated in this way, it is right to speak of these goddesses as the Two Dawns. When they appear isolated, unless there is a special reason for the contrary, Isis remains the Dawn, as in the myth where Horus strikes off her head, or in the 133rd chapter, which begins as follows: 'The Sungod rises from his horizon; the company of gods is with him, as the god comes forth who is in the secret dwelling. The mists fall away from the eastern horizon of heaven at the voice of Isis, who has prepared the way for the Sun-god.' And, on the other hand, Nephthys considered as the spouse of Set, the destroyer of Osiris, or as the mother of Anubis, 'who swallows his own father,' can only be identified with the Sunset.

"Hathor, 'the dwelling of Horus,' out of which he comes and into which he returns, stands both for the Dawn and the evening twilight.

"I thought it probable that Neith, the great goddess of Sais, and mother of the Sun-god Rā, who in various texts is identified with Isis, was one of the many names of the Dawn, not of Heaven, as has generally been thought. I ought to have spoken more positively. The passage I referred to in the Book of the Dead (114, 1, 2) is sufficient to support a decided assertion. The goddess herself says on the sepulchral canopi, *set ua semāsera rā neb*, 'I come at Dawn and at Sunset daily,' and I ought to have remembered that a papyrus of the Louvre says that 'the Sun-god Rā rises at the gates of the horizon at the prime portals of Neith.' Upon which M. Maspero says, 'En tant que déesse cosmique [*the Egyptians had no others*] Neith représentait la matière inerte et ténébreuse d'où le soleil sortait chaque matin.' I am pleased to find that on some important points I am not so far at variance with other Egyptian scholars as I thought when I delivered my Lectures. I am certainly not disposed to admit the general proposition, that the Egyptian goddesses represented *space*. But M. Pierret's doctrine, 'qu'elles personnifient la lumière du soleil ou l'espace *dans lequel il prend sa naissance et dans lequel il se couche*,' is very nearly my own view. I fear Egyptologists will soon be accused, like other persons, of seeing the Dawn everywhere. The ancient Egyptians at least saw these goddesses where we see them. 'Oh Shu, Amen Rā, Harmachis, self-sprung,' says a hymn, 'thy sister goddesses stand in Buchat, they uplift thee into thy bark.' Buchat, as Brugsch proved many years ago, is the place on the horizon where the sun rises.

"I am, I confess, compelled to see the Dawn, or rather the Two Dawns, in Shu and Tefnut, the two children of the Sun-god Rā. It may be quite true that in later times Shu represented Air, but this is only because the Dawn brings fresh breezes—Oriens afflavit anhelis. But in all the early texts Shu is the rising Sun. The Harris magical papyrus identifies Shu with 'the Sun travelling upwards at the prime of morning, whilst Tefnut, seated upon his head, darts her flame against his adversaries.' The myth, according to which Shu 'divided heaven from earth,' only means that at the dawning of the day heaven and earth, which were previously confused together in darkness, are clearly seen apart. And when it is added that 'he raised the heaven above the earth for millions of years,' what happens every day is, according to the well-known wont of myths, related as having occurred once. The expression *hotep shu*, implies that Shu is used for the Sunset as well as for the Dawn. Shu and Tefnut are called the Two Lions, but they are also represented by a single Lion, as though there were but a single divinity. In the tomb of queen Maāt-ka-rā, the two Eyes of Horus are said to be Shu and Tefnut—one being in the morning boat and the other in the evening boat of the Sun.

"As Tefnut etymologically seemed to represent some form

of *moisture*, I had conjectured that this was Dew rather than Rain, which is not one of the regularly recurring phenomena of Egypt. And Brugsch has recently come to a similar conclusion. This conjecture, however, scarcely does justice to the powers of Tefnut, who is always described as a fiery and even blood-stained divinity. It is fire that she *spits* against the adversaries. 'I am Tefnut,' she says, 'thundering against those who are kept on the earth, who are annihilated for ever.' She surely represents
'The sanguine sunrise, with his meteor eyes
And his burning plumes outspread,'
or the 'crimson pall of eve.'

"Both Isis and Nephthys shoot flames against the adversaries of Rā.

"The same may be said of the two Uræus goddesses, Uat'it and Nechebet, who are in fact but one goddess, who is herself identified with Hathor in a text published by M. Maspero, which adds that she consumes the adversaries with her flames.

"Sechet, the beloved of Ptah, is simply the fiery Dawn. 'She sendeth flames of fire in the face of the foes; whoever approaches sinks to ruin, she sendeth fire to burn their limbs.' She is distinctly identified with Neith in the Ritual (66, 9).'"

All the myths just mentioned are founded upon facts eternally recurring in regular and unvarying succession.

But the sky of Egypt, like that of all other lands, displayed phenomena which it was thought impossible to reduce to rule. The clouds with their varied aspects occupy a large portion of Egyptian mythology, but always in connection with and in subordination to some deity. There is no independent "meteorological myth."

The crimson or scarlet tints of dawn and sunset assume different mythological forms; sometimes as blood proceeding from the gods, sometimes as the blood of the enemies of the gods.

The Sun-god Rā hastens to his suicide, and *blood* flows from him.

Or he cut the foot of Hathor as he stretched his hand to bring her to him in his evening boat.

A third myth speaks of Isis, the Dawn goddess, as stanching the blood from the eye of the Sun-god Horus.

The blood of Isis, which is commemorated in one of the chapters of the Book of the Dead, is probably that which flowed when Horus smote off her head.

In other chapters the enemies of Osiris appear in the forms of birds, beasts and fishes, and the Sun-god washes in their blood. These enemies of the Sun are called Samiu or Sebiu. Their transformations, their slaughter and the effusion of their blood, represent the dissolution of the dark clouds into smaller ones, assuming fantastic forms, and coloured by the sun's rays in hues of crimson and scarlet.

But animal forms do not only represent the adversaries of the Sun-god. They are sometimes the cattle of Horus, "his oxen, his goats and his swine." And at other times Horus is a hunter, his greyhounds representing the light clouds rapidly skimming along under the influence of a steady breeze.

The Latin word *cirrus*, which signifies a lock of hair, is the scientific name of one of the commonest forms of cloud. The corresponding Egyptian word is *Nebtu*. And in several parts of the Book of the Dead, Nebtu appears as a demon who encounters the Sun-god in battle. And in a text of great antiquity he is called a son of Nut, that is, "a child of the sky."

The Samiu, who have already been mentioned as enemies of the Sun, and represent dark cloud, etymologically signify dark hair. The Samiu of Set exactly correspond to the πλό-καμοι ἑκατογκεφάλα Τυφῶ.

Hair is also the mythical equivalent of cloud when the overcast dawn is represented by Isis covering herself by letting her hair flow over her; also by the wig of Hathor, which covers the rising Sun-god Shu.

Clouds also appear as *serpents*, and the most important is the great dragon Apap, or rather Apepi, who in the later periods of Egyptian religion was confounded with Set. But Set represents Night, and in the olden days was called the great and living god and lord of heaven. Apepi never was called a god. He therefore represents, not a regularly occurring phenomenon, but an irregular and occasional one. He is the strong, dark storm-cloud, and is overcome by the fire and flinty sword of the Sun-god, and forced back into his subterranean cavern. One of his names is the Roarer; he is represented as blind, and another of his names, Ubar, signifies "the blind one," like the Latin Cacus or Cæculus.

The *tree* is another mythical representative of cloud, and never appears otherwise than as a joyful or beneficent phenomenon.

The light cloud under which the Sun rises is either the Persea-tree, beneath which the great Cat, which represents Rā, crushes the head of the Serpent; or it is the olive-tree of Ptah, or the tamarisk, or the willow on whose branches the *bennu* bird sits, or Isis suckles the infant Horus under bushes of marsh plants.

The beautiful green tints on the horizon at daybreak and at sunset are mythologically represented by "the sycamore of emerald," through the midst of which the Sun-god advances into the firmament. Green, no less than crimson or gold, was to the Egyptians a characteristic colour of the Dawn. The

Lion of Dawn had a green cap or mantle. The "golden Hawk" has wings of green. One of the names of the Dawn is *Uat'it*, which signifies "the green one," just as *l'alba* or *l'aube* signifies "the white one." One of the names of the Dawn-god Shu is *neshem*, "green felspar," and the green colour of the frog is a clue to the meaning of the ancient goddess Heqet.

Another mythological sycamore is that of Nut. This tree in the sky, which yields both wind and water, is no other than the rain-cloud.

I have ventured to identify the bright girdle of Rā (Todt, 110, 4) with the Rainbow. The Bow which is mentioned in another chapter of the Ritual, and from which the Sun-god is said to shoot forth, is not the Rainbow, but (as I have pointed out) the Moon's crescent.

The Tortoise is so deadly an enemy to the Sun-god that on each of the four gates of heaven it is written, "Life to Rā, death to the Tortoise!" There are, I believe, the strongest reasons for supposing that the Tortoise stands for an Eclipse. The Egyptians already knew, when the Book of the Dead was composed, that the moon's light was derived from the Sun, whom they addressed as "shining from the moon;" but they did not know that the Eclipse was *neb maāt*, as obedient to fixed law as the sun and stars, and they never deified it.

Such is the summary of the principal results of this inquiry. I concluded my paper on the subject with saying, that "if I am not entirely mistaken, a key is now at our service which, if intelligently used, will gradually open to us all, or at least most of, the mysteries of the Book of the Dead." Since these lines were written, however, a whole Ritual, consisting of a long series of mythological texts, has been discovered, vying in antiquity with the Book of the Dead. Though found in the pyramids of the fifth and sixth dynasties, they are manifestly much more ancient. They contain the same mythology as the Book of the Dead, and a great deal also which is not found there. But the interpretation of all these texts depends upon one and the same key; and to those who cannot understand that as Râ is the Sun of to-day, Osiris is the Sun of yesterday, who was overcome by Night in the person of Set, who in his turn was vanquished by Horus, the son and heir of Osiris, and that Osiris and Horus, like Râ, Ptah and Tmu, are originally but names of the Sun, the solution of all Egyptian mythology must be mere arbitrary guesswork.

It is not without surprise that I have found myself described by more than one distinguished critic as being a partizan of the view of "primitive henotheism," and my surprise is not diminished by finding that the same view is attributed to Professor Max Müller. "Primitive henotheism" appears to me to be a contradiction in terms. Henotheism, as I understand it, is but a stage of polytheism, and cannot possibly be primitive. Nor have I anywhere put forth the opinion that the Egyptians commenced with monotheism, or that their most ancient religion was pure and perfect. I said, indeed, that no one was better entitled to be heard upon the subject than so eminent a scholar as the late M. de Rougé, but while admitting the general accuracy of his facts, I respectfully suggested a very different interpretation of them.

There are two distinct and independent currents in the history of human thought, which very soon unite and are confounded together; but it is a grievous error to attempt to derive one from the other. One of these currents is the mythological, the other is the religious.

Mythology as such has nothing whatever to do with religion. It has its origin in the more or less picturesque utterance of man in presence of nature. When the clouds rose up like immense mountains, one above the other, obscuring the sky, it was said that the earth-born powers, the Titans, were piling up Pelion over Ossa in their war upon Zeus. The word *seb* in Egyptian means both "the earth" and a "goose." When the sun rose, it was said that the great cackling goose had laid an egg. This was only one of the many mythological ways of expressing sunrise. In none of these myths is there any religious idea whatever; nor from them can any religious idea be derived, any more than pure principles of morality could be derived from myths which represent a god as being the "husband of his mother," and another as striking off his mother's head, while another great god is said to have slain his brother, to have eaten his eye or swallowed his head.

But just as the purest and most delicate notions of morality are found expressed in the early writings of the Egyptians, so do we also find among them the consciousness of their dependence upon a divine power, eternal, infinite, ubiquitous and self-existent, wise and good.

It was by wholly different and independent exercises of thought that the Egyptian mind gave birth to its mythology, to its practical system of ethics, and to those notions of pure religion which I have just mentioned. Mythology did not make the religion, but it mixed with it and corrupted it at a very early date—as soon, in fact, as appellatives grew into proper names, and proper names led to personification, and personification fostered, and finally implied, the belief in living beings of infinite might, by whom some at least of the attributes of divinity might reasonably be claimed.

Henotheism, which is a phenomenon recurring in the histories of so many independent religions all over the world, is the result of an attempt to harmonize popular polytheism with the necessary conclusions of human reason with reference to the unity of the divine power.

Professor Lieblein could not have supposed that in asserting the identity of Egyptian religion during some thousands of years I intended to deny that new gods had been introduced into the pantheon, or that new conceptions had been attached to the names of the oldest gods. The addition of new gods to a pantheon is as natural as the addition of new saints to the calendar. Such additions do not necessarily imply the least change in a religion. And my Lectures furnish numerous instances in which the gods have attributes applied to them which did not originally belong to them. But I do not believe, as Professor Lieblein seems to believe, that the sublimer portions of the Egyptian religion are the result of a process of development or elimination from the grosser. Sublime and gross proceed from separate mines of thought. This is not the place to reply in detail to all the criticisms of Professor Lieblein, which are sometimes based on a misconception of my meaning, as when he thinks it necessary to protest against the ridiculous assertion "that Egyptian civilization and religion have remained unchanged through the course of time"! On those points in which we really differ, I beg to assure my learned critic that in "boldly deciding the difficult and far-reaching question as to the influence of Egyptian upon foreign thought, as, for instance, on the Hebrew or Greek religions or philosophies," I was not speaking rashly, or without due study of the subject. I have all my life been an attentive student of the history of religious and philosophical thought. When I was a University Professor, I delivered lectures on the history of Greek Philosophy, and in discussing the evidence respecting the origin of that philosophy it was impossible for me to arrive at any other conclusions than those of Ritter, in one of the best chapters of his History, of Brandis and of Zeller. Greek philosophy is essentially a flower of Hellenic origin, and not traceable to any other soil. When one speaks of the Jewish-Greek philosophy of Philo, it is not meant that Jewish thought influenced the Greek, but the converse. As for times more recent than Philo, no one, of course, questions the conquest both of Greece and Rome by "oriental teaching" in the form of Christianity.

Professor Lieblein points to the mythological names Io, Themis and Kerberos, as "all having an unmistakeable Egyptian stamp," to the worship of Zeus-Ammon, to the Greek and Roman worship of Isis and Serapis.

I do not see the unmistakeable Egyptian stamp upon the name Io. I do not know, and I am sure Professor Lieblein does not know, of any Egyptian story like that of Io; nor do I like to think that he connects her name with one of the Egyptian words signifying ox or cow, such as *aüa* or *aha*. But even this would not prove transmission of "religious ideas."

As to Themis, the stamp is so unmistakeably Hellenic and Indo-European, that the onus probandi lies upon those who insist upon another origin. Themis is etymologically akin to $\theta\epsilon\sigma\iota\varsigma$, $\theta\epsilon\mu\alpha$, $\theta\epsilon\sigma\mu\delta\varsigma$, $\theta\epsilon\mu\epsilon\nu\alpha\iota$ ($\tau\iota\theta\eta\mu\iota$). Between $\tau\iota\theta\eta\mu\iota$ and $\theta\epsilon\mu\iota\varsigma$ there is the same relation in sense as between our *lay* and *law*, or the German *setzen* and *Gesetz*. From the same root *dha* we have a large family of kindred words in Sanskrit and Zend, in Sclavonic, Teutonic and Keltic languages. Our English word *doom*, the Gothic *dôms*, the old High German *tuom*, the Swedish and Danish *dom*, are in the estimation of all good scholars derived from the same root, and are near relatives of the Greek Themis.

Kerberos is as certainly Indo-European. The difficulty here

lies in the choice of parentage. Has Professor Lieblein ever
seen the following words of Wilford (Asiatic Researches, III.
p. 408): "Yama, the regent of hell, has two dogs, according
to the Puranas, one of them named *Cerbura* and *Sabala*, or
varied; the other *Syáma*, or black; the first of whom is also
called *Triçiras*, or *with three heads*, and has the additional
epithets of *Calmâsha*, *Chitra* and *Cirmira*, all signifying
stained or spotted"? Has Professor Lieblein any parallel
Egyptian *myth* to produce? I think not; but even if he had,
the Egyptian origin of Cerberus would not be proved thereby.
The Indo-European origin must first be disproved or made
doubtful. Now it is indeed probable, as Kuhn thinks, that
Wilford's pundit explained the name *Çabala* by *Karbura*,
without that being the dog's real name. Anyhow, here is an
Indo-European etymology which fully explains the myth of
Kerberos. And very excellent Sanskrit scholars admit this
etymology. It is given as a probable one in Benfey's Sanskrit-
English Dictionary, p. 164, under the word *karbura*. Benary
finds a Greek etymology for the name, and Professor Max
Müller (*Chips*, II. p. 183) explains it as connected with the
Sanskrit *çarvara*, which must have had the original sense of
dark or pale. "Kerberos, therefore, in Greek would have
meant originally the dark one, the dog of night, watching the
path to the lower world." *Çabála*, with which Professor Max
Müller connects *çarvara*, is the Vedic epithet of the dog of
Yama.* The nearest corresponding Egyptian myth is that of
the jackal Anubis, who swallowed his own father Osiris. The
Āmām of the Egyptian Amenti, who sits before the throne of

---

* The dogs of Yama have four eyes (çvānau caturakshaû çabálau),
Rig-veda, x. 14, 10. The same four-eyed animal occurs in the Zend-
Avesta, Fargard, viii. 18, 48.

Osiris, is not a dog. It is a creature of threefold nature, like the Greek Chimaera. As the latter is

πρόσθε λέων, ὄπιθεν δὲ δράκων, μέσση δὲ χίμαιρα,

so is the former drawn and described as having the head of a crocodile, the hind parts of a hippopotamus, and the middle (including the fore-legs) of a lion. And, like the Greek Chimaera, the Egyptian "eater of the dead" mythologically represents some form of darkness, which is everywhere associated with Hades—*anārambhaṇe tamasi* of the Rig-veda (i. 182, 6; vii. 104, 3), the "Endless Darkness" of the Zend-Avesta, the Hellenic Erebos.

No one will deny that Isis and Amon were Egyptian divinities, and that they were worshipped by Greeks of the later periods. But when the Greeks adopted foreign gods, they Hellenized them. This is not what I meant when I denied the transmission of religious ideas from Egyptians to Greeks. I do not believe that Serapis was an Egyptian god. According to all ancient accounts, his statue was brought to Alexandria from Sinope in the time of the Ptolemies, and his worship seems to have been confined to the Greeks and Romans. It is found principally, as Wilkinson says, "in cities founded or greatly frequented by them, as Alexandria, Canopus, Antinoopolis and Berenice, in small Roman towns of the Oasis, in the Nitriotis, or in quarries and stations in the deserts, where he was also invoked under the names of Pluto and Sol Inferus." The identification of Serapis with Osiris-Apis is a mere etymological conjecture, which is not in the least supported by the Greek or Roman types of him known to us through coins and monuments.

It is in vain that I look here for evidence of transmission of "religious *ideas*." Nor do I see "*manifestly* the Egyptian doctrine of hell's fire and torturings" in a passage quoted by Professor Lieblein from the fourth book of Maccabees.* There is undoubtedly a doctrine of hell there, but it is no more Egyptian than it is Brahmanic or Buddhist or Greek. The Egyptian doctrine is far more like that which is contained in the forty-third section of the Vishnu-smriti, and yet no one will suspect that Egyptian and Hindu doctrines are otherwise than absolutely independent of each other. Each religion has a hell of its own. Professor Lieblein also assumes not only that the writer of the Jewish work in question borrowed his doctrine from the Egyptians (and this he does from the mere fact of the book being written in Alexandria), but that the doctrines of all other Jews, Palestinian and Babylonian as well, were borrowed from a work never esteemed canonical by Jews or Christians, and never sufficiently read to justify the notion of its being the source of the popular Jewish doctrine of which it furnishes a proof. If I had to look for the inspiration of an Alexandrian Jew beyond the traditions of his own religion, I should rather look to Homer and Plato for such notions as Tartarus and the fiery stream of Pyriphlegethon than to the Egyptian Amenti. But the real explanation of the matter is, that when two religions agree in admitting the notion of retribution for sin in the future life, they are very likely to agree in some remarkable points of detail, and that without any borrowing. One of the most remarkable features of the Egyptian doctrine is that of the *balance* in which human actions are weighed. But this balance is also found in the Çatapatha-Brâhmaṇa.

I have thought it well to speak at some length on these

---

* I understand a passage quoted by Prof. Lieblein from the " Book of Hades," not as referring to the punishment of wicked *men*, but to the annihilation of the mythical enemies of Râ.

objections of Professor Lieblein, partly from sincere respect to so estimable a scholar, but also because it is most desirable that no misunderstanding should exist as to the real points in discussion, or the method and principles by which right conclusions may be arrived at.

As Professor Lieblein argues that the Egyptians began with nature-worship (which is a mixture of religion and mythology), and gradually rose to a higher conception of the divine power, so, on the other hand, did the late M. de Rougé, and so now do his able successors of the French school, M. Pierret, M. Grébaut, and others, depending chiefly upon texts of the henotheistic period, argue that the Egyptian religion was essentially monotheistic, though disfigured by polytheistic imagery. The opposite parties necessarily admit each other's facts, but in the analysis of these facts they are, I believe, equally in error, because neither party seems to me rightly to apprehend the nature of mythology.

It would be very ungrateful of me to finish this Preface without offering my sincere thanks for the exceedingly kind way in which these Lectures have been noticed, both here and abroad, in literary organs representing every variety of theological opinion. My thanks are also due to those of my learned colleagues in Egyptology who have honoured my book with their countenance, and specially to Dr. Karl Piehl, an admirable Egyptian scholar, who has published a translation of the book in the Swedish language.

TABLE OF CONTENTS.

LECTURE I.

THE SOURCES OF INFORMATION RESPECTING THE ANCIENT EGYPTIAN RELIGION.

	PAGE
Early Christians on the Egyptian worship	1
Heathen writers on the same subject	2
How far can such evidence be relied upon	4
Modern attempts at investigation	9
Decipherment of hieroglyphic writing	11
Dr. Young	12
Champollion	14
His successors	19
Recovery of the ancient language	20
Publication of Egyptian texts	22
Most of the texts are of a religious nature	26

LECTURE II.

ANTIQUITY AND CHARACTERISTICS OF EGYPTIAN CIVILIZATION.

Egyptian chronology depends upon monuments recording contemporary facts	32
Monuments mentioning the year of a reign	33

	PAGE
Monuments furnishing evidence of a succession of reigns	34
Royal lists and their verification by the monuments	37
Royal list of Abydos	38
Evidence of the reality of sovereigns named	39
Omissions of this list	41
Genealogies	46
Manetho	47
Absolute dates	48
Egyptian monarchy anterior to 3000 B.C.	49
Pre-historic antiquity of human race in Egypt	50
Egyptian ethnology	53
Language	55
Art	61
Moral code	71
Castes	78
Monogamy	79

LECTURE III.

THE GODS OF EGYPT.

Identity of the religious institutions from first to last	80
Temples	82
Triads and enneads	83
Local character of Egyptian worship	83
The deities innumerable	85
Mean notions concerning these deities	86
Simplification of the list	87
Is the religion really monotheistic?	89
Evidences as to the meaning of the word Nutar	93
The Power	100
The Powers	103

	PAGE
Myth and legend	104
Râ and his family	109
Osiris and his family	110
Horus	113
Set	115
Thoth	116
The reign of Law	119

LECTURE IV.

COMMUNION WITH THE UNSEEN WORLD.

Sepulchral rites	124
The tombs and their inscriptions	127
The ka or genius	147
Souls, shadows, apparitions	152
Possession	154
Dreams	155
Oaths	157
Angels	158
Destiny	159
The king's divinity	161

LECTURE V.

THE RELIGIOUS BOOKS OF EGYPT.

The Book of the Dead	172
Beatification of the dead	179
The renewed existence "as upon earth"	180
Transformation	181
Identification with Osiris and other gods	184

	PAGE
Amulets	191
Words of power	192
Moral doctrine	194
Other sacred books	200

LECTURE VI.

Religious Books and Hymns: Henotheism, Pantheism and Materialism.

	PAGE
Lamentations of Isis and Nephthys	204
Book of glorifying Osiris	205
Book of the Breaths of Life	207
Rhind papyri	209
Magical literature	210
True notion of God	215
Henotheism	217
Pantheism	230
Materialism	239
Influence of Egyptian upon foreign thought	243
Conclusion	249

THE
RELIGION OF ANCIENT EGYPT.

THE SOURCES OF INFORMATION

RESPECTING THE

ANCIENT EGYPTIAN RELIGION.

THE religion of ancient Egypt is known to us through authentic records of various kinds, extending through a period of not less than three thousand years. It may have been in existence for many centuries anterior to the earliest of the monuments which have been preserved. Its origin is a matter, not of history, but of speculation. Its last centuries coincide with the first centuries of the Christian religion which gradually supplanted it. During this period the zoolatry, or worship of the sacred animals, was the feature which chiefly attracted the notice of the Christian apologists who have made any observations upon the subject.

Early Christians on the Egyptian Worship.

Clement of Alexandria, one of the most learned and philosophical of the Greek Fathers, introduces his

B

account of the Egyptian worship in a chapter against the use or abuse of finery by Christian ladies.[1] He compares those ladies who elaborately decorate their outside and neglect the soul, in which the image of God should be enshrined, to the Egyptians, who have magnificent temples, gleaming with gold, silver and electrum, and glittering with Indian and Ethiopian gems. "Their shrines," he continues, "are veiled with gold-embroidered hangings. But if you enter the penetralia of the enclosure and, in haste to behold something better, seek the image that is the inhabitant of the temple, and if any priest of those that offer sacrifice there, looking grave and singing a paean in the Egyptian tongue, remove a little of the veil to show the god, he will furnish you with a hearty laugh at the object of worship. For the deity that is sought, to whom you have rushed, will not be found within, but a cat, or a crocodile, or a serpent, or some such beast, unworthy of the temple, but quite worthy of a den, a hole or the dirt. The god of the Egyptians is revealed; a beast rolling on a purple couch."

Heathen Writers on the same Subject.

The language of Origen is very similar to that of Clement. That Christian and Jewish controversialists should have felt the utmost disdain for the Egyptian

---

[1] Paedagog. iii. c. 2.

worship is natural enough, but this disdain was fully shared by many of their heathen contemporaries. "You are never done," says Clement to the latter, "laughing every day of your lives at the Egyptians." He then quotes a Greek philosopher, Xenophanes of Colophon, who tells the Egyptians, "If you believe these brutes to be gods, do not mourn or bewail them; if you mourn or bewail them, do not any more regard them as gods." The comic writers of Greece had already made themselves merry upon the subject. Antiphanes, one of the most fertile and celebrated Athenian poets of the Middle Comedy, jests at the cleverness of the Egyptians who consider the eel as equal to the gods. Anaxandrides, another famous Athenian comic writer, tells the Egyptians: "I never could be your ally, for neither our customs nor our laws agree. They differ widely. You worship an ox, but I sacrifice him to the gods. You consider the eel a mighty demon; we think him by far the best of fish. You do not eat swine flesh, and I am particularly fond of doing so. You worship a dog, but I thrash him whenever I catch him stealing meat. Here the law is, that integrity of all their members is required of priests; with you, it appears, they must be circumcised. You weep if you see a cat ailing, but I like to kill and skin him. A shrew-mouse is an object of great consideration with you, not of the least with me." Timokles, in a play called "The Egyptians," asks, "How is it possible for an ibis or a dog to save you? For when men have sinned against the gods whom all acknowledge, whom will the altar of a cat repel by its terrors?"[1]

Classical scholars are familiar with the Satire commonly attributed to Juvenal: "Who does not know what kinds of monsters demented Egypt worships? One part adores the crocodile, another quakes before the ibis gorged with serpents. The golden image of a sacred long-tailed ape glitters where the magic chords resound from mutilated Memnon, and ancient Thebes lies in ruin, with her hundred gates. There whole towns venerate cats, here a river fish, there a dog, but no one Diana. It is impiety to violate and break with the teeth the leek and onion. O holy races, to whom such deities as these are born in their gardens!"[2]

It is not wonderful that, with such evidence before them, many writers should at the present day speak of the Egyptian religion as one of the lowest and grossest forms of nature-worship, as consisting in what is commonly called African fetishism, or at least as being based upon it.

How far can such Evidence be relied upon?

Yet the external aspect of a religion as presented to strangers is not often one that is to be trusted. We

---

[1] These comedians are quoted in Athen.: Deipnos. vii. p. 299.
[2] Juvenal, Sat. xv. 1. Mr. Lewis's translation.

have but to remember the accounts of the Jewish religion and of its history which have been left us by heathen writers, and the judgments which the most enlightened of these writers passed upon Christianity in the earliest and purest days of its existence. Christianity was not only considered as an *exitiabilis superstitio*, but was popularly supposed to involve the worship of a brute animal.[1] Do you think the prejudices of men holding such opinions would have been weakened had they accidentally heard of "the Lamb of God who taketh away the sins of the world," or read in the Apocalypse of the Lamb with seven horns and seven eyes who is the Lord of lords and King of kings, and represented as receiving the worship of the four beasts, the four-and-twenty elders, and innumerable angels?

A Roman soldier, according to the historian Diodoros, incurred the furious wrath of an Egyptian village by the slaughter of a cat. But the fury of a Mohammedan population may at this day be aroused by an attack upon its wild dogs; and there are, or till very

---

[1] The Christians were popularly supposed to worship the ass, but this worship was naturally imagined to have been derived from the Jews, who worshipped not only the ass, but the swine. "Judaeus licet et porcinum numen adoret;" Petronius Arbiter, p. 224 : Berlin, 1842. See Gill's *Notices of the Jews and their Country by the Classic Writers of Antiquity*, and an essay of Geiger (*Juden u. Judenthum nach d. Auffassung d. Schriftsteller d. Alterthums*) in the *Illustrirte Monatshefte für die gesammten Interessen des Judenthums* of Oct. 1865.

lately were, numerous Christian populations which resented the slaughter of doves or pigeons as impious and sacrilegious. Yet neither Moslems nor Christians have ever worshipped dogs or pigeons.[1]

It is in the nature of things that persons living outside a religion, especially if they are not inclined to it, cannot understand it or its symbols unless their inquiries are conducted under conditions which are generally considered superfluous or wrong. Men are rarely conscious of the prejudices which really incapacitate them from forming impartial and true judgments on systems alien to their own habits of thought. And philosophers who may pride themselves on their freedom from prejudice may yet fail to understand whole classes of psychological phenomena which are the result of religious practice, and are familiar to those alone to whom such practice is habitual.

There is distinct evidence that the absurdity which the Egyptian religion presented to strangers disappeared on closer acquaintance with it. Philo, the philosophical

---

[1] Yet Mr. Herbert Spencer, *Sociology*, p. 354, after quoting a remark of Mr. McLennan that the dove is almost as great a god among the ancients as the serpent, says, "that the still extant symbolism of Christianity shows us the surviving effect of the belief in the ghostly character of the dove." N'est ce pas chercher midi à quatorze heures? Even if the schoolboy authorities on which Mr. McLennan relies were not absolutely worthless, surely the belief in the gospel narrative would be sufficient to account for the symbolism of the dove among populations who in their heathen condition had never heard of the dove as a divinity.

Jew of Alexandria, tells us that foreigners coming for the first time into Egypt knew not what to do for laughter at the divine beasts, but that the universal superstition finished by overpowering them also. Apollonios of Tyana, according to his biographer Philostratos, decidedly condemned the Egyptian system as absurd and ridiculous. But the form which his objections assume is quite inconsistent with the notion of fetishism. He takes it for granted that the beasts are not deities, but symbols of deity. "If you place a hawk or an owl or a wolf or a dog in your temples to represent Hermes, Athene or Apollon, the beasts and birds may derive dignity from such representations, but the gods will lose theirs." "I think," said Thespesion, "you slight our mode of worship before you have given it a fair examination. For surely what we are speaking of is wise, if anything Egyptian is so; the Egyptians do not venture to give any form to their deities, they only give them in symbols which have an occult meaning that renders them more venerable." Apollonios, smiling at this, said, "O ye sages, great indeed is the advantage you have derived from the wisdom of Egyptians and Ethiopians, if you find anything worthy of your worship in a dog, an ibis or a goat; or if you think such creatures fit to represent your gods. . . . . . If what the mind discovers couched under such symbolical figures is entitled to greater veneration, surely the condition of the gods in Egypt would be more highly respected if no statues whatever were erected to them, and if theology was treated in a different manner, with a little more wisdom and mystery. .... The mind forms to itself a something which it delineates better than what any art can do; but in the present instance you have taken from the gods the very power of appearing beautiful either to the eye or to the understanding."[1]

I do not quote this conversation as in any way deserving to be considered authentic, but only as evidence that the Egyptian worship of animals was considered even by grave opponents as symbolical, and not as pure fetishism. Celsus is quoted by Origen as distinctly denying the worship by the Egyptians of brute creatures of a day (ζώων ἐφημερίων). And some Christian Fathers even admit that the symbolical worship of animals denotes a higher stage of culture than the worship of inanimate images, stocks and stones, or of deities whose actions are inconsistent with the most elementary notions of morality. Porphyry[2] explains the animal worship from a Pantheistic point of view. All living creatures in their degree partake of the Divine essence, and "under the semblances of animals the Egyptians worship the universal power which the gods have revealed in the various forms of living nature."

---

[1] Vit. Apollonii, vi. 19.   [2] De Abstinentia, iv. c. 9.

Modern Attempts at Investigation.

After all, the religion of the Egyptians was not confined to the worship of the sacred animals. Herodotos, Plato and other classical writers, mention Amon, Osiris, Isis, Thoth, Neith and other divinities; and the belief in the soul's immortality is not only decidedly ascribed to the Egyptians, but is said to have been first taught by them. What relations did the various parts of this religion bear to each other? Was the religion in its later ages identical with the primitive religion of the country? Had there been advance or retrogression? The solution of these and many other obvious questions was quite impossible until very recently. The learned Brücker, in his Critical History of Philosophy, and Jablonski, in his Pantheon Aegyptiacum, have with indefatigable industry put together all the evidence that can be found in Greek and Latin writers. But they had no means of testing this evidence. No history can be learnt with certainty except from evidence contemporaneous with the events recorded; no religion can be studied with profit except in the very words of its own votaries. But the knowledge of the Egyptian language had not only actually perished, but the key to the decipherment of its writings was supposed to be irrecoverably lost. The hieroglyphic characters, consisting of representations of the sun, moon, animals, plants and other objects, either natural or artificial, which are painted or sculptured upon so many Egyptian monuments, were indeed looked upon as symbols under which the mysteries of the religion had been concealed from the vulgar, and several attempts were made to explain them. All these efforts, however, were destitute of any scientific basis. The most elaborate attempts proceeded from the learned Jesuit, Athanasius Kircher, who is not without merit as one of the restorers of Coptic; but his enormous folios upon hieroglyphic inscriptions are mere memorials of a frightful amount of time and thought elaborately wasted. Every hieroglyphic sign was supposed to represent an idea; and groups which we now know to stand for the names and titles of the Roman emperors Vespasian, Titus and Domitian, are converted into long sentences of mystical rubbish. Even at the beginning of the present century, the Chevalier Palin indulged in dreams not unworthy of Athanasius Kircher. Dr. Birch has briefly described his views as follows. He "did not hesitate to assert that it was only necessary to translate the Psalms of David into Chinese, and write them in the ancient characters of that language, in order to reproduce the Egyptian papyri, and that these contained many Biblical books."

Spurious monuments served the purposes of these interpreters quite as well as genuine ones. In the "Isiac table" Kircher discovered a variety of sacred mysteries favourable to Christianity; Pignorius read in it precepts of moral and political wisdom. Another critic (Jablonski) considered it as a calendar of festivals; whilst a fourth attempted to persuade the learned world that "these characters described the properties and use of the magnet, and of the mariner's compass."

Decipherment of Hieroglyphic Writing.

The discovery of the Rosetta stone put an end to all this guess-work. Most of you have probably seen this stone in the British Museum. It is a tablet of black basalt, about three feet long by about two and a half wide, and was erected in honour of Ptolemy Epiphanes, 193 years before Christ. The inscriptions upon it are in three distinct characters, the third of which is Greek. The Greek text consists of a decree in honour of the king, and it is expressly stated in the last line that this decree is to be engraved on the tablet, τοῖς τε ἱεροῖς καὶ ἐγχωρίοις καὶ ἑλληνικοῖς γράμμασιν, "in the sacred characters, in the vernacular and in Greek." The tablet is unfortunately mutilated, great part of the hieroglyphic portion is lost, and so is the end of the Greek. Fifteen lines of the enchorial or (as it is now generally called) demotic part have lost their first letters or words.

The conditions of the problem to be solved were now of a very definite kind. The inquirer, instead of guessing at the sense of the hieroglyphic text, had the sense supplied to him. His problem lay in dividing the hieroglyphic text into groups or words corresponding to the Greek words. The problem would be completely solved if each Egyptian group were successfully analyzed and read, the verification of the result being found in the facility of reading and interpreting other texts by means of the alphabet and vocabulary thus obtained.

Several of the most eminent scholars in Europe attempted the problem, and some of them even with partial success. The great orientalist Silvestre de Sacy determined the demotic groups corresponding to Ptolemy, Berenike, Alexander and other proper names; and the Swedish scholar Akerblad already, in the year 1802, even drew up a phonetic alphabet of the demotic characters, which is remarkably correct as far as it goes. The complete key to the decipherment of Egyptian was, however, not revealed to the world till the publication of Champollion's letter to M. Dacier in the September of 1822.

Dr. Young.

It is even to this day a common habit of Englishmen to couple the name of their countryman Dr. Thomas Young with that of Champollion, as sharing with him the glory of this discovery. No person who knows anything of Egyptian philology can countenance so gross an error. Dr. Young was indeed a man of extraordinary genius, but the true direction of it was long unrecognized by those very countrymen of his who ridiculously put him forward as a rival of Champollion. "It fell to his lot," as Professor Tyndall has said, "to discover facts in Optics which Newton's theory was incompetent to explain; and he finally succeeded in placing on an immovable basis the Undulatory Theory of Light." Helmholtz, a kindred genius, thus speaks of him: "His was one of the most profound minds that the world has ever seen." But it is not true that he discovered the key to the decipherment of hieroglyphics, or even that his labours assisted Champollion in the discovery. When the key was once discovered and recognized as the true one, it was found that one or two of Young's results were correct. But there was nothing in his method or theory by which he or any one else could distinguish between his right and his wrong results, or which could lead him or any one else a single step in advance. Young was certainly right in assuming that the first two signs in the hieroglyphic name of Ptolemy[1] were P and T, but his next step was a failure, and so was the next after that. He did not succeed in analyzing this royal name or that of Berenike. All his other attempts were simple failures. "He mistook Autokrator for Arsinoe, and Cæsar for

---

[1] That the oval rings contained royal names was first pointed out by the Danish scholar Zoega, who was also the first in modern times to assert that some hieroglyphic characters were phonetic.

Euergetes." "His translations," says Dr. Birch, "are below criticism, being as unfounded as those of Kircher." Besides being unable to identify more than a very few alphabetic characters, he failed to recognize the nature of determinatives, no less an essential part of the key than the phonetic.

Champollion.

Champollion's discovery was of a very different nature. Besides the two kinds of Egyptian characters which are used on the Rosetta stone, there is a third, commonly called the hieratic. The hieroglyphic characters, with their accurately elaborate designs of animals, plants and other objects, are very suitable for monumental inscriptions, but very unsuitable for the ordinary purposes of life; and the Egyptians had from the earliest times used a tachygraphic or cursive character which is a rough and abridged form of the hieroglyphic. The stones of the great Pyramid bear notes upon them in this character which were already written in the quarry. At a much more recent period (some seven centuries before Christ), the character was still further abridged and debased, and assumed the form now called demotic, and this is the second character on the Rosetta stone. A great many documents in our museums are written in this character. Long before he suspected the real nature of Egyptian writing, Champollion had patiently studied the relations be-

tween its three different kinds, and had discovered the
essential identity of the three, demotic being a debasement of the hieratic, the hieratic a debasement of the
hieroglyphic. Through M. Dacier he had presented
two dissertations to the French Académie des Sciences,
one on the hieratic and a second on the demotic character. His enemy Klaproth asserts that he suppressed
the dissertation on the hieratic character for fear of its
telling tales against him, and showing his need of
Young's guidance. I do not know that it is true that
Champollion tried to suppress this " Mémoire ;" but if
he did, it surely was not for the purpose malignantly
asserted by Klaproth and ignorantly repeated in this
country. The dissertation in question is a very excellent work, chiefly consisting in *plates*, wherein passages
of the Book of the Dead written in hieroglyphics are
placed side by side with the same passages copied from
hieratic manuscripts, and the identity is made apparent
to the most unlearned eye. And if, as Klaproth asserts,
Champollion had wished to destroy all trace of certain
passages which occur in his text, he would certainly
not have repeated them, as he does, in his letter to
M. Dacier. But the most important step in his progress
was discovering the identity of certain demotic characters, the alphabetic nature of which had been demonstrated by Akerblad, with the corresponding hieratic
ones, and consequently with their hieroglyphic ori-
ginals. If any one has a right to be named in con-

junction with Champollion, it is not Young, but Akerblad, to whom he does full justice (as he does indeed to Young himself) at the very beginning of his letter to M. Dacier. But in 1822,[1] Champollion had not only one bilingual inscription before him, but two, the obelisk of Philæ having been found, with an Egyptian inscription and also a Greek one containing the name of Cleopatra, which offered special facility for decipherment, two of the letters in it being alike, and others being the same as in the name of Ptolemy. But in discussing this question, it must not be forgotten that the key to hieroglyphic decipherment does not consist in recognizing the phonetic nature of this or that sign, but in the knowledge of the simultaneous use of both phonetic and ideographic signs, not only

---

[1] That Champollion never thought of hieroglyphic characters as phonetic till after Young's publication, is one of Klaproth's unscrupulous assertions which has been thoughtlessly repeated by some who should have known better. It has been refuted by M. Champollion-Figeac, who in the *Revue Archéologique* of 1856, 1857 and 1858, has produced abundance of evidence from his brother's writings between the years 1808 and 1814. In his *Mémoire sur les Ecritures Egyptiennes*, read on Aug. 7, 1810, before the Society of Sciences and Arts of Grenoble, Champollion strongly insists upon the necessity of phonetism, for otherwise how could foreign names, for which no symbolism existed, be expressed in writing? "L'inscription de Rosette présente les noms Grecs de Ptolémée, Bérénice, Arsinoe, Pyrrha, d'Aréia, de Diogènes, d'Aétes, d'Alexandre, etc.; ils ne pouvaient être exprimés dans la partie hiéroglyphique de ce monument, si ces hiéroglyphes n'avaient, comme nous l'avons dit, la faculté de produire des sons."

in every line, but in nearly every word, and of the law of this use. And neither Akerblad, nor, since the language had ceased to be spoken, had any one else before Champollion a notion of this.

The truth of Champollion's alphabet was demonstrated by its enabling one to read the name not only of Ptolemy and Cleopatra, but of all the Persian, Greek and Roman sovereigns of the country. And, what was far more important still, the meanings of many hieroglyphic groups, on being read according to his system, were immediately known from the Coptic vocabulary. Champollion's hypothesis that the old Egyptian language was identical with Coptic, though a very imperfect one, and productive even at the present day of many errors among those who discard it, was not fatally wrong, for Coptic is in fact a later stage of the language in which the hieroglyphic texts are written, and the vocabulary of the latter is full of words which are as intelligible to the Coptic scholar as the infinitives of Latin verbs are to a mere Italian scholar. The remaining years of his short life were spent in copying, studying and interpreting Egyptian texts. The amount of work accomplished by him in eight years is almost incredible. He not only laid the foundations of a Grammar and Dictionary, but illustrated the history and religion of ancient Egypt by the translations and analyses of short but authentic texts, opening an entirely new world to the historical student, and convincingly proving that scarcely a single page which had hitherto been written upon Egyptian history or religion deserved the least credit. A splendid work which he had begun on the Egyptian Pantheon was even discontinued in consequence of the fresh information on the Egyptian religion which he was perpetually discovering.

During his lifetime, Champollion had many opponents and detractors, but not a single person can be named who in the slightest degree contributed to the modification or development of his views. Whatever corrections he adopted resulted from his own studies. His immediate disciples did not advance a step beyond what they learnt from him. One of them, Salvolini, was guilty of the infamous wickedness, after his master's death, of using the manuscripts of the latter for the purpose of winning glory for himself at the expense of the generous friend who had lent him his most valuable papers. It was not till 1837, several years after the death of Champollion, that his philological system was subjected to a thoroughly scientific criticism by Dr. Lepsius in his Letter to Rosellini, in which the obviously erroneous portions of the system were eliminated, the relations between the Coptic and the old Egyptian languages were set in a truer light, and a more accurate method of transcription was adopted.

His Successors.

For a good many years after this, Egyptian archaeology was chiefly cultivated by *dilettanti*, whose knowledge of the language seldom extended beyond the decipherment of royal names. Whole systems of Egyptian chronology have been devised by men incapable of reading and understanding a single line of Egyptian. Till 1850, the only genuine scholars who can be mentioned in addition to Lepsius, are Mr. Birch and Dr. Hincks in this country, M. Emmanuel de Rougé in France, and Dr. Brugsch (then a very young man) in Germany. But every one of these was a scholar of more than average ability, and has left his mark for ever upon the science. The important discoveries of M. Mariette belong to the next period, as also do the first works of M. Chabas and Mr. Goodwin, two scholars whose translations of some of the most difficult texts in the language caused the study of it to advance with gigantic strides. Since 1860, and particularly since the foundation in 1863 at Berlin of a journal in which everything connected with the language or archaeology of ancient Egypt might be discussed, the number of highly distinguished scholars has greatly increased. A very valuable journal of the same kind was founded in Paris in the year 1872. The names of Dümichen, Lauth, Ebers, Stern, Eisenlohr, Wiedemann, Bergmann and Reinisch in Germany and Austria, Pleyte in Holland, Lieblein in Sweden, Golenischeff in Russia, Déveria, J. de Rougé, Horrack, Maspero, Lefébure, Pierret, Grébaut, Robiou, Baillet and Rochemonteix in France, Naville at Geneva, Rossi, Szedlo and Schiaparelli in Italy, are authorities familiar to every Egyptologist. To these I must add Canon Cook and Professor Lushington in this country.

Recovery of the Ancient Language.

It is not without a melancholy feeling that I enumerate these names (many of them belonging to dear and valued friends), for the hand of death has already thinned our ranks, and some of us are growing old and disabled. The spell, however, is broken; the language of ancient Egypt has really been recovered—slowly, it is true, and step by step. The decipherment of a language does not at once put us in possession of a language. The ancient Etruscan writings are read with ease, but they are as unintelligible as ever. The relationship between Coptic and old Egyptian happily enabled Champollion to find the meanings of many words and the general sense of entire inscriptions. But the old Egyptian vocabulary, besides representing an earlier stage of the language, is very much more extensive than the Coptic, and the greater part of the words which compose it had to be recovered, one after another, by an inductive process. The truth of the vocabulary which has thus gradually been built up is verified by its enabling us to read and understand entire documents of every kind. This alone ought to be considered sufficient proof, for no imaginary vocabulary can possibly adapt itself to the needs of an indefinite number of texts. But sceptics who are incapacitated by the imperfect acquaintance with the processes of philological science from feeling the force of this proof, may at least be referred to the confirmation of our vocabulary by the bilingual inscription of Canopus. In 1866, Dr. Lepsius discovered a tablet at San, in Lower Egypt, of the same nature as the Rosetta stone; that is to say, containing inscriptions in old Egyptian, demotic and Greek, but much more considerable in extent and quite perfect. The sense of this tablet, according to the vocabulary already received among Egyptologists, exactly agreed with that given by the Greek text. And the truth of the Grammar is proved in the same manner. Already in 1860, M. de Rougé declared that there was no kind of Egyptian text the translation of which might not be undertaken if only the necessary pains were employed. We are now able to read and understand not only the splendid and accurate texts of the public inscriptions, but the wretched scrawls of manuscripts in the cursive character. And some scholars—Mr. Goodwin, for instance, and M. Chabas, and before them Dr. Birch and M. de Rougé— have successfully translated texts so frightfully mutilated that in many places only fragments of letters were visible. But their familiarity with the cursive character enabled them to restore the text with an accuracy of which no competent critic can entertain a doubt. When I speak of our being able to read and comprehend the language, you will not understand me as implying that all Egyptologists are equally learned and skilful. Nor are all Egyptian texts equally easy of translation.[1] As in all languages, some are very easy and others extremely difficult. There is one long and most interesting document, of which I shall have occasion to speak later on, which will, I fear, long continue to baffle the efforts of translators.

Publication of Egyptian Texts.

The progress of the study was greatly retarded at first by the difficulty of obtaining authentic copies of

---

[1] Other questions than those of a purely philological nature often arise in reference to the texts translated. I do not quarrel with the translations given by M. de Rougé and other scholars of the great texts describing the invasion of Egypt in the time of Seti II. But I have always considered the identification of the foreign invaders with the Achaeans, Tyrrhenians, Sardinians and Sicilians, as in the highest degree improbable. Nor do I believe that the Danai or the Pelasgi have been really identified under hieroglyphic spelling. When we reflect that Deutschland is called Allemagne in French and Germany in English, that the people called Dutch by us are called Hollandais by the French, that the Greeks only knew themselves as Hellenes, that the name Egypt was unknown to the inhabitants of that country, and that its real name, *Kamit*, was unknown to Greeks and Romans, we should be very cautious in identifying names on the mere strength of similarity in sound.

Egyptian texts. Almost all the old copies, not even excepting those made by Belzoni, are absolutely worthless. Science is insatiate, and its wants can never be adequately supplied, yet much has been done, both through the unassisted efforts of private individuals and through the munificence of governments and public bodies. The collection of published Egyptian texts which can be relied upon is now very considerable. To the plates contained in the Description de l'Egypte published in 1809 by the French government, as the result of a great scientific expedition, must be added the collections of Champollion, Rosellini and Prisse d'Avennes, Burton's Excerpta Hieroglyphica, Sharpe's Egyptian Inscriptions, Dr. Leemans' Monuments Egyptiens du Musée de Leide, Ungarelli's Obelisks, the magnificent Denkmaeler of Lepsius, the Hieratic Papyri of the British Museum, and many other splendid publications bearing the names of Lepsius, Chabas Bonomi, Rhind, Brugsch, Dümichen, Mariette Bey, E. de Rougé, Rossi and Pleyte, Naville, Ebers and Stern, Maspero, Guyesse, Golenischeff, Bergmann, Wiedemann and others. Some of these costly works reproduce the original text in facsimile; in some of them the accuracy of the copy is secured by photography.

But large as is the collection of these texts, it is but a fragment of the texts actually in existence. Mariette Bey has published four folio volumes of plates from the temple of Denderah alone, but he gives them only as a selection. To copy the whole would, he says, be the work of years. Dr. Dümichen has published another folio volume of texts of special interest, selected from the same temple, without interfering with those published by M. Mariette. Every square foot of the walls is in fact covered with picture or text. I had the pleasure of passing some time, one or two years ago, at Qurna, on the left bank of the Nile, near Thebes, with a great scholar, who had spent much time in copying the inscriptions of a single tomb; but though he worked indefatigably and rapidly, he was compelled to come away leaving a great part of his intended work unaccomplished. Would that we might rely upon the zeal of future labourers for the completion of such tasks as the present generation is unable to perform! Unfortunately the monuments are rapidly perishing, and there are no effectual means of arresting the progress of destruction. The tombs are convenient abodes for Arab families, who destroy the paintings and inscriptions either by the dense smoke of their fires or by actually pulling down walls. I was taken to see the "Lay of the Harper," one of the most interesting remains of Egyptian poetry, which was published a few years ago by Dr. Dümichen; but we found the walls on which the poem was written a mere heap of ruins. But the vandalism of European and American travellers is most fatal to the monuments. There is, or rather was, a famous picture at Benihassan which was formerly thought to represent Joseph presenting his brethren to Pharaoh. An English lady has been heard to request her guide to cut out for her the face of Joseph.

But this destruction in some form or other has been going on for centuries. Abd-el-Latif, a learned Arabian writer of the middle ages, tells us in his description of Egypt that the ruins of Memphis in his time extended half a day's journey in every direction, and that, in spite of the removal for building purposes of immense masses of materials, its ruins presented to the spectator a re-union of marvels sufficient to confound the intelligence, and which the most eloquent man would vainly undertake to describe. He then proceeds to give a very intelligent account of these marvels, which must have been scarce less astounding than those still to be seen at Thebes. But of Memphis there is at present hardly a trace left. And other great cities known to ancient travellers have disappeared with their monuments. Mummy-cases and coffins with most interesting inscriptions have for centuries been used as fuel. And innumerable manuscripts have suffered the same fate.

In speaking of our stock of information respecting the ancient world, Mr. Grote says that "we possess only what has drifted ashore from the wreck of a stranded vessel." If this be true with reference to such a literature as that of Greece, with its immortal poets, historians, orators and philosophers, how immeasurably more true is it of Egypt! Yet if we only look to quantity, the stock of original and trustworthy materials actually in existence illustrative of the religion of ancient Egypt, is more extensive than the corresponding materials extant for the religions of Palestine, Greece or Rome. Neither Romans nor Greeks have left any sacred books. They have left poetry of the highest order, but no psalms or hymns, litanies or prayers, as the Egyptians have so largely done. No people certainly were more remote than the Egyptians from the idea that religion could exist without outward forms of worship. In studying their religion, we have to deal, not with a mere sentiment, but with a vast and complicated system of beliefs and institutions, resulting from their view of man's relations to the unseen world.

Most of the Texts are of a Religious Nature.

Of the many thousands of texts which have been rescued from destruction and made accessible to us, there are extremely few which do not bear directly upon the subject of the present Lectures. There are two reasons for this. The first is to be found in the fact that the Egyptians were among the most religious of the ancient nations. Religion in some form or other was dominant in every relation of their lives. One of the most extensive Egyptian works which has been recovered is the great medical papyrus published by Dr. Ebers. That work, however, though a medical one, and descending to minute details about cosmetics and even to receipts against vermin, is essentially a religious book. The medical prescriptions are subordinate to the prayers or religious observances which give them their efficacy. If we wish to keep clear of religion in studying Egyptian literature, we shall have to confine ourselves to mathematics. There is on the staircase of the British Museum a papyrus treating of various kinds of mathematical problems, and I confess that in studying it I was surprised to find it of so purely secular a character as it really is. It is only at the very end that we meet at last with a mention of prayers for fine weather and a high Nile.

But the principal reason why most of the documents which have come down to us are of a religious character is, that all the ancient monuments of Egypt have perished except some which were necessarily of a religious nature—the temples and the tombs. The palaces of kings and nobles have utterly disappeared. Our knowledge of Egyptian civil architecture is derived from paintings in the tombs. Many texts of historical interest have been preserved, but their original intention was not historical, but religious. For us, the royal texts of Karnak, Abydos and Saqâra, are of historical value; but they have a purely religious meaning on the walls where they were found. We should in all probability never have recovered the Annals of Tehutimes III. except for the splendid donations to the god of Thebes which they commemorate. All the objects in our museums and other collections which seem to belong to civil or domestic life, have only been preserved by being buried in the tombs. On examining what appears to be a mere trinket, you will often find a prayer for the departed. And this is the case with the papyri, all of which would infallibly have perished had they not been deposited in tombs, and by the deep dry sand of the desert been rendered inaccessible to external influences. It is only accidentally that documents of a purely secular character have been preserved, and fragments of Greek and Coptic literature have in like manner been recovered from tombs. The information which we possess about Egyptian history is entirely derived from the public inscriptions on the walls of the temples, and accidental details contained in the funereal inscriptions of private individuals.

The first step to be taken in the endeavour to obtain light out of these materials is classification, and the most essential kind of classification at starting, is that of the order of succession. We shall never understand the development of the Egyptian, or of any other religion, if our ideas are uncertain as to the order in which the phenomena which represent it stand towards

each other in reference to time. The speculations of
the ablest men are sure to fail if their chronology is
fatally wrong. I remember the time when men talked
gravely and learnedly of reminiscences of primeval
revelation respecting the Trinity and other Christian
doctrines, as having been preserved, though in a very
corrupt state, in the Hindu traditions about Trimûrti.
Some, on the other hand, perhaps suspected that the
Christian doctrine might have been derived through
some unknown channel from a Hindu source. It is
now acknowledged by all scholars that the Hindu doctrine in question is extremely modern; the first traces
of it are to be sought more than fourteen hundred
years, not before, but after, the Christian era. The
work upon India of P. Von Bohlen used to be considered a decisive authority respecting the influence of
Indian upon Egyptian culture. No such influence can
any longer be admitted. Many of you have probably
read Mr. McLennan's articles on the Worship of Animals and Plants. In order to show that the ancient
nations passed through what he calls the Totem stage,
which he says must have been in pre-historic times, he
appeals to the signs of the Zodiac. "The Zodiacal
constellations figured on the porticos of Dendera and
Esne in Egypt are," he says, "of great antiquity."
The authority for this statement is a passage from
Chambers' Encyclopaedia, to the effect that "Dupuis,
in his *Origine des Cultes*, has, from a careful investi-

gation of the position of these signs, and calculating precession at the usual rate, arrived at a conclusion that the earliest of them date from 4000 B.C. M. Fourier, in his '*Recherches sur la Science*,' makes the representation of Esne 1800 years older than M. Dupuis." Mr. McLennan is here more than half a century behind his age. Every tourist on the Nile in possession of Murray's Handbook, knows that both Dupuis and Fourier were ludicrously mistaken.[1] The Zodiacal representations in question, far from being of great antiquity, belong to the very latest period of Egyptian workmanship; they are not anterior to the Christian era or the Roman domination; they were borrowed from the Greeks, and were entirely unknown to the ancient Egyptians.

It is not sufficient to be in possession of trustworthy witnesses; it is also necessary to know the limit within which alone their evidence is really available. I am obliged, therefore, to say something about Egyptian chronology, especially as the current opinions on the subject are very vague and inaccurate. I shall not, however, detain you by entering into any of the questions which are still at issue between learned men who have given their attention to them, but will simply explain to you the nature of the undisputed evidence

---

[1] All Mr. McLennan's statements about the ancient nations are based on equally worthless authorities. He goes for his facts to Bryant and to Lempriere's Dictionary.

upon which we assign *relative* dates to the various periods of Egyptian civilization, and which imperatively demand that a very early date indeed should be assigned to the origin of that civilization.

ANTIQUITY AND CHARACTERISTICS

OF

EGYPTIAN CIVILIZATION.

Egyptian Chronology depends upon Monuments recording Contemporary Facts.

I PROMISED to explain the kind of evidence which compels us to assign a very remote antiquity to Egyptian civilization—so remote indeed as to appear simply fabulous to men whose studies of ancient history have been confined to Greece and Rome, and who know how very soon historical evidence fails at the distance of a few centuries from the Christian era. Such men are not unnaturally inclined to suspect us of uncritically attaching importance to exaggerated or even fictitious numbers handed down by untrustworthy authorities. Such a suspicion is entirely without foundation. There is not a single Egyptian monument known which in its bearings upon chronology is liable to the charge of numerical exaggeration. The monuments, as a rule, never speak except of contemporary events. There are a few instances in which a temple built by an ancient sovereign is said to have been repaired or rebuilt by another, but the interval between the two sovereigns is unfortunately never stated.

Monuments mentioning the Year of a Reign.

Although Mena is the first of the Egyptian kings, and is repeatedly named, dates are never reckoned from his or from any other era, but are given by the year of the reigning king. This is never so high as to justify a doubt. We can certainly conceive the case of a forged inscription on a tombstone, saying that John Smith died on the 9th September, 1876, or (were such the custom of the country) in the 39th year of Queen Victoria; but unless good reasons for rejecting such a statement are produced, the law of historical evidence compels us to admit it. Most of the documents upon which we rely for Egyptian chronology are of this simple nature, and no one who has seen the tombs or buildings from which they have been taken, can dream for an instant that these inscriptions are less trustworthy than those in an English churchyard.

The manifest defect for chronological purposes of such inscriptions is, that the last monumental year which happens to be preserved to us of a king is not necessarily the last of his reign. An error of several (perhaps of many) years is possible in each reign when there is no direct evidence to the contrary. But the error is at all events not on the side of exaggerated numbers.

Monuments furnishing Evidence of a Succession of Reigns.

Still more important than the monuments which mention the year of the king, are those in which two or more sovereigns of the same period are mentioned, especially if their succession or other precise data are given. Such is the treaty made in the twenty-first of his reign between Rameses II. and the king of the Cheta, wherein Rameses II. calls himself the son of Seti I., who in his turn is called the son of Rameses I.[1] There is a very large number of inscriptions belonging to personages who have been born in one reign and died in another, or who have served several kings in succession. And the inscriptions of the same period naturally confirm one another, or supply details which were missing.

Thus, to take the case of the eighteenth dynasty, the sepulchral inscriptions of Aahmes, the son of Abana,[2] gives the account of a naval officer who served three sovereigns one after the other,—Aahmes I., Amenhotep I. and Tehutimes I. (commonly called Thothmes or Thoth-

---

[1] "Records of the Past," Vol. IV. p. 25. [2] Ibid. Vol. VI. p. 5.

mosis). His father, the same inscription tells us, served the king Sekenen-Rā. Another well-known inscription, now in the Louvre at Paris,[1] begins the tale of its hero in the reign of Aahmes I., and ends it in that of Tehutimes III. The tablet of Nebuaiu, now in the Museum at Bulaq, gives thanks to Tehutimes III. and his son Amenhotep II., who had honoured Nebuaiu. King Amenhotep II. himself, on a tablet at Amada, speaks of Tehutimes III. as his father. And a third and independent witness, Amenemheb,[2] tells us that Tehutimes III., in whose service he was, died on the last day of the month Phamenoth, in the 54th year of his reign, and that he was succeeded by his son Amenhotep II. The entire succession of the dynasty is established on a large mass of evidence of the same kind, as may be seen at length in an excellent dissertation of Dr. Wiedemann.[3] And the chronology of other periods has been established in like manner.

The most remarkable series of inscriptions which has been utilized for chronological purposes consists of the inscriptions relating to the Apis bulls, whose wonderful tombs were discovered by M. Mariette. One of these sacred animals was born in the twenty-eighth year of king Sheshonk III., lived twenty years, and died in

---

[1] "Records of the Past," Vol. IV. p. 7. [2] Ibid. Vol. II. p. 59.
[3] "Geschichte der achtzehnten ägyptischen Dynastie bis zum Tode Tutmes III.," in the *Zeitschrift der Deutschen Morgenländischen Gesellschaft*, Bd. xxxi.

the second year of king Pamai. Another Apis was born in the twenty-sixth year of Taharqa, and died in the twentieth year of Psammitichus I. A hundred and sixty-eight tablets in honour of this one Apis have been found, fifty-three of which are dated. Another Apis, born on the nineteenth day of the month Mechir, in the fifty-third year of Psammitichus I., lived sixteen years, seven months and seventeen days, and died on the sixth Paophi of the sixteenth year of Necho II. This bull was succeeded by another, born on the seventh Paophi of the sixteenth year of Necho II., lived seventeen years, six months and five days, and died on the twelfth day of the month Pharmuti, of the twelfth year of king Apries.

As documents of this kind bring us down past the time of Cambyses and even into the Ptolemaic period, that is, into a period of well-ascertained chronology, we are able, by means of the Apis inscriptions alone, to go back from Cambyses to the first year of Taharqa, about seven hundred years before Christ, the limit of possible error being two or three years at the utmost. And with Taharqa (the Tirhaka of Scripture), who was the last king of the twenty-fifth dynasty, begins, as Brugsch observes, the *latest* period of the history of the Pharaohs.

Royal Lists and their Verification by the Monuments.

The first kind of monuments which I have described is useful as furnishing the highest ascertainable monumental year of a reign; the second kind enables us besides to determine the order of succession of reigns. Both these kinds of monuments are contemporaneous with the persons and events mentioned upon them. But besides these, there are monuments giving long lists of sovereigns, all of whom cannot have been contemporaneous. Such are the famous tablets of Abydos, that of Saqâra,[1] the chamber of Karnak, and some others. The royal hieratic canon of Turin (which is unfortunately in so mutilated a condition as practically to be of little use, and which enumerates many kings and gives the lengths of their reigns) is a document of the same historical character, at least from the point of view from which I am now looking at the matter.[2] In the chamber of Karnak, Tehutimes III. is represented as making an offering to sixty-one of his royal prede-

---

[1] Mariette, "La table de Saqqarah," in the *Revue Archéologique*, 1864, II. 169.

[2] It differs from the rest in being a professedly historical document. The others may rather be compared to lists of saints in Catholic litanies. That royal names should occur in this way in the prayers of private persons, as in the tablet of Saqâra, is not wonderful, when we learn from the Book of the Dead (ch. 136, l. 14) that the pious dead are in the company of the kings of the North and of the South.

cessors, whose names are given. At Abydos, Seti I., together with his son Rameses, then heir-apparent, offers incense to no less than seventy-six kings.[1]

Royal List of Abydos.

You will at once understand the importance of such a monument, if it can be relied upon, when I remind you that the Israelites in bondage are said to have been employed in building the treasure cities (as the Hebrew *meschenoth* is commonly translated), or rather sanctuaries, of Pithom and Rameses. It may be considered absolutely certain that no place in Egypt ever had the name of Rameses till the appearance of the celebrated hero of the name, who is actually represented on this monument as the son and heir-apparent of Seti I. The name of the place is as significant as the names of Alexandria, Antioch, Ptolemais, Seleucia, Washington or Napoleonville. The name of Rameses is a very peculiar one, the latter part of it consisting of the reduplicated form of the verb *mes*, not of the simple form, like the names Rames, Aahmes, Tehutimes, Chonsumes, and I do not believe any instance

---

[1] Dümichen, "Die Sethostafel von Abydos (mit Abbildung)," in the *Zeitschrift für ägyptische Sprache und Alterthumskunde*, 1864, p. 81. Devéria, "La nouvelle table d'Abydos, comparée aux autres listes royales de l'ancienne Égypte, redigée sous les Ramessides ou antérieurement," in the *Rev. Archéologique*, 1865, I. 50, and Mariette, "La nouvelle table d'Abydos," *Rev. Arch.* 1866, I. 73.

of it will ever be found more ancient than that of
Rameses I., the grandfather of the great conqueror.
Now if this tablet of Abydos is correct, seventy-six
kings, that is, very many more kings than can be
counted in English history, must have reigned over
Egypt before the first books of the Bible were written.
But if we go back in English history to Ethelred II.
in 976, we shall find that not more than forty-four
sovereigns have reigned during a thousand years, and
the average length of an Egyptian king's reign cannot
be shown to be shorter than that of an English sovereign.

Evidence of the Reality of Sovereigns named.

But are the names on the tablet of Abydos names of
real personages, or are they (or at least some of them)
as imaginary as the kings of Britain, beginning with
Brutus, as reported by Geoffrey of Monmouth, or the
kings of Scotland, beginning with Fergus I., whose
portraits adorn the walls of Holyrood? There is but
one way of settling the question, and that is by looking
out for evidence which will confirm or contradict that
given by these royal lists. As far as the test of verification has been applied to these lists, there is no
reason whatever for distrusting them. Instead of admitting sovereigns who have never lived, they have
for certain reasons omitted many, the existence of whom

is quite certain. The intention of the tablets was not historical or chronological, but simply devotional, and the selection and arrangement of names consequently vary, though the most considerable names are the same in all.

M. de Rougé has carefully studied all the monuments which belong to the first six dynasties.[1] The earliest monuments that can be found belong to king Seneferu, the 20th on the list of Abydos; and from this king till the 38th on the list, the evidence is complete, and the order of succession thoroughly established by independent inscriptions contemporaneous with the sovereigns of whom they speak. There is, for instance, the tomb at Gizeh of a queen who graced the courts of king Seneferu and the two kings who followed him. Two officers have left inscriptions which say that they had served the kings Unas and Teta. The great inscription of Una[2] begins by saying that this officer served Teta, and ends with his services under Merenrā. This king was succeeded by his brother Neferkarā (No. 38 of the list). The tomb of the mother of these royal brothers still exists. She was the wife of Pepi-Merirā (No. 36), several monuments of whom are known; one of them, in Wádi Maghārah in the peninsula of Mount

---

[1] "Recherches sur les monuments qu'on peut attribuer aux six premières dynasties de Manethon:" Paris, 1866.

[2] "Records of the Past," Vol. II. p. 1.

Sinai, is dated in the eighteenth year of his reign. No period in any history that can be named is better authenticated by contemporary monuments.

The same truth may be asserted of the twelfth dynasty, which in the tablet of Abydos is represented by Nos. 59 to 65. The number of monuments accurately dated belonging to this period is very considerable. They are all perfectly consistent with one another, and leave no doubt as to the length of each reign and of the whole dynasty. It is to this dynasty that the splendid tomb of Nahre-se-Chnumhotep at Benihassan belongs. His inscription mentions the first four sovereigns as having honoured three successive generations of his family.

Omissions of this List.

Let me now speak of the omissions of this tablet, which I have selected in preference to others in consequence of its being the longest and the most intelligible as to its arrangement.

The most beautiful monuments of the eighteenth dynasty were raised by the powerful queen Hatshepsu, daughter of Tehutimes I., who associated her with him. She reigned for some years either alone or in conjunction with her brothers Tehutimes II. and Tehutimes III. successively; but her name and memory were persecuted by the latter, who resented her dominion over him during the years of his minority. Her name does not appear on the tablet of Abydos. There is also an interval between the reigns of Amenhotep III. and Hor-em-heb, which chronologically is filled up by the period of the sun-disk worshippers. Amenhotep III. was followed by a king, the fourth of the same name, who dropped it when he assumed that of Chut-en-Aten, as the founder of a new religion, which had but a very partial and short-lived success. His attempts at reformation led to his exclusion from the lists of the legitimate kings. There is monumental evidence of one or two reigns of short duration before that of Hor-em-heb, who broke up the monuments of Chut-en-Aten, and used them in the construction of his own. It is not out of place to mention the fact that the first information we obtained about this abortive attempt at the transformation of the Egyptian religion, was derived from blocks of one of the propyla of Karnak, which Mohammed Ali had brutally pulled down, that the stones might be broken up and roasted to quick-lime, in order to furnish stucco for his saltpetre works. Mr. Perring, an English architect, who was there, was surprised to find that the faces of the stones, which had been placed inwards and covered with cement, were sculptured with hieroglyphics of the same perfect execution as those which had been engraved on them after their arrangement in the new building. This appropriation, of which there are many instances, by one sovereign of materials bearing the name and inscriptions of one of his predecessors, is always of value as determining the question of priority in time.

The omission of the heretical sovereigns is easily accounted for, and Seti may have shared the dislike of Tehutimes for queen Hatshepsu. But no satisfactory explanation has yet been given of the omission of a large number of names between the end of the twelfth and the beginning of the eighteenth dynasty. The immediate passage on the tablet from one of these dynasties to the other, cannot mean that the king numbered 65 was followed by the king numbered 66, who is Aahmes I. The important inscription of the naval officer Aahmes, son of Abana, which has already been quoted, mentions king Sekenen-Rā as the predecessor of Aahmes I. Sekenen-Rā is as thoroughly historical a personage as any one of our own sovereigns. There were even three kings of the name, and their tombs have actually been found at Thebes. On the other hand, the tablet of Ameni-senb, now in the Louvre, belongs to the reign of a king anterior to the eighteenth dynasty, but later than the twelfth, as it records the restoration of a temple at Abydos founded by Usertsen I.[1] The interval between the twelfth and the eighteenth

---

[1] Commonly called Usertesen, or still more erroneously Usirtasen. *Usert* is a feminine noun, and *sen* is a pronominal suffix, in allusion to the child's parents, like *ef*, *es* and *ári*.

dynasty must have been very considerable. The time immediately preceding the eighteenth dynasty was the period of the foreign domination generally known as that of the Hyksos, or the Shepherd kings. So much is certain, but it is absolutely impossible to ascertain from Egyptian records when this period began, and how long it lasted. The 511 years which are ascribed to it by Manetho, as quoted by Josephus, are neither to be simply accepted nor rejected, but must remain subject to future verification. The only evidence from Egyptian sources which bears upon the subject is a monument of Rameses II., dated from the four hundredth year of one of these kings of foreign origin. But a considerable number of native kings must have reigned between the last king of the twelfth dynasty and the beginning of the foreign invasion. There are numerous inscriptions which prove that sovereigns powerful in the north of Egypt had extended their dominion to the very heart of Nubia. The monuments of Thebes, southern Egypt and Nubia, might be consistent with the hypothesis of a Hyksos kingdom in the north, but the presence of equally important monuments of the Sebekhoteps at Bubastis and Tanis, kings whose names occupy an important place in the chamber of Karnak, would alone be sufficient to overthrow this hypothesis. There is in the Louvre a magnificent colossal statue in red granite of Sebekhotep III., with reference to which M. de Rougé says: "A single statue of this excellence and of such a material shows clearly that the king who had it executed for the decoration of his temples or palaces had not yet suffered from the invasion of the Shepherds. It is evident that under his reign Egypt was still a great power, peacefully cultivating the arts." Perhaps the most interesting monument of this period is the colossal statue of the king Semench-ka-Rā (the eighteenth king of the thirteenth dynasty, according to the royal Turin papyrus), on the right shoulder of which one of the foreign kings has had his name engraved in hieroglyphic characters.

Of the kings of the eleventh dynasty, only two (Nos. 57 and 58) appear on the tablet of Abydos. Very interesting inscriptions belonging to their reigns are still extant; but other kings bearing the name of Antuf and Mentuhotep are known to us, not only by inscriptions, but by their coffins in our museums. Of Mentuhotep III., dates have been found as high as his forty-third year. And a tablet has been found representing him as being worshipped by his successor, Antuf IV. There is a very interesting fact connected with one of the monuments of this dynasty. Many years ago,[1] Dr. Birch translated a papyrus, now in the

---

[1] In the *Revue Archéologique* of 1859. See Dr. Birch's paper "On the Tablet of Antefaa," in the *Transactions of the Society of Biblical Archaeology*, Vol. IV. p. 172.

British Museum, describing a judicial inquiry concerning robberies committed in the royal tombs at Thebes. The tombs of the kings are described as having been inspected. In one of these tombs the king Antuf-āa is reported to be represented on a tablet accompanied by his hound Behkaa. This tomb has quite recently been discovered by M. Mariette at Drah-abu'lneggah, with the picture of the king, and the dog's name Behkaa written over the picture of the animal. The inscription on the tablet is dated from the fiftieth year of the king.

Evidence like this proves that there is no exaggeration in the list of Abydos. It does not aim at presenting a complete list of kings. It only mentions those for whom Seti had a special devotion. The disappearance of Memphis and other great cities is quite sufficient to account for the absence of monumental evidence for some of the reigns. It is very probable that the earliest kings left no monuments. But for nearly every king on the tablet who is unrepresented by monumental evidence, we can produce another king omitted by the tablet, but whose reign is proved by unimpeachable evidence.

Genealogies.

The evidence of such genealogies as are found in the tombs leads to chronological results very similar to those derived from the succession of the kings. These genealogies have nothing fabulous about them, like

those against which Mr. Grote cautions his readers;
they are as completely matter of fact as any recorded
on the tombstones of our own churchyards.[1]

Manetho.

A great many writers who have treated of Egyptian
chronology have endeavoured to utilize the names and
numbers given in the fragments of Manetho. There
is not the slightest reason for questioning the fact that
Manetho had access to authentic historical records;
and if his work were still extant, it would be of invaluable service to us. As it is, we are indebted to him
for the notion of the division into dynasties with local
origins, all of which have been accurately verified.
But his work has unfortunately been lost, and the few
fragments of it which remain, and which give but an
imperfect notion of the whole, have been preserved by
writers who do not appear to have observed strict
accuracy in their quotations, and they have clearly in
some instances quoted him at second-hand. The late
Dr. Hincks, who had given great attention to the

---

[1] The funereal tablets often mention the name of the father and mother and some other near relatives of the departed. One tablet seldom goes back three or more generations. And the longest genealogy which has been recovered appears to be defective rather than otherwise. Dr. Lieblein's "Dictionnaire des noms hiéroglyphiques" contains an invaluable collection of these family records arranged in chronological order.

subject, has pointed out a series of deliberate falsifications of Manetho's lists made by the early Christian and perhaps by Jewish chronologers for the purpose of bringing these lists into harmony with the Old Testament, or rather with fanciful interpretations of the Old Testament. He does not attribute these falsifications to dishonest motives, but to "mistakes or injudicious attempts to correct mistakes."

Absolute Dates.

It was once generally supposed (and I have myself written in favour of the supposition[1]) that absolute dates might be detected on the monuments. The heliacal risings of certain stars were calculated by M. Biot as fixing the reign of one king in 1300 B.C., and of another king in the year 1444. But I no longer believe that the Egyptian texts really bear out the interpretation which furnishes the data of these cal-

---

[1] On "The Earliest Epochs of Authentic Chronology," in *Home and Foreign Review*, 1862, p. 420. M. Biot, in his "Mémoire sur quelques dates absolues," and after him M. Romieu and Dr. Gensler, have dealt with the Egyptian calendars as if they recorded the *risings* of certain stars. But the text of the calendars distinctly speaks of the *transits* of the stars, and *never* of their risings. I have discussed this question in the *Chronicle*, 25 Jan. 1868, and in the *Transactions of the Society for Biblical Archaeology*, Vol. III. M. E. de Rougé has a very important "Note sur quelques conditions préliminaires des calculs qu'on peut tenter sur le calendrier et les dates égyptiennes," in the *Revue Archéologique*, 1864, Vol. II. p. 81.

culations. Dr. Dümichen,[1] Dr. Lauth[2] and other scholars have written in favour of other fixed dates which they believe can be determined astronomically. But whether these dates are right or wrong (and I am unwilling to express an opinion on questions which I have not personally investigated), matters but little for our present purpose. The essential point upon which I wish to insist is, that the Egyptian monarchy, according to the most moderate calculation, must have already been in existence fifteen hundred years at the very least, but probably more than two thousand years, before the book of Exodus was written.

Egyptian Monarchy anterior to 3000 B.C.

The composition of the book of Exodus, however, cannot unfortunately be considered a fixed date. The opinion which used to be universally received, that Moses is the author of the Pentateuch, must assuredly be abandoned. I am quite ready to admit that the

---

[1] "Die erste bis jetzt aufgefundene sichere Angabe über die Regierungszeit eines ägyptischen Königs aus dem alten Reich, welche uns durch dem medicinischen Papyrus Ebers überliefert wird:" Leipzig, 1874.

[2] "Aegyptische Chronologie, basirt auf die vollständige Reihe der Epochen seit Bytes-Menes bis Hadrian-Antonin durch drei Sothisperioden = 4380 Jahre." See also a paper of M. Chabas, "Détermination d'une date certaine dans le règne d'un roi de l'ancien empire en Egypte," in the *Mémoires présentés à l'Académie des inscriptions et belles lettres*, 1877.

co-existence in the Pentateuch of the documents called Elohistic and Jehovistic is in itself no argument against the authorship of Moses. But the fact that these documents continue to run through the book of Joshua furnishes an argument which admits of no reply. The book of Joshua and the book of Exodus are parts of one and the same work, and the historical allusions in the book of Joshua have compelled some of the commentators who pride themselves most upon their orthodoxy (Matthew Henry, for instance), to refer the authorship of it to times subsequent to the foundation of the Hebrew monarchy.

But though the book of Exodus as a whole may not be the work of a contemporary, there is really no reason for doubting the accuracy of the statement about Pithom and Rameses. Egyptian history renders it most probable that Moses was a contemporary of the great Rameses. The exodus of the Israelites cannot with any probability be brought lower down than 1310 years before Christ, and it is about 2050 before this that I would place the lowest limit for estimating the beginning of the historical Egyptian monarchy. The date of the Great Pyramid cannot be more recent than 3000 B.C.

Pre-historic Antiquity of Human Race in Egypt.

This is undoubtedly a great and venerable antiquity, but it is after all very inferior to the antiquity of the human race in Egypt, as demonstrated by the operations suggested by Mr. Leonard Horner to the Royal Society, and carried out at first at its expense, and finally at the cost of Abbas Pacha, between the years 1851 and 1854. Ninety-five pits were sunk at different spots into the alluvial soil of the Nile valley. "Although," Professor Ansted tells us,[1] "it cannot be regarded as a matter about which there is no dispute, all the evidence that exists seems to point to five inches per century as fully representing the average amount of elevation given by the Nile mud to the bed of the Nile and the surrounding country covered by the annual inundation." "The average can hardly under any calculations have exceeded five inches per century during the last several centuries, whilst from the mere effects of long-continued pressure the beds must become compact at some depth below than they are near the surface, and the rate of thickness ought to become gradually less the deeper we penetrate." In the course of the operations, remains showing the handiwork of man were brought up from considerable depths: sculptured granite, architecturally carved limestone, human and animal figures, coloured mosaic, vases, jars, a copper knife, and at very great depths—fifty, sixty, or even seventy-two feet—bricks and fragments of pottery. At thirty-three feet and a half, a tablet with

---

[1] "Geological Gossip," p. 190.

inscriptions was found. There is not a single geologist who does not at once infer from these facts an enormous lapse of time during which the human race must have inhabited Egypt. Geologists are not more deficient in common sense than other men, and they are quite ready to allow that accidental circumstances may have contributed to bury some articles deeper than others; and their conclusions are not drawn from this or that experiment, but from the cumulative evidence derived from nearly a hundred experiments made over a very extensive area of land.

In reply to the objection that the artificial objects might have fallen into old wells which had afterwards been filled up, Sir Charles Lyell says:[1] "Of the ninety-five shafts and borings, seventy or more were made far from the sites of towns or villages; and allowing that every field may have had its well, there would be small chance of the borings striking upon the site even of a small number of them in seventy experiments."

I remember being once asked about these operations, and when I had described them, one of my friends came up to me and said in a voice of solemn warning and protest, "If what you have been saying is true, Christianity is a mere fable." I could only reply, "No; it only shows that your conception of Christianity involves something fabulous." Whatever claim a

---

[1] "Antiquity of Man," p. 38, 1873.

religion may have to a divine authority, that claim cannot be extended to its theology, which is nothing else but a system of reasoning upon two sets of data, namely, those furnished by the religion itself, and those furnished by the science of the day. Biblical chronology as understood by Usher, Petavius or other learned men, depends not upon the Bible only, but also upon the data of profane chronology as understood in their days, and the latter chronology was built in great part upon statements of Greek and Latin writers which at the present day are known to be absolutely worthless.

Egyptian Ethnology.

The boring instruments which had to be employed at great depths in the operations of which I have been speaking, necessarily brought up everything in fragments. There is therefore no proof that the Egyptians known to us from history were descended from the pre-historic men whose existence was first brought to light by these operations. But the very proximate probability of such a descent might have suggested itself to ethnologists, who have persisted in looking for the ancestors of the Egyptians among races the very existence of which cannot be traced very far back. At all events, the view is now entirely abandoned according to which the Egyptians came down the Nile from the more southern regions of Africa. It has been most conclusively proved that they gradually advanced from north to south, and the earliest Ethiopian civilization is demonstrably the child, not the parent, of the Egyptian. Most scholars now point to the interior of Asia as the cradle of the Egyptian people. I will only say that the farther back we go into antiquity, the more closely does the Egyptian type approach the European. This is the opinion of Mariette Bey and of Dr. Birch, and the same opinion was most powerfully expressed by Professor Owen at the Oriental Congress held in London in 1874. In reference to one specimen, Professor Owen said: "With English costume and complexion, this Egyptian of the Ancient Empire would pass for a well-to-do sensible British citizen and ratepayer." And of another he said: "The general character of the face recalls that of the northern German; he might be the countryman of Bismarck." In reference to another hypothesis which had been proposed, he observed: "Unknown and scarce conceivable as are the conditions which could bring about the conversion of the Australian into the Egyptian type of skull, the influence of civilization and admixture would be still more impotent in blotting out the dental characteristics of the lower race. The size of crown and multiplication of fangs are reduced in the ancient Egyptian to the standard of Indo-European or so-called highly civilized races. The last molar has the same inferiority of size."[1]

Language.

It is in vain, I believe, that the testimony of philology has been invoked in evidence of the origin of the Egyptians. The language which has been recovered belongs to a very early stage of speech, and is not, or at least cannot be shown to be, allied to any other known language than its descendant the Coptic. It is certainly not akin to any of the known dialects either of North or of South Africa, and the attempts which have hitherto been made towards establishing such a kindred must be considered as absolute failures. A certain number of Egyptian words, such as *i*, "go," *tā*, "give, place," have the same meaning as the corresponding Indo-European roots. And a few other Egyptian words sound very like Semitic words of the same meaning. But the total number of words in the Egyptian vocabulary which have the appearance of relationship either with the Aryan or with the Semitic stock turns out, after passing through the necessary process of sifting, to be extremely small. A consider-

---

[1] *Transactions of the Second Session of the International Congress of Orientalists*, held in London, 1874, p. 355 and following. Professor Owen here discusses the doctrine put forth by Professor Huxley upon "the Geographical Distribution of the chief Modifications of Mankind," in the *Journal of the Ethnological Society of London*, Jan. 1871.

able number of words have certainly passed from one language into another, but all these have to be deducted. Those who talk of Egyptian having its root in Semitic, or say that its grammar is Semitic, must mean something quite different from what these words imply in the mouth of some one well versed in the science of Language. I once heard a learned Jew compare Hebrew with Portuguese. All that he meant to say was, that it preferred the letter *m* where the kindred languages took *n*, as the Portuguese language often does in contrast with its sister languages, the Spanish, French and Italian. And those who speak of Egyptian grammar as being Semitic are clearly thinking of some peculiarities of it, in forgetfulness of very much more important ones. It would be quite easy, under such conditions, to discover Finnish or Polynesian affinities.

The Egyptian and the Semitic languages belong to quite different stages of language, the former to what Professor Max Müller calls the second or Terminational, the latter to the third or Inflexional stage. In the Terminational stage, two or more roots may coalesce to form a word, the one retaining its radical independence, the other sinking down to a mere termination. The languages belonging to this stage have generally been called agglutinative. Now the Egyptian language has indeed reached this stage as regards the pronominal and one or two other suffixes. But in all other respects it most nearly resembles the languages of the first or

Radical stage, in which there is no formal distinction between a root and a word. The agglutination between an Egyptian word and its pronominal suffix is of the lightest possible kind; a particle may, and often does, intervene between them. An English critic reviewing Rossi's Grammar a few weeks ago, preferred that of Brugsch's to it in consequence of the paradigms of verbs which are to be found in the latter. He might with equal wisdom have found fault with both for omitting the declensions. My own criticism would have been very different. There is, I believe, too much paradigm in Rossi's Grammar. There are no paradigms at all in Egyptian; and those who have inserted such things into their Grammars (I say it with the utmost deference to such admirable scholars as E. de Rougé and Brugsch) have been led astray by their efforts to find in Egyptian what exists in other languages. But each kind of language has its own processes. Hebrew and Arabic verbs can as little be thrown into moods and tenses corresponding to the Greek or Latin verbs, as you can find Pual or Hithpahel forms in French or English. Personal endings are indispensable to the Indo-European and to the Semitic verbs. The Egyptian verb is unchangeable, and has no personal ending properly speaking. The suffix which is sometimes added to it is not really a personal ending. It is put instead of a subject; and when the subject is expressed, the pronominal suffix is and must be omitted. It would be as impossible in Hebrew, or in any other Semitic language, to suppress the personal ending, which is an essential part of the word in which it occurs.

One of the chief differences between the Egyptian language on the one hand and the Indo-European and Semitic on the other, is, that the distinctions between roots, stems and words, can hardly be said to exist at all in the former. The bare root, which in the languages of the third stage lies, as it were, below the surface, and is only revealed by its developments to scientific inquiry, is almost invariably identical in Egyptian with the word in actual use. From one Aryan or Semitic root, which is itself no part of speech and has but an abstract existence, verbs, nouns, adjectives, adverbs and other parts of speech, are derived. The actual Egyptian word, taken by itself, is in very many instances no part of speech, but within the limits of the notion which it represents is potentially noun, verb, adjective, adverb, &c. The notion expressed by an Egyptian word is only determined, as that of a verb in the strict sense (verbum finitum), by the presence of a subject. When no subject (that is, noun or pronoun) is expressed, we may indeed have a "verbum infinitum," but this is grammatically a noun or an adjective. How can a language of this description be called Semitic in its grammar?

There are three different ways in which a verb may be connected with its subject, but these are wholly irrespective of time or mood, so that grammarians who have introduced these forms into their paradigms call them "Present-Past-Future," first, second or third. They might add, "Indicative-Potential-Conjunctive," and so forth. The Egyptian verb is often accompanied by an auxiliary, and is grammatically subordinate to it; and the combinations formed by these auxiliary words with the verbal notion enable the language to express meanings equivalent to those expressed by our Indo-European tenses and moods. But this is very different from what is meant by paradigm.

I have just spoken of the grammatical subordination of a verb to its auxiliary. This is almost the only kind of grammatical subordination which exists in the language, and the consequence of it is fatal to anything like beauty of construction in the form of the sentences. It seems unfair to judge of the capabilities of a language of which almost the entire literature has perished. How could we judge of the capabilities of the Greek language had all its poetry and oratory been lost, and nothing remained but its inscriptions? Yet enough remains to show what the structure of the Egyptian sentences must necessarily have been; we possess several narratives of considerable length and of different dates, a great many hymns, and the heroic poem of Pentaur, which was considered sufficiently important to be engraved on the walls of at least four temples— Abydos, Luqsor, Karnak and Ipsambul—at one of the periods of the greatest glory of Egypt. It is evident that prose sentences like those of Plato, Demosthenes, Cicero or Burke, or poetical ones like those of Sophocles, Euripides or Horace (not to mention any other names), are as impossible in Egyptian as they are in Hebrew or Arabic. Whatever beauty there is in Egyptian composition (and there often is considerable beauty) is derived either from the thought itself or from the simplicity of the expression, not from the artistic variety or structure of its periods. M. Renan[1] has made very similar remarks upon the structure of the Semitic sentence (which, however, admits of much greater variety than the Egyptian, and does not suffer in narratives from the perpetual repetition of the same auxiliary verb), and he has inferred from it the inferiority of the Semitic mind to the European with reference to certain branches of intellectual development. I have little doubt that M. Renan is right to this extent, that certain languages as vehicles of thought are inferior to others, and that as long as men are confined to the inferior vehicle of thought, they are unable to raise themselves to the level of others who enjoy a more efficient instrument. It is difficult to conceive the Egyptians as otherwise than incapacitated by their language from profound philosophy. It is hardly pos-

---

[1] "Histoire Générale et système comparé des langues Sémitiques," livre i. chap. i. p. 21. The whole chapter is to the point.

sible to read a page written in an Indo-European
language, from Sanskrit to Keltic, without coming
across some kind of dialectic process of which I do not
remember a single trace in an Egyptian text.

Art.

But if the Egyptian mind must be considered as
inferior in some branches of intellectual development,
the world of Art, not indeed in its full extent, but in
many aspects, ranging from mere elegance and pretti-
ness to real beauty and sublimity, was revealed to it
at a very early period indeed. Those who know
Egyptian art only through our northern museums can
have no adequate conception of what it really is or was.
Almost all the objects in our museums have suffered
by frequent locomotion, atmospheric influences, or other
deleterious causes. You should see the freshness of
the articles contained in the museum at Bulaq, which
seem to have just come from the hand of the artist, or
inspect some of the tombs which have not yet suffered
from the vandalism of the moderns, or see the magnificent temples whose ruins have as yet escaped
destruction. But, even on the spot, imagination must
come to our aid if the past has to be realized.

Many of us have seen the Pyramids, and, as Dean
Stanley says, "One is inclined to imagine that the
Pyramids are immutable, and that such as you see them

now, such they were always. Of distant views this is true; but taking them near at hand, it is more easy from the existing ruins to conceive Karnac as it was than it is to conceive the Pyramidal platform as it was. The smooth casing of part of the top of the second Pyramid, and the magnificent granite blocks which form the lower stages of the third, serve to show what they must have been all from top to bottom; the first and second, brilliant white or yellow limestone, smooth from top to bottom, instead of those rude disjointed masses which their stripped sides now present; the third, all glowing with the red granite from the first cataract. As it is, they have the barbarous look of Stonehenge; but then they must have shone with the polish of an age already rich with civilization, and that the more remarkable when it is remembered that those granite blocks which furnish the outside of the third and inside of the first must have come all the way from the first cataract. It also seems, from Herodotus and others, that these smooth outsides were covered with sculptures. Then you must build up or uncover the massive tombs, now broken or choked up with sand, so as to restore the aspect of vast streets of tombs like those on the Appian Way, out of which the Great Pyramid would rise like a cathedral above smaller churches. Lastly, you must enclose two other Pyramids with stone precincts and gigantic gateways; and, above all, you must restore the Sphinx as he (for it must never be forgotten that a female Sphinx was almost unknown) was in the days of his glory."[1]

I may perhaps appear open to the suspicion of over-estimating the arts of ancient Egypt. I therefore cannot do better than refer you to the mature judgment of one who has written the History of Architecture[2] with consummate knowledge, ability and taste.

"No one can possibly examine the interior of the Great Pyramid," says Mr. Fergusson, "without being struck with astonishment at the wonderful mechanical skill displayed in its construction. The immense blocks of granite brought from Syene—a distance of 500 miles—polished like glass, and so fitted that the joints can hardly be detected. Nothing can be more wonderful than the extraordinary amount of knowledge displayed in the construction of the discharging chambers over the roof of the principal apartment, in the alignment of the sloping galleries, in the provision of ventilating shafts, and in all the wonderful contrivances of the structure. All these, too, are carried out with such precision that, notwithstanding the immense superincumbent weight, no settlement in any part can be detected to the extent of an appreciable fraction of an inch. Nothing more perfect, mechanically, has ever been erected since that time, and we ask ourselves in vain, how long it must have taken before men acquired such experience and such skill, or were so perfectly organized, as to contemplate and complete such undertakings."

The walls of the most ancient tombs are decorated with pictures.

---

[1] "Sinai and Palestine," p. lvii.
[2] See also the whole fifth book of Mr. Fergusson's "Illustrated Handbook of Architecture."

"In all these pictures the men are represented with an ethnic and artistic truth that enables us easily to recognize their race and station. The animals are not only distinguishable, but the characteristic peculiarities of each species are seized with a power of generalization seldom, if ever, surpassed."

"More striking than even the paintings are the portrait statues which have recently been discovered in the secret recesses of these tombs; nothing more wonderfully truthful and realistic has been done since that time till the invention of photography, and even that can hardly represent a man with such unflattering truthfulness as these old coloured terra-cotta portraits of the sleek rich men of the Pyramid period."

I now turn to the pages describing the buildings at Thebes.

"Though the Rhamession is so grand from its dimensions, and so beautiful from its design, it is far surpassed in every respect by the palace temple at Karnac, which is perhaps the noblest effort of architectural magnificence ever produced by the hand of man.

"Its principal dimensions are 1200 feet in length, by about 360 in width, and it covers therefore about 430,000 square feet, or nearly twice the area of St. Peter's at Rome, and more than four times that of any mediæval cathedral existing. This, however, is not a fair way of estimating its dimensions, for our churches are buildings entirely under one roof; but at Karnac a considerable portion of the area was uncovered by any buildings, so that no such comparison is just. The great hypostile hall, however, is internally 340 feet by 170, and with its two pylons it covers more than 88,000 square feet, a greater area than the cathedral of Cologne, the largest of all our northern cathedrals; and when we consider that this is only a part of a great whole, we may fairly assert that the entire structure is among the largest, as it undoubtedly is one of the most beautiful, buildings in the world.

"We have thus in this one temple a complete history of the style during the whole of its most flourishing period; and either for interest or for beauty it forms such a series as no other country and no other age can produce. Besides those buildings mentioned above, there are other temples to the North, to the East, and more especially to the South, and pylons connecting them, and avenues of sphinxes extending for miles, and enclosing walls and tanks and embankments—making up such a group as no city ever possessed before or since. St. Peter with its colonnades and the Vatican make up an immense mass, but as insignificant in extent as in style when compared with this glory of ancient Thebes and its surrounding temples.

"The culminating point and climax of all this group of buildings is the hypostile hall of Manephthah.... No language can convey an idea of its beauty, and no artist has yet been able to reproduce its form so as to convey to those who have not seen it an idea of its grandeur. The mass of its central piers, illumined by a flood of light from the clerestory, and the smaller pillars of the wings gradually fading into obscurity, are so arranged and lighted as to convey an idea of infinite space; at the same time, the beauty and massiveness of the forms, and the brilliancy of their coloured decorations, all combine to stamp this as the greatest of man's architectural works, but such a one as it would be impossible to reproduce except in such a climate and in that individual style in which and for which it was created."

There is one more quotation from which I am unable to refrain.

"In all the conveniences and elegances of building they seem to have anticipated all that has been in those countries down to the present day. Indeed, in all probability, the ancient Egyptians surpassed the modern in those respects as much as they did in the more important forms of architecture."

True artistic power may display itself in a gem as well as in the design of a cathedral. The precious materials of which Egyptian jewellery was composed have naturally contributed to their destruction in former times, but there are still extant trinkets of marvellous beauty. A few years ago some peasants near Thebes dug up the coffin of the queen Aahhotep, wife of king Kames. This king's name is one of those which does not occur in the tablet of Abydos, but he is known from different records, and his picture is found at Qurnah in a tomb of the eighteenth dynasty. Queen Aahhotep was the ancestress of this dynasty. Her coffin contained treasures of jewellery, which were brought to Paris at the last General Exhibition, and are now objects of wonder and admiration to all who visit the Museum at Bulaq. Between the linen coverings, precious weapons and ornaments were found, daggers, a golden axe, a chain with three large golden bees and a breastplate, and on the body itself a golden chain, with a scarabaeus, armlets, a fillet for the brow and other objects. Two little barks in gold and silver, bronze axes bearing the name of her husband Kames, and great bangles for the ankles, lay immediately upon the wood of the coffin. The jewellers of Paris could not have produced more exquisite workmanship.

I must not omit to tell you that, to the practised eye of an archaeologist, every object of Egyptian art bears upon it as well defined a date as a mediaeval church window or porch. The astonishing identity which is visible through all the periods of Egyptian art is consistent with an immense amount of change, which must exist wherever there is life. There are periods of splendour, progress and deterioration, and every age has its peculiar character. Birch, Lepsius or Mariette, would at once tell you the age of a statue, inscription or manuscript, without looking at the text which actually mentions the exact date.

Painting, as understood in these later centuries, was entirely unknown to the Egyptians, though they had coloured pictures; but the harmony of colours was thoroughly understood by them, and their employment of colour in architecture or generally in decoration puts our modern efforts to shame. "They were aware" (as Sir Gardner Wilkinson says) "that for decorative purposes the primary colours should predominate, and that secondary hues should be secondary in quantity and in position; their most usual combinations were therefore blue, red and green; and a fillet of white or yellow was introduced between them to obviate that false effect which is apt to convert red and blue into purple when placed together in immediate contact. When yellow was introduced, a due proportion of black was added to balance it, and for each colour was sought its suitable companion; or if certain colours occasionally predominated in a part of the wall, the balance was restored by a greater quantity of others elsewhere, so that the due proportions of all were kept up, and the general effect was a perfect concord."

The earliest monuments show the use of a great variety of musical instruments—flutes, pipes, harps, guitars, lyres and tamburines—and they give representations of concerts in which human voices are combined with the sounds of several instruments.[1] My learned friend Dr. Dümichen, himself an admirable musician, in noticing the presence not only of a monkey, but of hounds, at a concert in the tomb of Ptahhotep, is very much tempted to doubt the musical taste of that great dignitary of the fifth dynasty, and to suppose that he preferred the accompaniments of his canine friends. There is, however, I believe, reason to suppose that the picture is intended to represent dogs from the spirit-land, whose ears are no doubt attuned to the harmony of sweet sounds.

The Egyptians were not, as used on very insufficient evidence to be supposed, a sad or morose people. Their religion at least does not appear to have been "designed to make their pleasures less." The description of their

---

[1] See Wilkinson, "Ancient Egyptians," Vol. I. p. 431; Carl Engel, "Music of the Most Ancient Nations," p. 180; and Lauth, "Ueber altägyptische Musik," in the *Sitzungsberichte* of the Munich Academy, 3rd July, 1869.

festivals given by classical writers is fully corroborated by authentic testimony, and the national tendency, at least in the prosperous times of the monarchy, was towards excess in the exercise of conviviality. Great quantities of wine, both native and foreign, were consumed; and beer-houses, if we may judge by the frequency with which they are inveighed against in the papyri, must have been as serious a pest in the time of the great Rameses as they are in the England of the nineteenth century. The point of the story which Herodotos tells about the representation of a dead body in a coffin being carried round and shown to the guests at entertainments, lies in the final words uttered by the bearer: "Cast your eyes on this figure; after death, you yourself will resemble it; drink then, *and be happy*." I think it would be easy to quote English, French or German drinking-songs containing the same moral. The element of mournfulness is introduced merely for the purpose of bringing out the convivial sentiment into stronger relief. It is possible that Herodotos makes allusion to a song of which several copies or fragments of copies have reached us. It is called the Song of King Antuf—a monarch of the eleventh dynasty, whom I have already mentioned—and it says:[1]

"Fulfil thy desire while thou livest. Put oils upon

---

[1] "Records of the Past," Vol. IV. p. 117.

thy head, clothe thyself with fine linen adorned with precious metals . . . . yield to thy desire—fulfil thy desire with thy good things whilst thou art upon earth, according to the dictation of thy heart. The day will come to thee when one hears not the voice,—when the one who is at rest hears not their voices. Feast in tranquillity; seeing that there is no one who carries his goods with him."

Another poem which has been preserved, "The Lay of the Harper," is very similar in its tone: "Let odours and oils stand before thy nostril. Let song and music be before thy face, and leave behind thee all evil cares. Mind thee of joy till cometh the day of pilgrimage, when we draw near the land which loveth silence."[1]

It is impossible to read these scraps of poetry without being reminded of a passage in the book of Ecclesiastes, written, in the person of Solomon, by some one living in the last century of the Persian domination in Palestine. It begins: "Go thy way; eat thy bread with joy, and drink thy wine with a merry heart, for God accepteth thy works. Let thy garments be always white; and let thy hand lack no ointment." And it ends—"for there is no work, no device, nor knowledge, nor wisdom in the grave, whither thou goest."[2]

---

[1] "Records of the Past," Vol. VI. p. 129. [2] Eccles. ix. 7, 8, 9.

And if it be true that the Preacher in another portion of his work reminds the young man to whom he is addressing himself that for all these things God will bring him into judgment, not less true is it that the Egyptian harper also sang:

"Mind thee of the day when thou too shalt start for the land to which one goeth to return not thence. Good for thee will have been a good life; therefore be just and hate iniquity; for he who loveth what is Right shall triumph."

Moral Code.

The triumph of Right over Wrong, of Right in speech and in action (for the same word signifies both Truth and Justice) is the burden of nine-tenths of the Egyptian texts which have come down to us. Right[1] is represented as a goddess ruling as mistress over heaven and earth and the world beyond the grave. The gods are said to live by it. Although funereal inscriptions are less to be depended upon when they describe the virtues of the deceased than when they give the dates of his birth and death, they may at least be quoted in evidence of the rule of conduct by which actions were estimated. We are not obliged to believe that this or that man possessed all the virtues

---

[1] The primitive notion implied by the word *maât* seems to be the geometrical one "right," as in "right line," as opposed to χ*ub*, "bent," "perverse." *Maât* as a noun is the "straight rule," "canon."

which are ascribed to him, but we cannot resist the conviction that the recognized Egyptian code of morality was a very noble and refined one. "None of the Christian virtues," M. Chabas says, "is forgotten in it; piety, charity, gentleness, self-command in word and action, chastity, the protection of the weak, benevolence towards the humble, deference to superiors, respect for property in its minutest details, . . . all is expressed there, and in extremely good language." In confirmation of this, I will add that the translators of the Bible and of the early Christian literature, who were so often compelled to retain Greek words for which they could discover no Egyptian equivalent, found the native vocabulary amply sufficient for the expression of the most delicate notions of Christian ethics.

The following are specimens of the praises which are put into the mouth of departed worthies:

"Not a little child did I injure. Not a widow did I oppress. Not a herdsman did I ill-treat. There was no beggar in my days; no one starved in my time. And when the years of famine came, I ploughed all the lands of the province to its northern and southern boundaries, feeding its inhabitants and providing their food. There was no starving person in it, and I made the widow to be as though she possessed a husband."[1]

---

[1] Inscriptions of Ameni, *Denkm.* ii. pl. 121.

Of another great personage it is said that, in administering justice, "he made no distinction between a stranger and those known to him. He was the father of the weak, the support of him who had no mother. Feared by the ill-doer, he protected the poor; he was the avenger of those whom a more powerful one had deprived of property. He was the husband of the widow, the refuge of the orphan."[1]

It is said of another[2] that he was "the protector of the humble, a palm of abundance to the destitute, food to the hungry and the poor, largeness of hand to the weak;" and another passage implies that his wisdom was at the service of those who were ignorant.

The tablet of Beka,[3] now at Turin, thus describes the deceased:

"I was just and true without malice, placing God in my heart and quick in discerning his will. I have come to the city of those who dwell in eternity. I have done good upon earth; I have done no wrong; I have done no crime; I have approved of nothing base or evil, but have taken pleasure in speaking the truth,

---

[1] Tablet of Antuf, Louvre, c. 26. I quote from M. de Rougé's *Notice des Monuments*, p. 88.

[2] British Museum, 581. This text, of which a copy is given in Sharpe, "Egyptian Inscriptions," Vol. II. p. 83, is a difficult one, and would repay a careful study.

[3] Published, with a translation and commentary by M. Chabas, in the *Transactions of the Society of Biblical Archaeology*, Vol. V. p. 459.

for I well know the glory there is in doing this upon earth from the first action (of life) even to the tomb.... I am a Sahu who took pleasure in righteousness, conformably with the laws (*hapu*) of the tribunal of the two-fold Right. There is no lowly person whom I have oppressed; I have done no injury to men who honoured their gods. The sincerity and goodness which were in the heart of my father and my mother, my love [paid back] to them. Never have I outraged it in my mode of action towards them from the beginning of the time of my youth. Though great, I have acted as if I had been a little one. I have not disabled any one worthier than myself. My mouth has always been opened to utter true things, not to foment quarrels. I have repeated what I have heard just as it was told to me."

Great stress is always in these inscriptions laid upon the strictest form of veracity; as, for instance, "I have not altered a story in the telling of it." The works of charity are commonly spoken of in terms which are principally derived from the Book of the Dead.

"Doing that which is Right and hating that which is Wrong, I was bread to the hungry, water to the thirsty, clothes to the naked, a refuge to him that was in want; that which I did to him, the great God hath done to me."[1]

---

[1] Dümichen, *Kalenderinschriften*, xlvi.

"I was one who did that which was pleasing to his father and his mother; the joy of his brethren, the friend of his companions, noble-hearted to all those of his city. I gave bread to the hungry; ... I received [travellers?] on the road; my doors were open to those who came from without, and I gave them wherewith to refresh themselves. And God hath inclined his countenance to me for what I have done; he hath given me old age upon earth, in long and pleasant duration, with many children at my feet, and sons in face of his own son."[1]

God's reward for well-doing is again mentioned in the great inscription now at Miramar[2] in honour of a lady who had been charitable to persons of her own sex, whether girls, wives or widows.

"My heart inclined me to the Right when I was yet a child not yet instructed as to the Right and Good. And what my heart dictated I failed not to perform. And God rewarded me for this, rejoicing me with the happiness which he has granted me for walking after his way."

We are acquainted with several collections of Precepts and Maxims on the conduct of life. Such are the Maxims of Ptahhotep contained in the Prisse Papyrus, the Instructions of Amenemhāt, and the

---

[1] Bergmann, *Hieroglyphische Inschriften*, pl. vi, l. 8.
[2] Ibid. pl. viii, ix.

Maxims of Ani; and fragments of other important works are preserved in the Museums of Paris, Leyden and St. Petersburg. The most venerable of them is the work of Ptahhotep, which dates from the age of the Pyramids, and yet appeals to the authority of the ancients. It is undoubtedly, as M. Chabas called it,[1] in the title of the memorable essay in which its contents were first made known, "The most Ancient Book of the World." The manuscript at Paris which contains it was written centuries before the Hebrew lawgiver was born, but the author of the work lived as far back as the reign of king Assa Tatkarā of the fifth dynasty. This most precious and venerable relic of antiquity is as yet very imperfectly understood. Its general import is clear enough, and some of the sections are perfectly intelligible; but the philological difficulties with which it abounds will for many years, I fear, resist the efforts of the most accomplished interpreters.[2] These books are very similar in character and tone to the book of Proverbs in our Bible. They inculcate the study of wisdom, the duty to parents and superiors, respect for property, the advantages of charitableness, peaceable-

---

[1] "Le plus ancien livre du monde," in the *Revue Archéologique* of 1857.

[2] M. Chabas has fully explained the nature of these difficulties in the *Zeits. f. ägypt. Spr.* 1870, p. 84 fol. Dr. Lauth's essay in the *Sitzungsberichte* of the Academy of Munich, 1869 and 1870, is very valuable, and I confess myself to be greatly indebted to it; but even the best portions of it can only be accepted provisionally.

ness and content, of liberality, humility, chastity and sobriety, of truthfulness and justice; and they show the wickedness and folly of disobedience, strife, arrogance and pride, of slothfulness, intemperance, unchastity and other vices. It is only through a lamentable misunderstanding of the text that some scholars have discovered anti-religious, epicurean or sceptical expressions.[1]

The same morality is taught in the romantic literature which sprung up at a very early period and continued to flourish down to the latest times. It is an interesting question, but one which cannot as yet be answered with certainty, whether or no the moralizing fables about animals attributed to Æsop are really of Egyptian origin? The Egyptian text of at least one of these fables is contained in a papyrus of the Leyden collection, but it is in " demotic," not in the early language of the country.

I have laid before you some of the characteristic

---

[1] " Let thy face be white (i.e. enjoy thyself) whilst thou livest; has there issued from the coffin (μαχερα chest) one who has entered therein?" This hasty translation by Mr. Goodwin (*Zeitschr.* 1867, p. 95) does not deserve the success it has enjoyed, and I do not believe the author of it would have published it, had his attention been called in time to such difficulties as these: 1, the Egyptian preposition *en* cannot stand at the end of a sentence; 2, it never means "therein;" 3, the word μαχερα is never found in the sense of "coffin," but in that of "chest of provisions;" 4, the sentiment in question is absurdly out of place in the context where the words occur.

features of Egyptian civilization, and I ought not to conclude without alluding to two errors, one of which may be considered as entirely obsolete among scholars, whilst the other may claim the sanction of very high authority.

Castes.

As long as our information depended upon the classical Greek authors, the existence of castes among the Egyptians was admitted as certain. The error was detected as soon as the sense of the inscriptions could be made out. A very slight knowledge of the language was sufficient to demonstrate the truth to the late M. Ampère.[1] Among ourselves, many men may be found whose ancestors have for several generations followed the same calling, either the army or the church, or some branch of industry or trade. The Egyptians were no doubt even more conservative than ourselves in this respect. But there was no impassable barrier between two professions. The son or the brother of a warrior might be a priest. It was perhaps more difficult to rise in the world than it is with us; but a man of education, a scribe, was eligible to any office, civil, military or sacerdotal, to which his talents or the chances of fortune might lead him, and nothing prevented his marriage with the daughter of a man of a different profession.

---

[1] "Des Castes dans l'ancienne Egypte," in the *Revue des Deux Mondes*, Sept. 1848.

Monogamy.

The high position occupied in ancient Egypt by the mother of the family, the "mistress of the house," is absolutely irreconcilable with the existence either of polygamy as a general practice, or of such an institution as the *harîm*. The plurality of wives does not appear to have been contrary to law, but it certainly was unusual. A few of the Egyptian kings had a large number of wives, but they appear in this respect to have followed foreign rather than native custom. The use of the word *harem* in the translation of hieroglyphic texts tends to produce an entirely erroneous conception of ancient Egyptian society. The word itself is harmless; but (to say the least) it confounds Egyptian with utterly foreign ideas, Arabian or Turkish; and when it is used to signify an establishment of concubines, I believe the translator has entirely misunderstood the Egyptian text.[1]

---

[1] Many excellent scholars have used "harem" as the translation of the Egyptian word χ*ent*. The most important passage which would justify this rendering is on the tablet of Pa-shere-en-Ptah. It is thus translated in Brugsch's Hieroglyphic Lexicon, p. 1093: "Es waren mir schöne Weiber, doch war ich bereits 43 Jahr alt ohne dass mir ein männliches Kind geboren war." I believe the passage is better understood if taken in connection with the corresponding passage on the tablet of the *wife* of Pa-shere-en-Ptah (Sharpe, "Egyptian Inscriptions," Vol. I. pl. 4). This lady says of her husband: "I had not borne to him a male child, but *daughters* only." He therefore means to say: "I had handsome *girls*, but I was already forty-three years old before a *boy* was born to me." The German "Frauenzimmer," if put into hieroglyphic orthography, would admit of the very determinative sign which leads to the notion of "shutting up."

THE GODS OF EGYPT.

Identity of the Religious Institutions from First to Last.

IT was quite unnecessary for the purpose of these Lectures that the sketch of Egyptian civilization which I laid before you in the last Lecture should be completed or filled up in detail. But in studying the phenomena which a religion presents, it is indispensable that we should understand certain conditions accompanying those phenomena. Men's thoughts are forced into certain channels and assume definite forms according to the nature of their occupations. It is not a matter of indifference whether we have to do with people in what is called the hunting stage, nomadic populations, agriculturalists or merchants; with men of hot or of cold climates; with savages or with men in the most advanced stages of culture. The religions and mythologies of such peoples differ very widely. Even among those professing the same religion, great differences must necessarily be found between men of highly educated and cultivated minds, and unpolished

THE GODS OF EGYPT. 81

men insensible to art or poetry of a high order. Now it is certain that at least three thousand years before Christ there was in Egypt a powerful and elaborately organized monarchy, enjoying a material civilization in many respects not inferior to that of Europe in the last century. Centuries must have elapsed before such a civilization became possible. Of a state of barbarism or even of patriarchal life anterior to the monumental period, there is no historical vestige. The earliest monuments which have been discovered present to us the very same fully developed civilization and the same religion as the later monuments. The blocks of the Pyramids bear quarry marks exhibiting the decimal notation, and are dated by the months of the calendar which was in use down to the latest times. You must remember that the calendars of other nations (Hebrews, Greeks and Romans) show great ignorance of the real length of the year. It was only after the conquest of Alexandria that the Roman calendar was reformed by Julius Cæsar. The political division into nomes (provinces, each of which had its principal deity) is as old as the age of the Pyramids. The gods whose names appear in the oldest tombs were worshipped down to the Christian times. The same kinds of priesthoods which are mentioned in the tablets of Canopus and Rosetta in the Ptolemaic period are as ancient as the Pyramids, and more ancient than any Pyramid of which we know the date. There is in the Ashmolean Museum at Oxford the monument of a man whose priestly office had been endowed by a king of the second dynasty. Excellent scholars like Dr. Hincks and Mr. Goodwin have ascribed the monument to this early date, and have considered it the most ancient of all dated monuments. This indeed cannot be proved; but there is no doubt whatever that it is the most ancient authentic monument recording a religious endowment.

Temples.

No temples of the ancient empire are extant at present, except perhaps the monument discovered some years ago in the neighbourhood of the great Sphinx; but no one can say whether this is a temple or a tomb. But this want of early temples is certainly owing to the destruction of the most ancient cities, like Memphis and Heliopolis. There is no reason for doubting the inscription first published by M. de Rougé, which says that Chufu or Cheops built his pyramid near a temple of Isis, and that he built or endowed a temple to Hathor; or the inscriptions at Dendera, which ascribe the restoration of its ancient temple to Tehutimes III., "according to the plan found in ancient writings of the time of king Chufu." There is every reason for believing that in the ancient empire great and splendid temples were built. But we must not take for granted that temples at this early period were places of worship in our modern sense of the term. At no period of the

Egyptian religion were the public admitted to the temples as worshippers. All the temples we know were royal offerings made to the divinity of the locality, and none but the priestly personages attached to the temple itself had free access to its precincts. But the image of the god and those of the divinities associated with him were often brought out in solemn processions, in which the entire population took part.

Triads and Enneads.

In the principal temple of each province, the chief deity was associated with other gods; hence the expression θεοι συνναοι of the Greek inscriptions; hence from an early period triads (consisting of the principal god, a female deity and their offspring), or enneads, consisting of nine gods. Thus at Thebes the triad consisted of Amon, Mut and Chonsu; at Abydos, of Osiris, Isis and Horus. No special importance was attached by the Egyptians to the number *three*, and it is a mistake to look for triads everywhere, for the number of gods varied according to the place; the number *nine* was much more frequent, and this is often nothing more than a round number, signifying either the gods of a locality or the entire Pantheon.

Local Character of Egyptian Worship.

As each deity was connected with some locality, his name was generally followed by a phrase indicating this relationship. A deity was said to be Lord of Abydos, mistress of Senem, presiding in Thebes, inhabiting Hermopolis; sometimes a particle was interposed between the name of the god and that of the town, as "Anubis from Sechem," "Neith of Sais;" sometimes one or more epithets were added, as "the mighty," "the beneficent," "the august;" sometimes the name of an animal which was the recognized symbol of the god, a bull, a ram or a lion. Special titles were given to divinities according to the place in which they were worshipped: Osiris, for instance, was called *che*, "the child," at Thebes; he was *ura*, "the great one," at Heliopolis; *ati*, "the sovereign," at Memphis. It happened frequently that in the same town one god was worshipped under different aspects, or as proceeding from different localities, and treated as though there were different divine persons of the same name. Chonsu in Thebes, under the name *nefer-hotep*, is entreated to lend his miraculous power to Chonsu in Thebes under the name *ari secher*. We read of Set the god of Senu, Set of Uau, Set of Un and Set of Meru. Other forms of Set are well known, but those I have cited are brought together in one inscription as children of the god Tmu. I find invocations in a very early inscription addressed to the Anubis of six different localities. Apis is the son of Ptah, of Tmu, of Osiris and of Sokari. Are all these fathers of Apis one person? Horus is the son of the goddess Isis, but he is also the son of the goddess Hathor. Isis must then be the same as Hathor, unless mythology is proof against logic. Let us admit this, and also that Seb, the father of Isis, is identical with Rā, the father of Hathor; but what shall we say on being told that Horus was born in Tattu (the Mendes of the Greeks), and also that he was born in Cheb? Geographical localities do not so easily lend themselves to identification. In a well-known text, Horus is called the son of Isis and Osiris, but shortly afterwards Seb is named as his father. Students of mythology will not be astonished or scandalized if they discover that Osiris is at once the father, brother, husband and son of Isis, and also the son of their child Horus. They will read a text on the alabaster sarcophagus of Seti I., now in the Soane Museum, which speaks of "the son who proceeds from the father, and the father who proceeds from his son," and if their studies are rightly conducted, the mystery will not be hard to understand.

The Deities Innumerable.

The Egyptian deities are innumerable. There were countless gods in heaven and below the earth. Every town and village had its local patrons. Every month of the year, every day of the month, every hour of the day and of the night, had its presiding divinity, and all these gods had to be propitiated by offerings. I several times made the attempt to draw up an index of the divine names occurring in the texts, but found it necessary to abandon the enterprize. What can all these gods mean?

Mean Notions concerning these Deities.

Nothing can be more clear than that under the name of God the Egyptians did not understand, as we do, a being without body, parts or passions. The bodies of the gods are spoken of as well as their souls, and they have both parts and passions; they are described as suffering from hunger and thirst, old age, disease, fear and sorrow. They perspire, their limbs quake, their head aches, their teeth chatter, their eyes weep, their nose bleeds, "poison takes possession of their flesh, even as the Nile takes possession of the land." They may be stung by reptiles and burnt by fire. They shriek and howl with pain and grief. All the great gods require protection. Osiris is helpless against his enemies, and his remains are protected by his wife and sister. Hathor extends her wings as a protection over the victorious Horus, or, as one form of the legend expresses it, "she protects him with her body as a divine cow;" yet Hathor in her turn needs protection, and even the sun-god Râ, though invested with the predicates of supreme divinity, requires the aid of the goddess Isis. All the gods are liable to be forced to grant the prayers of men, through fear of threats which it is inconceivable to us that any intelligence but that of idiots should have believed. There are many aspects of this religion, and some of them are extremely ridiculous. The very impulse, however, which prompts us to laugh at the religion of our fellow-men, ought to suggest a doubt whether we have really caught their meaning.

Simplification of the List.

We are tempted, in our bewilderment at the number of the gods, to ask whether the process of reduction is not applicable to them as well as that of multiplication. And we discover to our relief that such a process is actually suggested to us by documents of indisputable authority, which show that the same god is often known under many names. In the Litanies of the god Rā, which are inscribed on the walls of the royal tombs at Bibān-el-molūk, the god is invoked under seventy-five different names. A monument published in Burton's *Excerpta Hieroglyphica* gives the names, or rather a selection of the names, of Ptah, the principal god of Memphis. The Book of the Dead has a chapter entirely consisting of the names of Osiris. The inscriptions of the temple of Dendera give a long list of the names of the goddess Hathor. She is identified not only with Isis, but with Sechet at Memphis, Neith at Sais, Saosis at Heliopolis, Nehemauit at Hermopolis,

Bast at Bubastis, Sothis at Elephantine, and many other goddesses. These authorities alone are sufficient, almost at a glance, to convince us that not only are some inferior deities mere aspects of the greater gods, but that several at least of the greater gods themselves are but different aspects of one and the same.

Lepsius, in his Dissertation on the gods of the first order, has published several lists of these divinities taken from monuments of different periods, the most ancient list being taken from an altar of the sixth dynasty. On comparing these lists together, it is again plain that Mentu and Tmu, two of the great gods of Thebes, are merely aspects of the sun-god Rā. The entire list of the gods of the first order is easily reduced to two groups; the first representing the sun-god Rā and his family, and the second Osiris and his family. It is most probable that neither Ptah nor Amon were originally at the head of lists, but obtained their places as being chief divinities of the capitals Memphis and Thebes. Both these gods are identified with the sun-god Rā, and so indeed are all the chief local divinities. The whole mythology of Egypt may be said to turn upon the histories of Rā and Osiris, and these histories run into each other, sometimes in inextricable confusion, which ceases to be wonderful when texts are discovered which simply identify Osiris and Rā. And, finally, other texts are known wherein Rā, Osiris, Amon and all the other gods disappear, except as simple *names*, and the unity of God is asserted in the noblest language of monotheistic religion. There are many very eminent scholars who, with full knowledge of all that can be said to the contrary, maintain that the Egyptian religion is essentially monotheistic, and that the multiplicity of gods is only due to the personification of "the attributes, characters and offices of the supreme God."

Is the Religion really Monotheistic?

No scholar is better entitled to be heard on this subject than the late M. Emmanuel de Rougé, whose matured judgment is as follows:[1]

"No one has called in question the fundamental meaning of the principal passages by the help of which we are able to establish what ancient Egypt has taught concerning God, the world and man. I said *God*, not *the gods*. The first characteristic of the religion is the Unity [of God] most energetically expressed: God, One, Sole and Only; no others with Him.—He is the Only Being—living in truth.—Thou art One, and millions of beings proceed from thee.—He has made everything, and he alone has not been made. The clearest, the simplest, the most precise conception.

---

[1] "Conférence sur la religion des anciens Egyptiens, prononcée au Cercle Catholique, 14 avril, 1869," published in the *Annales de la Philosophie Chrétienne*, tome XX. p. 327.

"But how reconcile the Unity of God with Egyptian Polytheism? History and geography will perhaps elucidate the matter. The Egyptian religion comprehends a quantity of local worships. The Egypt which Menes brought together entire under his sceptre was divided into nomes, each having a capital town; each of these regions has its principal god designed by a special name; but it is always the same doctrine which re-appears under different names. One idea predominates, that of a single and primeval God; everywhere and always it is One Substance, self-existent, and an unapproachable God."

M. de Rougé then says that from, or rather before, the beginning of the historical period, the pure monotheistic religion passed through the phase of Sabeism; the Sun, instead of being considered as the symbol of life, was taken as the manifestation of God Himself. The second characteristic of the religion was "a mystery which does honour to the theological intellect of the Egyptians. God is self-existent; he is the only being who has not been begotten; hence the idea of considering God under two aspects, the Father and the Son. In most of the hymns we come across this idea of the Double Being who engendereth Himself, the Soul in two Twins—to signify two Persons never to be separated. A hymn of the Leyden Museum . . . . calls him 'the One of One.'

"Are these noble doctrines then the result of centuries? Certainly not; for they were in existence more than two thousand years before the Christian era. On the other hand, Polytheism, the sources of which we have pointed out, developes itself and progresses without interruption until the time of the Ptolemies. It is, therefore, more than five thousand years since, in the valley of the Nile, the hymn began to the Unity of God and the immortality of the soul, and we find Egypt in the last ages arrived at the most unbridled Polytheism. The belief in the Unity of the Supreme God and in his attributes as Creator and Lawgiver of man, whom he has endowed with an immortal soul—these are the primitive notions, enchased, like indestructible diamonds, in the midst of the mythological superfetations accumulated in the centuries which have passed over that ancient civilization."

Although some of the texts here alluded to have most probably a somewhat different meaning from that which M. de Rougé ascribes to them, the facts upon which he relies are in the main unassailable. It is incontestably true that the sublimer portions of the Egyptian religion are not the comparatively late result of a process of development or elimination from the grosser. The sublimer portions are demonstrably ancient; and the last stage of the Egyptian religion, that known to the Greek and Latin writers, heathen or Christian, was by far the grossest and most corrupt. M. de Rougé is no doubt correct in his assertion that in the several local worships one and the same doctrine re-appears under different names and symbols. But he does not venture to assert that at any time within the historical period the worship of one God was anywhere practised to the exclusion of a plurality of gods. He only infers from the course of history that, as polytheism was constantly on the increase, the monotheistic doctrines must have preceded it. Another conclusion, however, is suggested by the Egyptian texts to which he refers. The polytheistic and the so-called monotheistic doctrines constantly appear together in one context; not only in the sacred writings handed down by tradition, and subjected to interpolations and corruptions of every kind, but even more frequently in literary compositions of a private nature, where no one would dream of suspecting interpolation. Throughout the whole range of Egyptian literature, no facts appear to be more certainly proved than these: (1) that the doctrine of one God and that of many gods were taught by the same men; (2) that no inconsistency between the two doctrines was thought of. Nothing, of course, can be more absurd if the Egyptians attached the same meaning to the word God that we do. But there may perhaps be a sense of the word which admits of its use for many as well as for one. We cannot do better at starting than endeavour to ascertain what the Egyptians really meant when they used the word *nutar*, which we translate "god."

Evidence as to the Meaning of the word Nutar.

At first sight, the Egyptian language is less likely to throw light upon the subject than might be expected if it really belonged to the same stage of speech as either the Indo-European or the Semitic languages. In these languages almost every word is closely allied to several others connected together by derivation from a common root, and the primitive notion conveyed by the word in question can be illustrated by the signification of the kindred words and their root. Generally speaking, however, in Egyptian every word is isolated. There is no distinction between word, stem and root. The same Egyptian word may sometimes have different significations; but this, as a rule, only means that the one notion which is expressed by a word in Egyptian has no single word corresponding to it in English, French or German. It seldom happens that we can advance a step beyond such a fact as that the word *nutar* is rightly translated "god." I am glad, however, to be able to affirm with certainty that in this particular case we can accurately determine the primitive notion attached to the word. None of the explanations hitherto given of it can be considered satisfactory. That which I am about to propose will, I believe, be generally accepted by scholars, because it is arrived at as the result of a special study of all the published passages in which the word occurs. Such a study, as far as I am aware, has not yet been made, but if made by any other person it must necessarily lead to the same result.

The old Egyptian word *nutar* had already in the popular pronunciation suffered from phonetic decay, and lost its final consonant as early as the nineteenth dynasty, as we see by the inscriptions in the royal tombs at Bibān-el-molūk,[1] and it appears in Coptic under the forms *nuti*, *nute*. It is remarkable that the translators of the Bible into Coptic, who generally abstained from the use of old Egyptian words connected with religion, and used Greek words instead, nevertheless adopted this one as expressive of their notion of God.

There is another word, *nutra*, very frequently used either as verb or adjective, which is closely allied to *nutar*. The sense of "renovation" was first attached to it by M. E. de Rougé, on the strength of its final sign, which he considered as a determinative of signification. But this conjecture, which has been very generally accepted, is really without any solid foundation; the sign in question is here expressive of nothing more than the sound *tra*, and it will be found appended to all

---

[1] *Zeitschr. f. Aegypt. Spr.* 1874, p. 105, and M. Maspero's article in the *Mélanges d'Archéologie*, 1874, p. 140. The orthography of these popular forms is philologically of the highest importance. The form *nuntar* I reserved for a future study; M. Maspero published it with the rest, but no one appears to have noticed it.

words so ending, whatever be their meaning; as *hetra*, whether signifying "join," "horse," or "tribute;" *petra*, "behold;" *tra*, "season." Another more obvious sense, "sacred," "divine," may be justified by the Greek text of the tablet of Canopus, where *nutra* is translated ἱερὸς, as applied to the sacred animals. But this meaning, though a certain one, occurs but seldom in the Egyptian texts, and when it so occurs is, after all, only a derived meaning, as is in fact the case with the Greek ἱερὸς, the first sense of which is "strong," "vigorous."[1] The notion expressed by *nutar* as a noun, and *nutra* as an adjective and verb, must be sought in the Coptic *nomti*, which in the translation of the Bible corresponds to the Greek words δύναμις, ἰσχύς, ἰσχυρὸς, ἰσχυρόω, "power," "force," "strong," "fortify," "protect."[2]

The reason why the identification of the old form *nutar* with the more recent *nomti* as well as *nuti* has

---

[1] Ἱερός corresponds to the Sanskrit *ish-ira-s*, vigorous, from *ish*, juice, strength. See Curtius, *Zeitschr. für vergleichende Sprachforschung*, III. 154, and his "Griechische Etymologie," p. 372. Plutarch (Mor. 981 D) mentions this original physical sense of the word as maintained by certain persons, and the ὀστοῦν ἱερὸν, "os sacrum," is given as an example. Ἱερὰ νόσος, also called μεγάλη, is another striking instance. In the Homeric poems, this physical sense gives the true force to such expressions as Τροίης ἱερὸν πτολίεθρον, ἱερὴν πόλιν Ἠετίωνος, ἱερῷ ἔνι δίφρῳ, ἱερὸν μένος Ἀλκινόοιο, ἱερὴ ἲς Τηλεμάχοιο.

[2] The Alexandrians invented the barbarous word δυναμόω, which can always be used as a translation of the verb *nutra*.

hitherto escaped observation is, that the connecting link *nuntar* has either been unknown to scholars or disregarded by them. In *nuntar*, a process as well known to Egyptian as to Indo-European scholars has taken place.[1] The vowel of the first syllable has been strengthened by the addition of a nasal consonant. The old Egyptian word *heket* (beer) has by this process become *henke* in the Thebaic, and *hemki* in the Memphitic dialect.

The following examples will illustrate the usage of the word.

Large stones are often said to be *nutru*. This does not mean that they *grow* or that they are *divine*, but that they are *mighty*. In one of those paraphrases which are so common on the walls of Dendera, the unequivocal word *uru*, "great, mighty," is substituted for *nutru*.[2] *Sauit nutrit* is a "strong wall." A crypt is *aat nutrit*, a "strong-hold." *Three* of the chambers

---

[1] The change of *n* into *m* before *t*, as though the latter were preceded by a labial consonant, is not usual, but it is not without a parallel in other languages. Cf. χρίμπτω from root χρι, the Latin *tempto* and the Lithuanian *temptyva*, both the latter from root *ta*, nasalized *tan*. The observations of Curtius, "Gr. Et.," pp. 46 and 481, on the *m* in γαμεῖν and the Lithuanian *gim-ti*, appear to me to justify the form *tempto*, which Corssen rejects, though it occurs in the best manuscripts as well as inscriptions.

[2] Mariette, *Dendera*, I. pl. 67. So in the royal titles of the eighteenth dynasty, *nutra sutenit* of Tehutimes II. corresponds to the *uah sutenit* of Tehutimes III. and to the simpler *ur sutenit* of Chut en Aten.

of the temple of Dendera are said to be *nutru*. "Qu'est ce qu'une salle divine?" very pertinently asks M. Mariette. *Sat nutrit* is a "potent talisman." Seti I. in his titles is the "potent image," *sexem nutra*, of Chepera. *Nutra* is constantly brought into *parallelism* with words implying "might." "Great (*ura*) is the Eye of Horus, Mighty (*āu*) is the Eye of Horus, Strong (*nutra*) is the Eye of Horus, the Giver of Strength (*senutra*) is the Eye of Horus."[1] "A mighty wall to Egypt, protecting their limbs; his force (*pehti*) is like Ptah in prostrating the barbarians, a child of might (*sif nutra*) in his coming forth like Harmachis."[2] "He is strong (*ten-re*) in performing his duties to Amon-Rā, he is vigorous (*nutra*) in performing his duties to the sovereign, his lord." In the demotic text of the tablet of Canopus, *nutra* is translated by χu, which signifies, "strengthen, fortify, protect, invigorate." It has constantly this meaning in the hieroglyphic texts. "Thy body is fortified (*nutri-ta*), protected (χu-ta), restored (*sput-ta*)."[3] "Thy limbs are fortified (*nutri-ta*) by the Power (*sexem*) which is in heaven."[4] *Nutra men ma pet*, "strong and durable as heaven." *Nutra-f nut-ek er neken*, "He fortifies thy city against destruction." *Nutra-f Nutrit er nefu*, "He strengthens

---

[1] Sharpe, "Egyptian Inscriptions," Vol. II. p. 28.
[2] Duemichen, *Historische Inschr.* Vol. II. pp. 46, 12.
[3] J. de Rougé, *Inscriptions*, Vol. I. pl. 25.
[4] Sharpe, Vol. II. p. 92.

Nutrit against harm."[1] *Nutrit*, the name of a town (in this place equivalent to Dendera), has exactly the same meaning as Samaria, Ashdod, Gaza, Valentia, and many other names significant of strength. Religious purifications were supposed to give strength, and the verb *nutra* is therefore often found in parallelism with *āb* and *tur*, both of which have the sense of religious purification.

I will add one more illustration, which by itself might not be of much weight, but is really important when taken in conjunction with other evidence. The goddess Isis is distinguished among other divinities by the frequent epithet *nutrit*. When the inscriptions in her honour are written in Greek, she is most frequently called μεγάλη or μεγίστη.

There is yet another Egyptian word cognate to those we have been studying. *Nutrit* signifies "eye-ball." The notion here is of something fortified, protected, guarded. "Custodi me ut pupillam oculi:" "Keep me as the apple of the eye." The Arabic word *hadaqat*, which means the same thing, has an exactly similar etymology. And several other parallel instances might be cited.

The Egyptian *nutar*, I argue therefore, means Power, which is also the meaning of the Hebrew El. The

---

[1] Many of the examples occur in Mariette's *Dendera*, Vol. I. pl. 6, 46.

extremely common Egyptian expression *nutar nutra*[1] exactly corresponds in sense to the Hebrew *El Shaddai*, the very title by which God tells Moses that He was known to Abraham and Isaac and Jacob. "And God spake unto Moses, and said unto him, 'I am Jahve: and I appeared unto Abraham, unto Isaac and unto Jacob by *the name of* El Shaddai, but by my name Jahve was I not known to them.'" *Nutar nutra amtu heret* is "the Almighty Power which is in heaven." It is very remarkable that "Brahman in Sanskrit meant originally Power, the same as El. It resisted for a long time the mythological contagion, but at last it yielded like all other names of God, and became the name of one God."[2] But the Egyptian *nutar* never became a proper name. It was indeed restricted in its use, as far back as our knowledge of the language enables us to trace it, but it never ceased to be a common noun, and was applied indifferently to each of the powers which the Egyptian imagination conceived as active in the universe, and to the Power from which all powers proceed. Horus and Rā and Osiris and Set are names of individual finite powers, but a Power

---

[1] M. de Rougé, *Chrestomathie*, Fasc. iii. p. 25, translates this, "dieu devenant dieu," and says in a note, "On ne sait pas au juste le sens du verbe *nuter*, qui forme le radical du mot *nuter*, 'dieu.' C'est une idée analogue à 'devenir,' ou 'se renouveler,' car *nuteri* est appliquée à l'âme resuscitée qui revet sa forme immortelle."

[2] M. Müller, "Chips," Vol. I. p. 363.

without a name or any mythological characteristic is constantly referred to in the singular number, and can only be regarded as the object of that "sensus numinis," or immediate perception of the Infinite, which, like my learned predecessor Professor Max Müller, I consider "not the result of reasoning or generalizing, but an intuition as irresistible as the impressions of our senses."[1] The following instances are taken from the moral writings of which I spoke in the last Lecture.

The Power.

1. The Maxims of Ptahhotep.

They speak of "God forbidding" and "God commanding."

"The field which the great God hath given thee to till."

"If any one beareth himself proudly, he will be humbled by God, who maketh his strength."

"If thou art a wise man, bring up thy son in the love of God."

"The magnanimous man is the object of God's regard, but he who listens to his belly is scorned by his own wife."

"Thy treasure has grown to thee through the gift of God."

---

[1] "Science of Language," Second Series, p. 479, 7th ed.

"God loveth the obedient and hateth the disobedient."

A good son is spoken of as "the gift of God."

2. A papyrus of Leyden.[1]

"Happy is the man who eateth his own bread. Possess what thou hast in the joy of thy heart. What thou hast not, obtain it by work. It is profitable for a man to eat his own bread; God grants this to whosoever honours Him."

3. A papyrus at St. Petersburg.[2]

"Praised be God for all His gifts."

"God knows the wicked; He smites the wicked, even to blood."

4. The Maxims of Ani.[3]

"Whoso acts, God will raise his name above the sensual man."

"The sanctuary of God abhors [noisy manifesta-

---

[1] Published in Leemans' *Monuments Egyptiens du Musée de Leide*, Pap. i. p. 344, i.—vi. An account of it is given in Dr. Lauth's "Altägyptische Lehrsprüche," in the *Transactions of the Academy of Munich*, July, 1872.

[2] This is described by Dr. Golenischeff in Lepsius' *Zeitschrift*, 1876, p. 107.

[3] This very interesting book, published with the other papyri of Bulaq by M. Mariette, has been described by Brugsch-Bey in the *Zeitschrift*, 1872, and has been translated by M. E. de Rougé and M. Chabas. The version of the latter scholar is the most careful and exact, all the difficulties of the text being minutely considered and discussed. It occupies the greater part of the scientific journal *l'Egyptologie*, entirely written by M. Chabas.

tions?]. Pray humbly with a loving heart all the words of which are uttered in secret. He will protect thee in thine affairs; He will listen to thy words; He will accept thine offerings."

"In making thine oblation to God, beware of what He abhors. .... Exaggerate not the liturgical prescriptions; it is forbidden to give more than what is prescribed. Let thine eyes consider the acts of His wrath. Thou shalt make adorations in His name. It is He who granteth genius with endless aptitudes; who magnifieth him who becometh great. The God of the world is in the light above the firmament; His emblems are upon earth; it is to them that worship is rendered daily."

Another section is upon maternal affection. It describes the self-sacrifice of an affectionate mother from the earliest moments of the child's existence, and continues as follows: "Thou wast put to school, and whilst thou wast being taught letters she came punctually to thy master, bringing thee the bread and the drink of her house. Thou art now come to man's estate; thou art married and hast a house; but never do thou forget the painful labour which thy mother endured, nor all the salutary care which she has taken of thee. Take heed lest she have cause to complain of thee, for fear that she should raise her hands to God and He should listen to her prayer."

"Give thyself to God, keep thyself continually for

God, and let to-morrow be like to-day. Let thine eyes consider the acts of God; it is He who smiteth him that is smitten."

5. The author of the Maxims contained in the demotic papyrus of the Louvre.

"Curse not thy master before God."

It was in this style that in all periods of their history, in the earliest not less confidently than in the latest, the Egyptians spoke of the *Nutar* in the singular number. There can, I trust, be no doubt who that Power is which, in our translations, we do not hesitate to call God. It is unquestionably the true and only God, who "is not far from any one of us, for in Him we live and move and have our being," whose "eternal power and Godhead" and government of the world were made known through "that Light which enlighteneth every man that cometh into the world." In the extracts which I have quoted, and in many similar passages, we recognize the elements of true religion, free from all admixture of mythology. But if such be the Power, what are the "powers" (*nutriu*), and what are their relations to it?

The Powers.

In the formation of a theory of the universe, the notion of Power productive of results may, according as it is defined, lead to very different consequences. It may be conceived very much in the same sense as a

Cause, and lead, as the notion of Cause will always lead reflecting men, in spite of the protests of critical philosophers, to the admission of One First Cause or Power from which all others are derived. But, as we know equally well from the history of speculation, the notions of Power and Substance may be identified, and it is easy to imagine one universal Force in nature, in itself eternal and unchangeable, but manifesting itself in the most different forms. In both cases the result is Unity; Theistic in the first case, Pantheistic in the second. I shall have occasion to speak of the complete and final triumph of the latter of these conceptions. But the triumph did not take place till a comparatively late period, and till then the Egyptian religion may be considered as susceptible of either a Theistic or a Pantheistic interpretation. In either case the gods of the mythology represent the real or imaginary powers of the universe; and what these powers were in the most primitive conception entertained of them by the Egyptians, can only be discovered by the same scientific process which has been applied with such success to the mythology of the Indo-European races.

Myth and Legend.

The most common opinion held by the best scholars only a few years ago was, that however many gods the Egyptians might have, they had no mythology properly speaking. The only myth they were supposed to possess was that about Osiris, and even this was imagined to have been brought into shape through Hellenic influences. This opinion is altogether an erroneous one: it confuses the notion of myth with that of mythological tale or legend; and whilst the Egyptians really had an abundance of legendary tales, their myths are simply innumerable. The tale of Osiris is as old as Egyptian civilization itself; that is, very much more than two thousand years before Hellenic influences came into operation.

Several mythological tales of considerable extent are now well known to us. The legend of the revolt of the first men against the god Rā and his destruction of them was discovered by M. Naville in one of the tombs at Bibān-el-molūk. A long narrative of the victories of Horus was copied by the same accomplished scholar from the walls of the temple at Edfu. It is written in the style of the heroic annals of the kings of Egypt, and accounts for the names of geographical localities by the exploits of the divine warrior. The tale of Osiris, as told in the Greek work attributed to Plutarch, is made up out of several genuine Egyptian legends, and the wanderings of the widowed Isis formed the subject of many legendary narratives. But the religious texts are literally crowded with allusions to mythological legends, and these allusions, though they are necessarily obscure to us, must have been familiar to the Egyptians.

The mythological legend grew out of the myth, but must not be confounded with it. The myth was in Egypt, what it was everywhere else, a mere phrase, often consisting of not more than a single word, descriptive of some natural phenomenon, such as the rising or setting of the sun, the struggle between light and darkness, and the alternate victory of the one or the other. The science of Language has established the fact that all names were general terms; and one of the most eminent masters of the science[1] begins a work on "Proper Names" by laying it down as a first principle that for the etymologist there are *no* such things as "proper names," but only "appellatives." These appellatives, when applied to natural phenomena, are either such predicates as the most prosaic observer might use at the present day, or they are metaphorical. An early stage of language is always highly metaphorical, its terms being derived from sensuous perception, and being ill adapted to express abstract ideas. Many roots were required to express the different stages or determinations of a single notion. Even in reference to so simple a notion as that expressed by the verb *to see*, the Greeks had recourse to no less than three roots (in ὁράω, ὄψομαι, εἶδον), according as the action was considered as continued, completed or momentary. We ourselves say *I go*, but *I went;* je vais, nous allons,

---

[1] Pott, "Die Personennamen."

j'irai. As the motives for applying an appellative to a phenomenon are many, it is evident that many myths may refer to the same phenomenon under different names. And every myth which involves a metaphor naturally suggests a legend, which in its turn is susceptible of an indefinite amount of development in the hands of poets or other mythographers, long after the primitive meaning of the myth has been forgotten.

It is therefore only through a radical misconception of the nature of a myth that attempts can be made to discover a consistent system in the mythology of any country. One myth was originally quite independent of every other.

Another serious mistake is to suppose that all the details of a mythological legend are of equal importance. The Psalmist speaks of a tabernacle in the heavens set for the sun, whom he compares to "a bridegroom coming out of his chamber, and rejoicing as a strong man to run a race." Call the sun the Bridegroom or the Racer (and he is so named in several mythologies), and a series of images will at once be suggested correlative to each of these names, and adventures will be invented to suit them. But these details are no real part of the myth, and frequently conceal its true meaning. One of the chief difficulties in dealing with a myth lies in distinguishing the essential from the non-essential portions of the legend to which it has given rise.

On the other hand, the moment we understand the nature of a myth, all impossibilities, contradictions and immoralities disappear. If a mythical personage really be nothing more than a name of the sun, his birth may be derived from ever so many different mothers. He may be the son of the Sky or of the Dawn or of the Sea or of Night. He may be identical with other mythical personages which are also names of the sun, and yet be absolutely different from them, as the midday sun differs from the rising and from the setting sun, or the sun of to-day from that of yesterday. He may be the husband of his own mother without the guilt or stain of incest. All myths are strictly true, but they can only be harmonized when translated into the language of physical reality.

All phenomena which attracted sufficient attention furnished matter for myths. It had been remarked, for instance, that certain stars never set, whereas all others, after performing their course, sink below the horizon. The Egyptians expressed this by the myth of the Crocodile of the West which fed upon the Achmu Uretu (the setting stars).[1] Thunder and lightning, storm and wind and cloud and rain, were no doubt duly personified, but they occupy a very small part of the mythology, which is almost exclusively

---

[1] Todt. 32, 2. The translation of *aχmu uretu* by "restless" is inadmissible. See M. Chabas, "Papyrus Magique," p. 84. We have nothing here to do with planets and fixed stars.

concerned with the regularly and perpetually recurring phenomena. Whatever may be the case in other mythologies, "I look upon the sunrise and sunset, on the daily return of day and night, on the battle between light and darkness, on the whole solar drama in all its details, that is acted every day, every month, every year, in heaven and in earth, as the principal subject"[1] of Egyptian mythology.

Ra and his Family.

There can be no controversy about the meaning of Rā. Rā is not only the name of the sun-god, it is the usual word for sun. In other mythologies the sun-god is borne on a chariot or on horseback; in Egypt, his course across the sky is made in a boat. The sky (*Nu*) is accordingly conceived as an expanse of water, of which the Nile is the earthly representative. Rā is said to proceed from "Nu, the father of the gods."[2] His adversary is Apepi, who is represented as a serpent pierced with the weapons of the god. The conflict is not between good and evil, but the purely physical one between light and darkness. Shu and Tefnut are the children of Rā; Shu is Air, and Tefnut is some form of moisture, probably Dew.[3]

---

[1] Max Müller, "Science of Language," Second Series, p. 565.

[2] In the legend of the Destruction of Mankind, Rā calls before him Shu, Tefnut, Seb, Nut, and the fathers and mothers who were with him when he was still in Nu.

[3] See Preface.

Osiris and his Family.

The myth of Osiris, though much more elaborate, has the same meaning. Osiris is the eldest of the five children of Seb and Nut. "He is greater than his father, and more powerful than his mother." He wedded his sister Isis whilst they were yet in their mother's womb, and their offspring was the elder Horus. Set and Nephthys, another wedded pair, are their brother and sister. In this myth the antagonist of Osiris is Set, by whom he is slain, but he is avenged by his son Horus, and he reigns in the nether world, like the Indian Yama, and judges the dead from his throne in the hall of the Two-fold Right. And this he does daily.

The explanation of this myth exercised the imaginations of the ancients. The priests and poets of the eighteenth and nineteenth dynasties already identified Osiris with the highest of all Powers. In later times, as we see from the treatise ascribed to Plutarch, he was identified with various abstract "principles." By the help of the light which comparative mythology supplies, we are enabled to arrive at a truer sense of the myth.

The parents of Osiris are Seb and Nut, and about these there can be no mistake. Seb is the Earth, and Nut is Heaven. Seb is identified with the Earth in the older texts, and in the later ones "the back of

Seb" is a familiar term for the earth. Seb is also the Egyptian name for a certain species of goose, and in accordance with the *homonymous* tendency of the mythological period of all nations, the god and the bird were identified; Seb was called "the great cackler," and there are traces of the myth of a "mundane egg" which he "divided" or hatched. Nut is the name of a female goddess,[1] frequently used synonymously with the other names of the sky, and she is as frequently pictured with her arms and legs extended over the earth, with the stars spread over her body. The marriage of Heaven and Earth is extremely common in mythologies; what is peculiar to the Egyptian myth is that Earth is not represented as the Mother of all things, Θεῶν μήτηρ, ἄλοχ' Οὐρανοῦ ἀστερόεντος, but the Father,[2] and Heaven is here the Mother; though, as we have seen in speaking of Rā, Heaven was also conceived as a male power, like the Indian Varuna and the Greek Uranos. From the union of Seb and Nut sprung the mild Osiris, the Sun, and Isis, the Dawn, wedded before they were born, and the fruit of their marriage

---

[1] In the legend of the Destruction of Mankind, Nu and Nut address each other as father and daughter. But in the Book of the Dead, 42, 20, Unbu (one of the names of Osiris) issues from Nu, his mother being Nut.

[2] There is indeed a passage (Duemichen, *Hist. Inschr.* II. 44 e) in which Seb seems to be called the *mother* of Osiris. But as the words are immediately followed by "whom Nut brought forth," I suspect an error in the text.

was Horus, the Sun in his full strength. Set the destroyer is also the son of Seb and Nut, but his triumph is in the west; he is Darkness, and his spouse Nephthys, a deity of mixed character, is the Sunset. There are the traces of a legend according to which Osiris mistook Nephthys for his wife Isis. Nephthys, who loved him, encouraged the illusion, and from their embraces Anpu (Anubis) was born. Anubis, like his mother, is a deity of a mixed character, partly belonging to the diurnal, partly to the nocturnal powers. It is said of him that "he swallowed his father Osiris." I believe that he represents the Twilight or Dusk immediately following the disappearance of the sun.

I am quite aware that texts may be quoted to prove that Osiris is the Moon, but these texts belong to a pantheistic period in which the god was recognized under all forms.[1] It might rather be doubted whether the story of Osiris had not reference to the annual rather than to the daily sun. His death might be supposed to represent the reign of winter. Some of the Egyptian usages in commemoration of his death and resurrection, such as the sowing of plants and watching their growth, might be cited in support of this view. But the closer we look at these matters of

---

[1] A hymn at Dendera says: "Hail to thee, Osiris, lord of eternity! When thou art in heaven thou appearest as the sun, and thou renewest thy form as the moon." Mariette, *Dendera*, Vol. IV. 44 a.

detail, the less will they disturb our conviction that the victory of Set over Osiris is that of Night over Day, and the resurrection of Osiris is the rising of the Sun. And I do not think Osiris will be spoken of as *dead* throughout an Egyptian winter by any one who has had any experience of that delightful season.

There is a passage in the Book of the Dead[1] which says that "Osiris came to Tattu (Mendes) and found the soul of Rā there; each embraced the other, and became as one soul in two souls." This may be a mythological way of saying that two legends which had previously been independent of each other were henceforth inextricably mixed up. This, at all events, is the historical fact. In the words of a sacred text, "Rā is the soul of Osiris, and Osiris the soul of Rā."

Horus.[2]

But Horus also is one of the names of the Sun, and had his myths quite independently of Rā or Osiris. The most prominent ones in comparatively later times

---

[1] Ch. xvii. l. 42, 43.

[2] M. Lefébure has published several important essays illustrative of the myths of Osiris and Horus. I should be glad to find real evidence of allusions to lunar eclipses, but it is impossible to reconcile the lunar hypothesis about these myths with the most elementary astronomy. How can a lunar eclipse, for instance, regularly coincide with a fixed day in a month of thirty days? The synodical month is nearly of this length, but the eclipses depend upon the nodes.

described his victories over Set or the monster Tebha (the Typhon of the Greeks). But the victory of Darkness over Light was appropriately represented by the myth of the Blind Horus. An ancient text speaks of him as "sitting solitary in the darkness and blindness." He is introduced in the royal Ritual at Abydos, saying, "I am Horus, and I come to search for mine eyes." According to the 64th chapter of the Book of the Dead, "his eye is restored to him at the dawn of day." A legend contained in the 112th chapter of the same Book describes Horus as wounded in the eye by Set in the form of a black boar. Anubis fomented the wound, of which Horus appears at first to have thought him the author,[1] and according to another legend, Isis stanched the blood which flowed from the wound. But according to another account, Set swallowed the eye, and was compelled to vomit it from the prison in which he was confined, with a chain of steel fastened about his neck. The Eye of Horus is constantly spoken of as a distinct deity, terrible to the enemies of light.

The conflict of Light and Darkness is represented in many other mythical forms. The great Cat in the alley of Persea trees at Heliopolis, which is Rā, crushes the serpent. In most parts of Egypt the sun sets behind a mountain-range; it is only in the north that

---

[1] And he said, "Behold, my eye is as though *Anubis* had made an incision in my eye."—Todt. 112. Although Anubis in the sequel restores the eye, the allusion is clearly to his nocturnal power.

the body of Osiris is said to have been plunged into the waters. According to another legend, the crocodile Maka, the son of Set, devoured the arm of Osiris. Other disastrous mutilations are described as befalling Osiris, Rā, Horus and Set, in their turn. Set and the other powers of darkness assumed the forms of fishes. Horus pursued them, and Set was caught in a net.[1] Horus, on the other hand, was changed into a fish, and was saved by his mother Isis.

Set.

Set, though the antagonist of Light in the myths of Rā, Osiris and Horus, is not a god of evil. He represents a physical reality, a constant and everlasting law of nature, and is as true a god as his opponents. His worship is as ancient as any. The kings of Egypt were devoted to Set as to Horus, and derived from them the sovereignty over north and south. On some monuments, one god is represented with two heads, one being that of Horus, the other that of Set. The name of the great conqueror Seti signifies, "he that is devoted to Set." It was not till the decline of the empire that this deity came to be regarded as an evil demon, that his name was effaced from monuments, and other names substituted for his in the Ritual.

---

[1] Indra used a net as well as other weapons against his foes.

Thoth.

The Egyptian god Tehuti is known to the readers of Plato under the name of Thōyth. He is the Egyptian Hermes, and the name of Hermes Trismegistos is translated from the corresponding Egyptian epithet which is often added to the name of Tehuti. He represents the Moon, which he wears upon his head, either as crescent or as full disk; and as our word *moon* is derived from the root *mâ*, to measure, and "was originally called by the farmer the measurer, the ruler of days and weeks and seasons, the regulator of the tides, the lord of their festivals, and the herald of their public assemblies,"[1] we shall not be surprised if we find a very similar account of the etymology and attributes of Tehuti. There is no such known Egyptian word as *tehu*, but there is *texu*, which is a dialectic variety, and is actually used as a name of the god. This form supplies us with the reason why the god is represented as an ibis. As Seb is the name both of a goose and of the Earth-god, so is Techu the name of an ibis and of the Moon-god. Tehuti probably signifies, as M. Naville has suggested, the "ibis-headed." But it means something besides. *Techu* is the name of the instrument[2] which corresponds to the needle of the

---

[1] Max Müller, "Science of Language," I. p. 7.
[2] The instrument itself is a vase, and the primitive meaning of the word *texu* is to be "full;" hence the sense of drunkenness

balance for measuring weights. The ancient Egyptian cubit is called the cubit of Techu. He is called "the measurer of this earth." He is said to have "calculated the heaven and counted the stars," to have "calculated the earth and counted the things which are in it."[1] He is "the distributor of time," the inventor of letters and learning (particularly of geometry), and of the fine arts. Whatever is without him is as though it were not. All this is because the Moon is the measurer.

It is impossible, after this rapid, but, I trust, not deceptive glance at the myths of some of the chief Egyptian gods, to withstand the conviction that this mythology is very similar indeed to that of the Indo-European races. It is the very same drama which is being acted under different names and disguises. The god slays the dragon, or a monster blinds, maims or devours the god. What bright god is born from the embrace of Heaven and Earth, and who is his twin sister and spouse? Who are his two wives? Who is the "husband of his own mother"? Who is the divine youth who emerges from the lotus-flower? And what is the lotus? Which is the god who, having performed his course from east to west, is worshipped as the king and judge of the departed? Sanskrit

---

which it sometimes has. Dr. Duemichen has thoroughly illustrated the use of the word in his "Bauurkunde v. Dendera," and in the Zeitschrift, 1872, p. 39.

[1] See Brugsch, Zeitschrift, 1872, p. 9.

scholars who do not know a word of Egyptian, and Egyptologists who do not know a word of Sanskrit, will give different names to these personages. But the comparative mythologist will hardly hesitate about assigning his real name to each of them, whether Aryan or Egyptian. One of the most curious instances of the identification of myths is to be seen in a bas-relief at the Louvre, wherein the legend of our own St. George and the Dragon, which is at bottom the same as that of Indra and Vritra, is represented by Horus spearing a crocodile.[1]

The Lectures on the Science of Language delivered nearly twenty years ago by Professor Max Müller, have, I trust, made us fully understand how, among the Indo-European races, the names of the sun, of sunrise and sunset, and of other such phenomena, came to be talked of and considered as personages of whom wondrous legends are told. Egyptian mythology not merely admits, but imperatively demands, the same explanation. And this becomes the more evident when we consider the question how these mythical personages came to be invested with the attributes of divinity by men who, like the Egyptians, as we have seen, had so lively a sense of the divine. Here we are at once brought into contact with the notion of the reign of Law.

---

[1] "Horus et St. George d'après un bas-relief inédit du Louvre," by M. Clermont Ganneau, in the *Rev. Arch.* 1876, September and December.

The Reign of Law.

M. de Rougé, in the extract which I have read from his Lecture, quotes the Egyptian expression, "the Only Being, living in truth," "le seul Être, vivant en vérité." But the original words, *ānx em maāt*, mean very much more than "living in truth." A more grammatically exact translation would be, "who lives by truth," or "whose existence depends upon truth;" but "truth" is not the exact meaning of *maāt*. When speaking of the moral code recognized by the Egyptians, I used the word "Right" as including both Truth and Justice. But it now becomes necessary to define the term more precisely.

Maāt as a noun signifies a perfectly straight and inflexible *rule*. It is evidently, I believe, derived from the root *mā*, "to stretch out," or "hold out straight before one," "protendere," as in the act of presenting an offering, *mā hotep*.[1] "I have stretched out (*mā-na*) my hand, as the master of the crown," says the Osiris in the Book of the Dead.[2] "Tehuti has extended to her (*mā-nes*) his hand," is said in one of the texts at Dendera.[3] With this notion of stretching out are con-

---

[1] Sharpe and Bonomi, "Sarcophagus," pl. 8, lines 5 and 8.

[2] Todt. 40, 2, comp. with 12, 2.

[3] Other words connected with the same root are *maāt*, an offering, πρόθεσις, *mā* signifying that part of the forehead from which the horns project in cattle, *mā* a fair wind, and *mā* an extent of water.

nected, in the Egyptian as well as in the Indo-European and the Semitic languages, the notions of "straight, right, righteous, true, rule, row, order." Our own word *rule*, like the Latin regula and rectus, is derived from the Aryan root *arg*, from which we have in Sanskrit *ringe*, I stretch myself (like the Greek ὀρέγομαι), *rigus*, straight, right, righteous; *rāgis*, a line, a row; in Zend, erezu, straight, right, true, and as a substantive, finger.[1] In Gothic we have rak-ja (uf-rak-ja, stretch out), rach-ts, right, straight.[2] The Egyptian *maāt* is not only Truth and Justice, but Order and Law, in the physical as well as in the moral world. It is in allusion to the fixed and unalterable laws of nature (which of course were very imperfectly known to them) that the Egyptians used the expression *ānχ em maāt*, "living or existing by or upon rule," which, if not actually a term equivalent to divinity, is at least with them the attribute most constantly connected with it. It was in consequence of the persistent recurrence of the same physical phenomena in an order which never varied and was never violated, that the Sun and Moon and other powers,

---

[1] A finger is sometimes in Egyptian found as a "determinative" of *mā*.

[2] Curtius, "Gr. Et." p. 184. Compare Gesenius on the Hebrew עָרַךְ—"*ordine* s. *ad lineam disposuit, struxit*, nostr. *reihen, richten*, gr. τάσσω, τάττω (vic. אָרַךְ recta protendit, extendit, et in linguis indo-germ. *Reihe* [Reige, Riege] *reihen* intens. *rechen*; rego [non pro *reago* ut nonnulli volunt] *regula, rectus*." "עָרַךְ . . . *ordo, strues*."

even the days of the month and the twenty-four hours of day and night, became the great and everlasting gods.

There is another Egyptian expression extremely frequent in the religious texts, the accurate meaning of which has never been recognized. *Em shes en maāt* is now generally allowed to mean "rightly," "perfectly." But *shes* is the measuring *line* used by builders, and *em shes* signifies "ad amussim," "nach der Schnur," "au cordeau," "according to the line;" hence, "with the strictest accuracy." The whole expression therefore means, "according to the strict accuracy of Law," to which is constantly added, *hehu en sep*, "millions of times." *Maāt* is Law,[1] not in the forensic sense of a command issued either by a human sovereign authority or by a divine legislator, like the Law of the Hebrews, but in the sense of that unerring order which governs the universe, whether in its physical or in its moral aspect. This is surely a great and noble conception.

You will not be surprised to learn that Maāt is spoken of as a mythical personage. She is called mistress of heaven, ruler of earth and president of the nether world, which indeed is recognized as her special domain. She is called the daughter of Rā, but she

---

[1] The opposite notion to *Maāt*, considered as Law, is *asfet*, lawlessness, disorder, iniquity.

might as truly have been called his mother.[1] Each of the great gods is said to be *neb maāt*, literally, "lord or master of Maāt;" but it is equally said that "she knows no lord or master." If she is brought into closer connection with Thoth than with other gods, this is because Thoth is essentially the "Measurer;" and if certain texts speak of the winds as proceeding from either Thoth or Maāt, it is not because these personages are wind-gods, but because the cardinal points from which the winds come are naturally the domain of the god who has measured and mapped out the universe, and because the winds themselves are obedient to Law.

Such were the gods of Egypt. They were not the ghosts of ancestors or other dead men, or representatives of abstract principles, as ancient and modern philosophers have supposed, nor were they impure spirits or foul demons, as an uncritical though not unnatural interpretation of their Scriptures led the early Christian missionaries to imagine. "All the gods of the nations are nought," says the Psalmist; but the Greek and Latin translators used the word "daemonia," which in Christian times never meant anything but "devils." The gods of the Egyptian, as well as those of the Indian, Greek or Teutonic mythologies, were the "powers" of nature, the "strong ones," whose might was seen and felt to be irresistible, yet so constant, unchanging and

---

[1] She is so called in the inscriptions of Chut-en-Aten.

orderly in its operations, as to leave no doubt as to the
presence of an ever living and active Intelligence.[1]

---

[1] Much in this Lecture will be new, and perhaps appear doubtful,
to my learned colleagues in Egyptology, especially to those whose
studies have not led them into the field of Indo-European philology.
From the time of Champollion, the Egyptian language and literature
have been almost exclusively illustrated from Semitic, not to say
purely Hebrew, sources. This is a fatal mistake, though perhaps
inevitable at first. I have for years been humbly endeavouring to
bring the Science of Language to bear upon Egyptian philology,
and I trust this Lecture will at least induce some eminent scholars
to study the Egyptian by the light of other mythologies. M.
Lefébure has already done most valuable work in this direction.
M. Grébaut, though confining himself entirely to Egyptian mythology, has, in his "Hymne à Ammon-Râ," published in the *Bibliothèque de l'ecole des hautes études*, and in an article of the *Mélanges
d'Archéologie*, tome II. p. 247, demonstrated several important
truths, and he has very nearly approached the true conception
of Maāt. As regards the identification of certain deities, I have
very nearly been anticipated by M. Naville, who in his admirable work on the "Litany of the Sun," p. 38, is inclined to
consider Isis and Nephthys "comme personnifiant des êtres dont
chacun caractérisait plus particulièrement l'un des horizons ; peut
être l'étoile du matin et celle du soir, *ou encore le crépuscule du
matin et celui du soir ; les deux formules de la litanie se compren-
draient alors facilement*." But he puts Isis at the west, and
Nephthys at the east. [See Preface.]

COMMUNION WITH THE UNSEEN WORLD.

Sepulchral Rites.

A BELIEF in the persistence of life after death, and the observation of religious practices founded upon this belief, may be discovered in every part of the world, in every age, and among men representing every degree and variety of culture. Classical scholars are familiar with the terms of Inferiæ and Parentalia, names given by the Romans to the propitiatory offerings which they presented to the manes of their departed ancestors. The Greeks had their ἐναγίσματα. The worship of the Fravashis by the Iranians, and that of the Pitris by the Hindu, are evidences of the antiquity in the Indo-European family of this form of religion, many traces of which remain to this day in the practices of European nations. And the celebration of rites in honour of their ancestors is perhaps the most ancient institution of the oldest civilization now in existence, that of China.

The habits of savages without a history are not in themselves evidence which can in any way be depended upon. To take for granted that what the savages now are, perhaps after millenniums of degradation, all other people must have been, and that modes of thought through which they are now passing have been passed through by others, is a most unscientific assumption, and you will seldom meet with it in any essay or book without also finding proof that the writer did not know how to deal with historical evidence. Authorities are sure to be quoted which the historian knows to be worthless, and evidence in itself irreproachable will be completely misunderstood. The universality of a belief or practice, even among savages, would of course, if proved, be a very weighty fact, tending to prove that the belief or practice in question had its origin either in reason or in tradition. It is, however, impossible to exaggerate the value of Sir Henry Maine's protest against "the very slippery testimony concerning savages which is gathered from travellers' tales." "Much," he says, "which I have personally heard in India bears out the caution which I gave as to the reserve with which all speculations on the antiquity of human usage should be received. Practices represented as of immemorial antiquity and universally characteristic of the infancy of mankind, have been described to me as having been for the first time resorted to in our days through the mere pressure of external circumstances or novel temptations."[1]

Far more important than any single instance from the descriptions of modern savages is the ancient tomb of Aurignac. "If the fossil memorials," says Sir Charles Lyell, "have been correctly interpreted—if we have before us at the northern base of the Pyrenees a sepulchral vault, with skeletons of human beings consigned by friends and relatives to their last resting-place—if we have also at the portal of the tomb the relics of funeral feasts, and within it indications of viands destined for the use of the departed on their way to a land of spirits, while among the funeral gifts are weapons wherewith in other fields to chase the gigantic deer, the cave lion, the cave bear and woolly rhinoceros—we have at last succeeded in tracing back the sacred rites of burial, and, more interesting still, a belief in a future state, to times long anterior to those of history or tradition."[2]

But if from pre-historic we pass to historic times, we at once meet on Egyptian ground with an entire system

---

[1] "Village Communities," p. 17.

[2] "Antiquity of Man," p. 193, 1863. I leave the words of the above passage as they were delivered. I was not aware at the time that the evidence of M. Lartet had been contested, and that Sir Charles Lyell had in his last edition admitted this evidence to be doubtful. See the article of Mr. W. B. Dawkins, on "The Date of the Interment in the Aurignac Cave," in *Nature*, Vol. IV. p. 208.

of notions wonderfully (indeed, almost incredibly) similar to those entertained by our Indo-European ancestors. There is, however, no confirmation of Mr. Herbert Spencer's hypothesis, that the rudimentary form of all religion is the propitiation of dead ancestors. If the Egyptians passed through such a rudimentary form of religion, they had already got beyond it in the age of the Pyramids, for their most ancient propitiation of ancestors is made through prayer to Anubis, Osiris, or some other gods. The deceased is already described in the funereal inscription as "faithful to the great God." And in no case can it be proved that the propitiation of departed ancestors preceded a belief in divinity of some other kind.

The Tombs and their Inscriptions.

"The Egyptians," we are told by Diodoros, "call their houses hostelries, on account of the short time during which they inhabit them, but the tombs they call eternal dwelling-places." The latter part of this is strictly and literally true; *pa t'eta*, "eternal dwelling-place," is an expression which is met with at every instant in the inscriptions of the earliest period, descriptive of the tomb. The word *ānchiu*, which literally signifies the "living," is in innumerable places used emphatically for the "departed," who are enjoying everlasting life. The notion of everlasting life, *ānch t'eta*, is among the few words written upon the wooden coffin, now in the British Museum, of king Mykerinos, of the third pyramid. *Neb ānch*, "Lord of life," is one of the names given to the sarcophagus. In the very ancient inscription of Una, the coffin is called *hen en ānchiu*, "the chest of the living." It is only evil spirits who are spoken of in the sacred writings of the Egyptians as "the dead."

The ancient Egyptian tomb[1] consisted of three essential parts: (1) a chamber above ground, entered by a door, which appears to have always remained open; (2) a corridor, now commonly known as the *serdab*, in the interior of the masonry, containing statues of the deceased; and (3) a pit, sunk to a considerable depth through the rock, and communicating with the sepulchral vault hollowed in the rock, and containing the sarcophagus of the dead. The chamber (which sometimes consisted of several rooms) was the only part accessible to human foot. Its walls were often covered with pictures, but the most essential portion of it was a tablet invariably facing the east. At the foot of this,

---

[1] The most complete account of early Egyptian tombs is found in M. Mariette's article, "Sur les tombes de l'ancien empire qu'on trouve à Saqqarah," in the *Revue Archéologique*, 1869, Vol. I. pp. 7—22, 81—89, much of which is repeated in his admirable description of the Museum of Bulaq. See also Duemichen, "Ueber die Tempel und Gräber im alten Aegypten," the very interesting text of his *Photographische Resultate*, and Brugsch, "Die Aegyptische Gräberwelt." The *Journal Asiatique* of 1880 contains a very important "Etude sur quelques peintures et sur quelques textes rélatifs aux funerailles" by M. Maspero.

lying on the ground and made of granite limestone or alabaster, was a table for the offerings. The *serdab*, or corridor, was only accessible through a small aperture, through which the smoke of incense might be conveyed from the chamber to the statues which the solid walls concealed from sight. The representations upon the walls of the chamber reproduce the entire domestic and social life of the period. It is from these pictures that Sir Gardner Wilkinson has drawn up his admirable work on the Manners and Customs of the Ancient Egyptians, and described the Egyptian house, with its furniture, its gardens, its farm-yards, its vine-yards—the occupations of its owner and the amusements of his guests—the games within and out of doors, the hunting and fishing, the agricultural operations, the numerous arts, manufactures and trades—all of which are represented to the life. Short inscriptions accompany the pictures; the names of men, animals and other objects are written over them; descriptive titles are constantly given, such as "ploughing," "mowing," "the slaughter of a young bull;" sometimes scraps of dialogue occur, generally of a very trivial character. "Hold hard," a master says to his servant; and the lad replies, *Ari heset-ek*, "Thy will be done." One man says, "This donkey is wild;" and another replies, "I will tame him." A peasant is engaged in combing flax, and he says to another who brings him a fresh supply of stalks, "If you bring me eleven thousand and nine, I will comb them." The other man rather rudely replies, "Make haste, and none of your chatter, you prince of clodhoppers!" The tomb in which this dialogue occurs is rich in texts of the same kind. It was here that Champollion found the "Song of the Oxen." But all these representations are really subordinate to one end, and that is the worship of the departed. The slaughter of the ox or the antelope is not introduced for its own sake, but really as a sacrifice; and the pictures of men bearing joints are on the point, as they are sometimes actually represented, of offering them to the image of the deceased. An endowment was always intended to provide for the celebration of these propitiatory services, as well as for keeping the tomb in perpetual repair.

The usual form of inscription over the lintel of the tomb, and which is often repeated within the chamber, is as follows:

"A royal table of propitiation grant Anubis, who dwells within the divine house. May sepulture be granted in the nether world, in the land of the divine Menti,[1] the ancient, the good, the great, to him [the

---

[1] In later times this name was written *Amenti*, and was supposed to be derived from the word *amen*, "conceal." This meaning is implied in the royal tombs at Bibān-el-molūk. But in the oldest tombs the name is distinctly written *Menti*, and the name of the presiding divinity χent menti. See *Denkmäler*, ii. pl. 45, 48, 101.

departed] who is faithful to the great God. May he advance upon the blissful paths upon which those advance who are faithful to the great God. May the funereal oblations be paid to him at the beginning of the year, on the feast of Tehuti, on the first day of the year, on the feast of Uaka, on the feasts of the Great and of the Small Heat, on the apparition of Sechem, at the feast of *Uāh-āch*, at the feasts of each month and the half-month and every day."

Such is the ordinary formula, which however admits of variations and additions, especially in the later inscriptions. I will mention one or two not more recent than the sixth dynasty. One of them consists in the repetition of the words *em hotep*, "in peace," like the בשלם of the Hebrew and the *In pace* of the Christian funereal inscriptions. It is extremely frequent in Egyptian texts, and may really be the origin of the Jewish and Christian form of petition for the departed, though the primitive signification has been altered.

There is also a petition that the departed may "traverse the firmament," "in company with the perfect spirits of the nether world." The word *ba*, which I translate firmament, properly signifies "steel."[1] The notions of *blue* and of *steel* seem to have been associated in the Egyptian mind, and the colour of the sky sug-

---

[1] Cf. the Homeric σιδήρεον οὐρανὸν, *Od.* xv. 329, xvii. 565. We have already met with another conception of heaven, namely, as an ocean upon which the sun travels in his bark.

gested the notion of a metallic firmament. The word spirit is given as the translation of the Egyptian *chu*, but this name for the dead signifies "glorified one."

A third petition is, that the deceased should be proclaimed glorified, or, as we should say, canonized (*sechut*), by the ministers of religion, the *cher-heb* or the *smer*, priestly officials who are frequently named in the inscriptions, especially in connection with the rites of the dead. A considerable number of priests bearing these and other titles, representing various functions, took part in these ceremonies, but the presence of a priest was not always indispensable. The offerings might be made, or rather had to be made, by the sons and daughters and other members of the family of the deceased. The pictures in which no minister of religion is seen (and they are perhaps the most numerous), all either directly represent religious rites or preparations for them. The very games and dances are religious ceremonies. In the tomb of Tebahen, the statue of the deceased is represented as standing within a shrine, before which a table of propitiatory offerings is laid. Men are advancing up the inclined plane which leads to it, bearing fowls and legs of oxen. On one side, other men are kneeling, with sacrificial cakes or vases of water in their hands; whilst on the other side, women are performing a solemn dance, also in presence of a table of offerings. In the great tomb of Nahre-se-Chnumhotep at Benihassan, women are tumbling in presence of a solemn religious service, in which libations are being poured by the "*ka*-minister." The words written over the scene are part of a prayer which is supposed to be recited, "Let the gates of heaven be opened that the god may enter!"

The later form of the sepulchral inscriptions, as found on the tablets of our museums, is, more or less fully, as follows:

"A royal table of propitiation grant Osiris, dwelling in Amenti, Lord of Abydos [or of Tattu]:" other divinities are often added. "May he [or they] grant the funereal oblations, bread, beer, oxen, geese, wine, milk, oil, incense, wrappings, all gifts of vegetation, whatever heaven gives or earth produces, to enjoy the Nile, to come forth as a living soul, to come in and go out at the Ristat, that the soul may not be repulsed at the gates of the nether world, to be glorified among the favoured ones in presence of Un-nefer, to receive the aliments on the altars of the great God, to breathe the delicious breezes of the north wind, and to drink from the depth of the river." Then follows the name of the person, generally accompanied by that of his mother; but on almost all tablets after the time of Amenemhāt I., these celestial gifts are said to be given not to the person, but to the *ka* of the person,—an important expression which has been misunderstood till quite lately.

This prayer is called the *Suten-hotep-tā*, from its first words; and as we speak of saying an "Our Father," the Egyptian texts speak of "a son making a *Suten-hotep-tā*." The great tablet of Abydos has for title, "The making of a *Suten-hotep-tā*," &c., to the kings of Egypt by king Seti.

The greatest importance was attached to the permanence of the tomb, to the continuance of the religious ceremonies, and to the prayers of passers-by. We constantly find men praised for having made to live again the names of their father and mother or of their "fathers." There is a very common formula stating that the person who raised the tablet "made it as a memorial to his fathers who are in the nether world, that he built up what he found imperfect, and renewed what was found out of repair." In the great inscription at Benihassan, Chnumhotep says, "I made to flourish the name of my father, and I built the chapels for his *ka*. I caused my statues to be conveyed to the holy dwelling, and distributed to them their offerings in pure gifts. I instituted the officiating priest, to whom I gave donations in lands and peasants. I ordered funeral offerings for all the feasts of the nether world, at the feast of the New Year, at the beginning of the year, at the feast of the Little Year, at the feast of the Great Year, at the feast of the great joyful feast, at the feast of the Great Heat, at the feast of the Little Heat, at the feast of the five supplementary days of the year, at the feast of Shetat, at the feast of the Sand, at the twelve monthly feasts, at the twelve half-monthly feasts, at all the feasts of the plain and the mountain. If it happens that the priest or any other cease to do this, then may he not exist, and *may his son not sit in his seat.*"

The great inscription of Rameses II. at Abydos minutely relates the provision made by that sovereign for the worship of his father, Seti I.

"The most beautiful thing to behold," says Rameses, "the best thing to hear, is a child with a thankful breast, whose heart beats for his father. Wherefore my heart urges me to do what is good for Mineptah. I will cause them to talk for ever and eternally of his son who has awakened his name to life. My father Osiris will reward me for this with a long existence, like his son Horus. Let me do what he did, let me be excellent as he was excellent, for my parent, I, who am a scion of the sun-god Rā." . . . .

"Awake," he says to his father, "raise thy face to heaven, behold the sun, my father Mineptah, thou who art like God. Here am I who make thy name to live. I am thy guardian, and my care is directed to thy temple and thy altars which are raised up again. . . . . I set apart revenues for thee for thy worship daily, to be just towards thee. . . . . I appoint for thee the priests of the vessel of holy water, provided with everything for sprinkling the water on the ground. . . . . I dedicated to thee the lands of the south for the services of thy temple, and the lands of the north they bring to thee their gifts before thy beautiful countenance. I gathered together the people of thy service one and all, assigning them to the prophet of thy temple. . . . . I dedicated to thee ships with their freight on the great sea. . . . . I fixed for thee the number of the fields . . . . great is their number according to their valuation in acres. I provided thee with land-surveyors and husbandmen, to deliver the corn for thy revenues."

He proceeds to enumerate the barks with their crews, labourers for the felling of wood, herds of all kind of cattle, tributes of birds, fishermen. The temple is provided with all kinds of guilds of handicraftsmen, men-servants and women-servants working in the fields.

"But I obtain by my prayers the breath of life at thy awaking. . . . . So long as I stay on earth, I will offer a sacrifice to thee. My hands shall bring the libations for thy name to thy [remembrance] in all thy abodes."[1]

It is only natural to suppose that the religious endowments here mentioned must in the course of years come to an end. There is, however, in the Louvre a monument which shows the astonishing length of time during which institutions continued

---

[1] Brugsch Bey, "History of Egypt," Vol. II. pp. 36, 40, English transl.

to be respected. The kings who built the Pyramids endowed a priestly office for the purpose of celebrating the periodical rites in their behalf. The same priest often officiated for several departed kings. The tablet of the Louvre shows that Psamtīk, son of Ut'ahor, who lived in the time of the twenty-sixth dynasty, was priest of Chufu or Cheops of the great Pyramid, and of two other sovereigns of the same period, who certainly had lived and endowed his office more than two thousand years before his time. We have actually the tombs of some of his predecessors who filled the office almost immediately after the death of the sovereign.

Innumerable inscriptions call upon the passers-by to invoke the gods in behalf of the departed. "O all ye who are living upon earth," "who love life and hate death," "you who are in the service of Osiris or of Anubis," "priest, prophet, scribe, spondist, ministrant, male or female, every man and every woman passing by this tomb, statue, tablet or shrine, whether you be passing northwards or southwards—as you desire to enjoy the favour of the king—or as you desire your names to remain upon earth, or to transmit your dignities to your children—or as you love and obey the gods of Egypt, or as you wish to be blest by the gods of your cities, or by your wish to possess a part of the divine abode of Osiris who dwells in Amenti—or to be faithful to the great God—or as you wish to flourish upon earth and pass on to the blessed—say a *Suten-*

hotep-tā," the entire formula being repeated, or merely (as an abbreviation) "thousands of oxen, geese, bread, beer," &c.

Such is the burden of all these funereal tablets. No one tablet contains all that I have quoted, and no two tablets are exactly alike, but all are made upon the same model and contain some portions of the whole. Many centuries after the construction of a tomb, Egyptian travellers have left a record upon its walls of the splendour of the sacred abode, of the abundance of the materials which they found provided for the fulfilment of the rites for the departed, and of their own repetition of the funereal formula.[1] The *Suten-hotep-tā* was supposed to have been delivered by divine revelation. An ancient text speaks of a "*Suten-hotep-tā* exactly corresponding to the texts of sacrificial offerings handed down by the ancients as proceeding from the mouth of God."[2]

It was most important that a man should have a son established in his seat after him, who should perform the due rites and see that they were performed by others; that he should, as it is expressed, "flourish in the children of his children." The duty of performing these rites comes immediately after that of worshipping the gods, in the enumeration of virtuous actions. It

---

[1] Champollion, *Notices*, Vol. II. pp. 423—425.
[2] *Denkm.* iii. pl. 13.

is enforced in the moral writings as well as in the theology of ancient Egypt.

"Give the water of the funereal sacrifice to thy father and mother who repose in the tomb; renew the water of the divine oblations..... Neglect not to do it, even when thou art away from thy dwelling. *Thy son will do it for thee in like manner.*"

These words are taken from the Maxims of Ani.

We find the following among the good wishes made for a person: "Mayst thou receive the lustral water from the hands of thy son each tenth day..... May every heir who offers the libation to his own father, contribute his offering of water to thy *ka*; and as he propitiates his father or buries his mother, may thy name be uttered together with his own father."[1]

On the other hand, the wish that a man may not have a son after him is the most terrible of imprecations.

"Whoever shall preserve this inscription," we read, "in the temple of Amon Rā, the Lord of Senneferet, he shall be favoured by Amon Rā, and his son shall be established in his place; but whosoever shall remove this inscription from the temple of Amon Rā, Amon Rā will curse him, and his son shall not be established in his place."[2]

---

[1] Louvre, Inv. 908.
[2] *Zeitschrift f. ägypt. Sprache*, 1871, p. 60.

Another text says:

"Whoso destroys this inscription, Bast, the great goddess of Bubastis, will annihilate him for ever; he will never have a son after him."[1]

The trustees of a religious foundation are threatened with the most tremendous penalties in case of their not carrying out the intentions of the founder; they are to "be delivered over to Sutech in the day of his wrath, whose serpent diadem will spit out flames of fire upon their heads, annihilating their limbs and consuming their bodies. May they not receive the reward of righteousness; may they not partake of the feast of the blessed; may the water from the spring of the river not refresh them; may it not come to pass that their posterity should sit in their place." But to faithful trustees the most splendid prospects are held out, one of which is, "Son of son, heir of heir, will be born to him." "May your bodies," they are finally told, "rest in the nether world of Amenti after a course of a hundred and ten years, and may the sacrificial gifts likewise be multiplied to you."

The inscription of Ptolemy, the son of Lagos, in the fourth century before Christ, ends as follows:[2]

"The land of Buto, whoever tries to plan the removal of any part thereof, may he incur the ban of those gods who are in Pe, may he be accursed by those who

---

[1] *Zeitschrift f. aeg..pt. Sprache*, 1871, p. 60.   [2] *Ib.* p. 8.

are in Tep, may he be in the flame of Aptaui in the day of her terrible wrath, may he have no son or daughter to give him the lustral water."

One of the most recent of the Ptolemaic tablets records the fulfilment of a promise made in a dream by the god I-em-hotep to Pasherenptah with reference to the birth of a son, and it contains the invocation, "Oh, all ye gods and goddesses who are unnamed, let a child remain in my place for ever and ever .... keeping alive the name of my house."

The lustral water offered upon earth to the dead had its counterpart in the other world. The most usual representation of this is the picture in which the goddess Nut pours out the water of life to the deceased, from the interior of a sycamore-tree. In a picture published by M. Chabas,[1] the deceased kneels before Osiris, and receives from him the water of life from a vessel under which is written ānch ba, "that the soul may live." The picture is taken from the mummy of a priest who lived twelve hundred years before Christ. But the same idea occurs in a Greek inscription found at Saqāra by Mr. C. Wescher. "She lived twenty-five years," the inscription says, "and Osiris beneath the earth gave her the refreshing water."[2]

Now let me remind you that the oblation of cakes

---

[1] *Revue Arch.* 1862, Vol. I. p. 370.
[2] *Ib.* 1864, Vol. II. p. 222.

and water is one of the five great ceremonies of the Hindus, and, as Professor Max Müller told you last year, that "without a son to perform the funeral rites, a Brahman believed that he could not enter into heaven." Here is undoubtedly a most remarkable coincidence between two religions which never came into contact. Nor can any even indirect influence of one upon the other be considered admissible. It is the logical process which has taken the same direction in both, and it can be traced in other branches of the Indo-European family.

Readers of ecclesiastical history will remember the fierce persecutions to which the first converts to Christianity were subjected in Persia, chiefly in consequence of the doctrines they held on the subject of virginity and celibacy, so much at variance with a religion which considered children as "a bridge leading to heaven;" but as this religion has special grounds of its own for condemning celibacy, over and above those which it derives from the Indo-European traditions, it is instructive to read Dr. Hearne's remarks on the traditions of Greece and Rome.

"The personal motives which led to marriage were in the early world very strong. The popular sentiment is emphatically expressed by Isaios when he says, 'No man who knows he must die can have so little regard for himself as to leave his family without descendants, for then there would be no one to render him the worship due to the dead.' A remarkable illustration of this sentiment occurs on a memorable occasion in Grecian history. When Leonidas arrived at the scene of his desperate defence of Thermopylæ, he was accompanied, says the historian, 'by the 300 men which the law assigned him, whom he had himself chosen from among the citizens, and who were all of them fathers with sons living.' According to modern notions, a forlorn hope would naturally be composed of men who had not given hostages to fortune. Such, however, was not the light in which the latter presented itself to the Greek mind. The human plant had flowered. The continuance of the house was secure. It was therefore comparatively of little moment what befel the man whose duty to his ancestors had been fulfilled. In the aspect of the case now before us, the fact that a man married or that he remained single, was not a matter which affected himself alone. The condition of his ancestors, the permanence of his household, depended upon his conduct. We cannot, therefore, doubt that celibacy was regarded as a deadly sin. Even the State, although it was slow to interfere in matters merely *privati juris*, lent its aid to enforce this primary duty. Solon prohibited celibacy. The laws of the Dorians, the most conservative of the Hellenes, contained similar provisions. Criminal proceedings might be taken, both at Athens and at Sparta, against those who married beneath them, and against those who did not marry at all. There is evidence that a prohibition to the same effect existed in early Rome."[1] I have thought it well to insist upon this feature of the Egyptian religion, in consequence of the importance attached to the celibate life in later times in four different religions: first, in the great system of Buddhism; secondly, in Judaism; thirdly, in Christianity; and fourthly, in Manicheism. Christian monasticism, as is well known, first grew up in Egypt, and was introduced into Europe through Christians from Egypt. But the monastic life and the word *monastery* already existed before Christianity among the Jewish ascetics, whose mode of life is described by the Alexandrian Philo.[2] It certainly was not from the Egyptian religion that monastic institutions were derived.[3]

It is no doubt extremely natural, when phenomena are discovered which bear close resemblance to each other, to look out for some historical connection be-

---

[1] "The Aryan Household : an Introduction to Comparative Jurisprudence," p. 71.

[2] Tom. II. p. 475, 15. Ἐν ἑκάστῃ δὲ οἰκίᾳ ἐστὶν οἴκημα, ἱερὸν, ὃ καλεῖται σεμνεῖον καὶ μοναστήριον, ἐν ᾧ μονούμενοι τὰ τοῦ βίου σεμνοῦ μυστήρια τελοῦνται. [Grave doubts have, quite recently, been raised against the genuineness of this treatise. Far graver doubts may be raised against the hypothesis that it was written by a Christian of the third century.]

[3] The Greek papyri speak of a class of persons called οἱ ἐν κατόχῃ, οἱ κατεχόμενοι, who led a cloistered life; that is to say, they were restricted to the precincts of the temple to which they were attached. But they were not ascetics or necessarily celibates.

tween them. But in the history of human thought, the supposition of such a connection frequently proves to be an illusion. No historical connection can possibly be admitted between the Egyptian and the Indo-European doctrines of the necessity of marriage, and all the doctrines in favour of religious celibacy may very probably turn out to be historically independent of each other. The late Professor Baur, of Tübingen, wrote an exceedingly able work, in which he endeavoured to trace the Manichean system to Buddhism.[1] His arguments were admitted by Neander and many other learned men; among others, by Dr. Pusey in this country. Admirable, however, as Baur's analysis of the Manichean system must be confessed to be, his conception of Buddhism was radically false. This is not to be wondered at, for the book was written before any authentic information on the subject of Buddhism was yet accessible, and the principles which in the Gnostic and Manichean systems were wrongly ascribed to Buddhism were taken from the Platonic, Neo-Pythagorean or some other Hellenic philosophy. And all attempts to discover Buddhist influences in Jewish or Christian theologies will, I am sure, prove equally abortive. What they have in common is human reason, working according to the same natural laws.

---

[1] I have discussed this question at length in an article on "Orientalism and Ancient Christianity," in the *Home and Foreign Review*, July, 1863, p. 151.

The question, however, is one which should be decided upon strictly historical evidence, independently of all dogmatic prejudice. Not a trace of the philosophic theories peculiar to the Buddhist canon has yet been discovered in any of the philosophic or religious systems of the Western world, and why should we be alarmed if it could be proved that the sublime precepts of humanity, purity, charity and unworldliness, inculcated by the moral code of Sâkya Muni had historically paved the way for Christianity?[1]

---

[1] " Le bouddhisme réformé, établi au Thibet sous la suprême direction du grand lama, a vivement excité la curiosité des Européens. Les premiers missionaires qui en eurent connaissance au dix-septième siècle, ne furent pas peu surpris de retrouver au centre de l'Asie des monastères nombreux, des processions solemnelles, des pélérinages, des fêtes religieuses, une cour pontificale, des colléges des lamas supérieurs, élisant leur chef souverain ecclésiastique et père spirituel des Thibétains et des Tartares en un mot une organisation assez semblable à celle de l'église romaine." Huc, " Le Christianisme en Chine en Tartarie et au Thibet," tome II. p. 9. The French philosophers of the last century inferred from this that Christianity was derived from Buddhism, and " que le culte catholique avait été calqué sur les pratiques lamaïques." But M. Huc shows that the most striking points of resemblance are owing to changes in the Tibetan worship since the time of Kubla Khan, in the thirteenth century, who had had frequent relations with Christian missionaries, and may have wished to imitate their institutions. The intercourse between the Mongolian conquerors and Western Christendom was very active at this period. Mongolian envoys repeatedly visited Rome, and some were present at the great Council of Lyons. Some points of resemblance are certainly more ancient, but it is worthy of notice that the resemblances are much more numerous as regards the Latin than as regards the Eastern churches. This would not be the case if Buddhism were the fountain-head. On matters such

I now come to another very remarkable point of coincidence between the Egyptian and the Indo-European religions.

The Ka or Genius.

When we speak of a man of genius, of a genius for poetry or for warfare, or of being inspired by the genius of the place, we are often forgetful of the original use of the word *genius*. The genius was a god, "sanctus et sanctissimus deus," as Servius calls him, in the religion of the Romans, worshipped with libations, incense and garlands of flowers. Every man had his own genius, which was to be propitiated by sacrificial offerings, and so had every god and even every locality. The genius was a sort of spiritual double of each individual. Men swore by their own genius, by the genius of Rome, of the gods, or of the emperor. Very similar facts are to be found in the Greek and in the Persian religions. The Fravashis in the religion of Zoroaster were heavenly types of created things, whether gods, men, mountains, streams or other objects, and formed a divine society, the guardian angels, as it were, of the good creation. Each individual thing was furnished with its Fravashi. On the Persian monuments, especially those of Persepolis, the king's Fravashi is repre-

---

as spiritual direction, both religions have developed very similar methods quite independently one of the other. In regard to the subject of the development of dogma, no history is more instructive than that of Buddhism.

sented standing close to the king, just as the royal *ka* is represented on Egyptian monuments down to the times of Vespasian. The notion was deeply rooted in all the branches of the India-European family, and has been preserved in many of the superstitions still current among us. You remember how in the novel of Waverley the Highland chieftain saw his own wraith. The water-wraith would in classical language be called the genius of the stream or of the billows, and this not in mere poetical phraseology, but in the severe prose of every-day life. The belief itself is not limited to the Egyptian and Indo-European families, but is nearly universal. "Everywhere," as Mr. Herbert Spencer tells us,[1] "we find expressed or implied the belief that each person is double; and that when he dies, his other self, whether remaining near at hand or gone far away, may return, and continues capable of injuring his enemies and aiding his friends." But the development of this belief among the Egyptians is in many of its details surprisingly similar to the corresponding process among Indo-Europeans.

The Egyptian word corresponding to the Latin *genius* is *ka*. Its original signification, as I have recently endeavoured to show, in a paper read before the Society of Biblical Literature,[2] is *image*. The use of the Greek

---

[1] *Fortnightly Review*, May 1, 1870, p. 537.
[2] *Transactions*, Vol. VI. pp. 494—508.

εἴδωλον and the Latin *imago* in the sense of ghost is well known.[1] The oblations which in the funereal formulæ are made to the *ka* of the departed are really made to his image. It is quite true that, as Dr. Hincks pointed out many years ago, the word *ka* was not introduced into the *Suten-hotep-tā* till the twelfth dynasty; but the word itself in its religious signification is as old as the language, as far back as we can trace it, and it enters with that signification into a large number of proper names of the earliest times;[2] so that at all events no new doctrine or practice was introduced when idolatry in the strictest sense of the term, namely, the worship of *idola*, was in so many words made part of the religious prayers of the Egyptians.

It is not to be supposed that so intelligent a people as the Egyptians were ignorant of the absurdity of

---

[1] Τῆλέ με εἴργουσι ψυχαί, εἴδωλα καμόντων.
Iliad, xxiii. 72.
Εἴδωλον Ἄργου γηγενοῦς. Æsch. Prom. 568.
Infelix simulacrum atque ipsius umbra Creusae
Visa mihi ante oculos, et nota major imago.
Æn. ii. 772.
Et nunc magna mei sub terras ibit imago.
Ib. vi. 464.

[2] The *hen ka*, or minister of the *ka*, is represented on the oldest monuments. In *Denkmäler*, ii. pl. 23, he occurs three times presenting offerings. In pl. 25 he is at the head of a procession of persons, each bearing offerings; he himself is pouring lustral water. Elsewhere he is represented offering incense; in pl. 58 he is doing so to statues of the departed.

propitiating the wooden or stone images of their ancestors or of themselves. It is the *living* image which is said to be worshipped, and was supposed to reside in the wood or stone. There is an ancient text[1] which, in reference to Ptah, the chief divinity of Memphis, whom the Greeks identified with Hephaestos as the inventor of the arts, distinctly speaks of the gods as being made through his agency to enter into their bodies, namely, their images of wood or stone.

When enumerating the experiences which tend to generate the belief in a double personality, Mr. Herbert Spencer speaks of the shadow which, following a savage everywhere and moving as he moves, suggests to him the idea of his duality, the shadow being perhaps considered as a specific something which forms part of him; and he adds:

"A much more decided suggestion of the same kind is likely to result from the reflection of his face and figure in water, imitating him as it does in his form, colours, motions, grimaces. When we remember that not unfrequently a savage objects to have his portrait taken, because he thinks whoever carries away a representation of him carries away some part of his being, we see how probable it is that he thinks his double in the water is a reality in some way belonging to him."

I quote these words in order to suggest to you the

---

[1] Sharpe, "Egyptian Inscriptions," Vol. 1. pl. 30.

kind of impression made upon a people who must have worked through a long course of years before they produced such marvels of life-like reality as some of the portrait sculptures of the age of the Pyramids. The art of sculpture was intimately connected with their religion, and its merits and demerits arise from this connection. It is not true, as is commonly supposed, that the Egyptians were not able, like the Greeks, to represent in sculpture motion and activity. They did this, and they did it wonderfully well, as small statues in the museum at Bulaq abundantly show; but most of the statues of this description have perished, like the private houses to which they belonged. But the statues of the gods and ancestors were intended to represent, not the concrete activity of a single moment, but the abstraction and repose of eternity.

As the Iranian Fravashi is represented accompanying the Persian king, so is the Egyptian *ka*, or royal living image or genius, depicted in numberless representations. As the Roman swore by the genius of the emperor, so did the Egyptian by the *ka* of his king. As the Roman appeased his genius, so is the Egyptian king frequently sculptured in the act of propitiating his own *ka*. Votive tablets are addressed to the royal *ka* in company with Ptah or other gods. Each of the gods had his *ka* or genius. And as the Persians, Greeks and Romans, had their local genius, so had the Egyptians. The *kau*, like the *genii*, *manes* and *lares* (who are radically identical), formed a whole class of divine beings, who are mentioned in thousands of inscriptions as "the *kau* who live everlastingly." A well-known and interesting tablet contains the prayer, "May I journey upon the everlasting road in company with the *kau* and glorified ones."[1]

Not the least curious coincidence between Egyptian and European thought is the use of the words *genius* and *ka* to express mental gifts. "Genius" is not used in this way in classical Latin, but by being made synonymous with *spirit*, and spirit being used as in the eleventh chapter of Isaiah ("the spirit of wisdom and understanding, the spirit of counsel and might, the spirit of knowledge, of the fear of the Lord"), genius has come to signify a divine gift. Now the Egyptian word *ka* had certainly acquired this secondary signification as early as the time of Rameses II.,[2] and I have but little doubt, though the proof is not absolute, that this signification already existed in the earliest times known to us.

Souls, Shadows, Apparitions.

The anthropology of the Egyptians was very different from that recognized in our modern systems of philosophy. We are in the habit of speaking of man as consisting of body and soul, the soul being considered

---

[1] *Denkm.* iii. 114.   [2] *Ib.* iii. 194.

the immaterial part of man. We should be astonished at a person calling himself a Christian and yet denying the immateriality of the soul. Yet this belief was not always recognized by the defenders of Christianity as a true one. M. Guizot shows, in his sixth Lecture on the History of Civilization in France, that the earliest doctors of the Church were strongly impressed with the conviction of the material nature of the soul, and that it was only by slow degrees that the opposite opinion prevailed. God alone was thought to be immaterial by nature, and it was only as relative to gross matter that angels, spirits and souls were allowed to be called immaterial or incorporeal.[1]

The disembodied personality of each individual was therefore supposed by the Egyptians to be provided with a material form and substance. The soul had a body of its own, and could eat and drink. We are unfortunately prevented, through want of materials, from accurately determining the relation between a man's *soul* and his *ka*. His shadow was also considered an important part of his personality, and was restored to him in the second life. The Book of the Dead treats the *shadows* as something substantial.

We shall not be surprised to find the belief in apparitions of the dead. There is a letter in one of the papyri of the Museum of Leyden in which a man com-

---

[1] Compare Petavius, De Angelis, I. iii. 12.

plains bitterly of the persistent annoyance caused to him by his deceased wife.[1]

Possession.

The most terrific form, however, of annoyance is that caused by what we commonly call possession. We are accustomed to hear of possession by evil spirits only, but this is because from a Christian point of view possession by spirits is necessarily incompatible with the goodness of the spirits; but the Greek δαίμων was not necessarily an evil spirit, nor was the Egyptian *chut*. There is an interesting inscription now preserved in the Bibliothèque Nationale at Paris, the translation of which was first given by Dr. Birch.[2] It records the possession by a spirit of the princess of Bechten, an Asiatic country which has not yet been satisfactorily identified. She was connected by marriage with the court of Egypt. Her sister had been married to one of the kings of the twentieth dynasty. She had fallen ill, and an Egyptian practitioner who, at her father's request, had been summoned to see her,

---

[1] "L'époux se plaint des mauvais procédés de l'épouse défunte dont à ce qu'il parait la mort ne l'a pas suffisamment debarassé." M. Chabas, in his Introduction to the Papyri of Leyden, p. 71. [The letter has been translated by M. Maspero, *Journal Asiatique*, 1880, p. 371.]

[2] The inscription has been repeatedly translated. [Dr. Erman has recently demonstrated the lateness of its date and its unhistorical character. But its value as a witness of the religious belief is not affected by this.]

declared that she was possessed by a spirit (*chut*) with which he was himself unable to cope. The image of the god Chonsu,[1] one of the divine triad of Thebes, was solemnly sent in his ark, accompanied by a talisman of the same god under a different title, for the purpose of exorcising the princess, and the spirit yielded at once to the superior divinity of such a god, who, speaking through his prophet, ordered that a sacrifice should be offered to propitiate the spirit. The inscription assures us that during the time that the god and the spirit were in presence of each other, the king of Bechten and all his army were in a state of excessive terror. The result, however, was so satisfactory, that he kept the Theban god by him for upwards of three years, and would probably never have allowed him to return, had he not been terrified by a dream; in consequence of which the god was sent back to Egypt with presents of great value.

Dreams.

The belief in dreams, as revelations from a world quite as real as that which we see about us whilst waking, was shared by the ancient Egyptians. The great tablet which is buried in the sand before the

---

[1] Chonsu is the moon, and one of his attributes is *hesb āhā*, the reckoner of time. [Etymologically, his name signifies "the hunter," and is applicable to the sun as well as to the moon; and I am inclined to the belief that Chonsu was originally a name of the sun. Some texts identify him with Ames, the ithyphallic Horus.]

great Sphinx at Gizeh, records a dream in which the god appeared to Tehutimes IV. whilst yet a prince, spoke to him as a father to a son, and promised him the kingdom, the white and the red crown, with the throne of Seb, and the earth in its length and breadth. This promise was made on the condition that Tehutimes should clear away the sand which then as now encumbered the mighty image of the god. King Mer-en-Ptah II. was encouraged by the god Ptah in a dream, and directed in his warfare against the northern invaders of Egypt.

One of the many valuable tablets found by Mariette Bey at Gebel Barkal is well known under the name of *Stèle du Songe.* It belongs to the Ethiopian period, and records an event which happened in the first year of a king (Nut) of the seventh century before Christ. "His Majesty had a dream in the night. He saw two serpents, one at his right hand and the other at his left. And when he awoke he found them not. Then he said, 'Let these things be explained to me at once.' And they explained them, saying, 'The land of the South is thine, and thou shalt seize the land of the North, and the two crowns shall be set upon thy head. The earth is given to thee in all its length and its breadth.'" The tablet proceeds to describe the accomplishment of the dream, and the king's gratitude as testified by his splendid donations.

I have already quoted the Ptolemaic tablet which

speaks of the fulfilment of a dream in which the god I-em-hotep promised a son to Pasherenptah.

Oaths.

The Egyptians invoked their deceased fathers and the gods in attestation of the truth of their assertions. Oaths were resorted to in legal investigations. The primitive sense of the word *ārqu*, which signifies to swear, is "bind." To "clear one's-self by an oath," is a recognized form of speech,[1] and it was no empty form, for the presence of the gods was strongly impressed upon the Egyptian mind. Even when the original meaning of a myth had not been entirely lost, the god was no longer identified with the physical phenomenon, but was supposed to be a living personal power connected with it. The absence of the sun was compatible with the presence of the sun-god Rā.

Presence of the Gods.

The presence of the gods is everywhere taken for granted, but the calendar of lucky and unlucky days contained in the Fourth Sallier papyrus, and translated by M. Chabas, supplies a large amount of evidence as to the popular belief in the immediate intervention of the gods in human affairs. The days of the year are marked as lucky or unlucky according as they com-

---

[1] See Brugsch, *Zeitschrift*, 1868, p. 73.

memorate events in the legendary history of the war between the powers of Light and those of Darkness. But there are incessant cautions about leaving the house or looking at certain objects on days when certain gods are visiting the earth. Whatever was seen on some days was sure to be of prosperous omen; on other days, the sight of a flame or of a rat, the touch of a woman or the getting into a boat, might prove fatal. "Do not go out of thine house at eventide," on the 15th Paophi; "the serpent that comes forth at even, whoever sees him, his eye is injured on the spot." On the 23rd of the month Choiak, a man is blinded if the eyes of certain deities fall upon him. On the 28th day of the same month it is unsafe to eat fish, because on this day the gods of Tattu assume the form of a fish. On the 11th Tybi, "Approach not any flame on this day; Rā is there for the purpose of destroying the wicked." On the 9th Pharmuti, "Do not go out by night; Rā is coming forth on his way to Haï-ren-sen." On the 24th Pharmuti, "Do not pronounce the name of Set aloud." The superstition of the Evil Eye naturally arose from a doctrine which led to such prescriptions. The Egyptian proper names bear distinct witness to the existence of this superstition.

Angels.

Our word angel is derived from the Greek ἄγγελος, which is the literal rendering of the Hebrew *malāch*, a messenger or envoy. This latter word is used in the Bible not only for human envoys, either of private individuals or of the king, but of supernatural beings sent by God to accomplish His purposes. The Egyptian language has a word (*aput*) which is used exactly in the same manner. It occurs repeatedly in the Book of the Dead, particularly in the sense of messenger of divine vengeance. The Maxims of Ani speak of the Angel of Death.

Destiny.

The notion of Destiny, which plays so important a part in Greek mythology, does not appear to have been foreign to Egyptian thought. In two of the romantic tales which have reached us, the Hathors appear in the character of the Fates of classical mythology, or the Fairies of our own folk-lore. In the tale of the Two Brothers, they foretel a violent death to the newly-fashioned spouse of Bata. In the tale of the Doomed Prince, "when the Hathors came to greet him at his birth, they said that he would either die by a crocodile, a serpent or a dog." Hathor, in the more recent theology of the texts of Dendera, is not only the Sun himself with feminine attributes, but the universal God of Pantheism. Mythologically, however, she is, even in these very texts, the daughter of Rā and mother of Horus. Like Isis, she is in fact the Dawn, which from different points of view may be considered either as the daughter or mother, sister or spouse, of the Sun. The Hathors, as represented in the pictures, have the appearance of fair and benevolent maidens; they are not the daughters of Night, like the Erinyes, but they are names of one and the same physical phenomenon, and are spoken of in very much the same relation to human destiny.

The Homeric poems constantly speak of the μοῖραι together with the ἠεροφοῖτις ἐρινύς. The Greek Moira has its counterpart in the Egyptian Shai. In the pictures of the Psychostasia which occur in many copies of the Book of the Dead, two personages are seated together; the male is called *Shai*, the female *Renenet*. They clearly preside over the *meschen*, or, as we should say, the cradle, of the infant. Several important texts, which he has quoted in his recent translation of the tale of the Doomed Prince, have induced M. Maspero to translate *Shai* fate, and *Renenet* fortune. I believe that the word *sha* means "divide, portion out;" hence *shai*, "the divider," and intransitively "the division, part, lot, fate." *Renenet*, as quoted by M. Maspero, may fairly be translated "fortune," but it has several other well-known meanings. It is used in the sense of "young" and "maiden;" and Renenet is the name of the goddess of the eighth month and of harvest. All these meanings can be harmonized if we think of the Greek ὥρα, ὡραῖος. Hora is the time *fixed by natural laws*,[1] the fitting time; it is also used in the sense of the spring or prime of life; ἡ ὡραία is the season of corn and fruit-ripening. The name Renenet is surely well chosen for a goddess presiding over birth. But she is also represented as suckling the infant Horus. And in whose lap can the Sun be nursed more fitly than in that of the Dawn?

The King's Divinity.

I must not quit this part of my subject without a reference to the belief that the ruling sovereign of Egypt was the living image and vicegerent of the sun-god. He was invested with the attributes of divinity, and that in the earliest times of which we possess monumental evidence. We have no means of ascertaining the steps by which the belief came to be established as an official dogma. It was believed in later times that the gods formerly ruled in Egypt; the mortal kings before Mena were called the "successors

---

[1] Compare the Hebrew עֵת "tempus .... spec. (1) de anni tempore (gr. ὥρα) .... (2) de tempore vitæ humanæ, max. de *juvenili* aetate puellæ .... Cf. עִדָּן juventus .... (3) *tempus justum*, ut gr. καιρός .... (4) *tempus* alicujus, i.e. *dies* alic..... i.e. tempus supremum *fatale* alic., interitus ejus." Gesenius. One of the kindred words is יָעַד "*indicavit, definivit, constituit,*" and the corresponding Arabic verb *w'ada*, "praesignificavit aliquid, pec. boni, sed passim etiam minatus est aliquid mali."

of Horus." But the kings who built the Pyramids and all the kings after them took the title of the "golden Horus;" Chāfrā and all after him were called "son of Rā" and *nutar āa*, "great god." The sun in his course from east to west divides the earth and sky into two regions, the north and the south. The king of Egypt, as son and heir of the Sun, assumed the title of King of the North and of the South; not, as has generally been thought, with reference to Egypt, but, as Letronne contended and as M. Grébaut has convincingly shown, with reference to the universe.

The sovereign of Egypt is always said to be seated upon the throne of Horus, and he claimed authority over all nations of the world. He was the "emanation" of the sun-god, his "living image upon earth." "All nations are subject to me," says queen Hatshepsu on her great obelisk at Karnak. "The god hath extended my frontiers to the extremities of heaven;" "the whole circuit of the sun he hath handed over (*mā-nef*) to her who is with him." "I have ordained for thee," says the god to Tehutimes III., "that the whole world in its length and in its breadth, the east and the west, should be thy mansion." Amenophis II. is the "victorious Horus, who has all nations subject to him, a god good like Rā, the sacred emanation of Amon, the son whom he begot; he it is who placed thee in Thebes as sovereign of the living, to represent him." The king himself says, "It is my father Rā who has ordained all these things. .... He has ordained for me all that belonged to him, the light of the eye which shines upon his diadem. All lands, all nations, the entire compass of the great circuit [of the sun], come to me as my subjects." "He made me lord of the living when I was yet a child in the nest. .... He hath given me the whole world with all its domains." The royal inscriptions are full of similar language, and in the temples all the gods are represented as conferring upon the kings whatever gifts they have to bestow. There is a long inscription which appears first in honour of Rameses II. at Ipsambul, and is again found elsewhere, but set up to glorify Rameses III. The god says to the king, "I am thy father; by me are begotten all thy members as divine; I have formed thy shape like the Mendesian god; I have begotten thee, impregnating thy venerable mother. .... Around thy royal body the glorious and mighty assemble festively, the high goddesses, the great ones from Memphis and the Hathors from Pithom; their hearts rejoice and their hands hold the tambourine and hymns of homage when they see thy glorious form. Thou art lord like the majesty of the sun-god Rā; the gods and goddesses are praising thy benefits, adoring and sacrificing before thine image." "I give to thee the sky and what is in it; I lend the earth to thee and all that is upon it." "Every creature that walks upon two or upon four legs, all that fly or flutter, the whole world I charge to offer her productions to thee."[1] The same texts assign to the king the fourteen *kas* of Rā. I have already explained the meaning of *ka*, which corresponds in this place to our word "spirit." But Rā was said to possess seven souls (*baiu*) and fourteen *kas*.[2] This explains the true meaning of the expression, "the souls of the king," which has puzzled many scholars. It is very frequently found and at a very early period. The king had the seven souls of Rā.[3]

That the sovereign in his official utterances should proclaim his divinity, is less to be wondered at than that private individuals should speak of him in the same style. But the doctrine was universally received. "Thou art," says an ode translated by M. Chabas and Mr. Goodwin, "as it were the image of thy father the Sun, who rises in heaven. Thy beams penetrate the cavern. No place is without thy goodness. Thy sayings are the law of every land. When thou reposest in thy palace, thou hearest the words of all the lands. Thou hast millions of ears. Bright is thy eye above

---

[1] I quote, with slight alteration, the excellent English version given in Madame Duemichen's translation of the "Flotte einer ägyptischen Königin."

[2] *Transactions of the Society of Biblical Archaeology*, Vol. VI. p. 501.

[3] It is quite true, as M. Grébaut says, *Mélanges d'Arch.* Vol. III. p. 60, "que le singulier [*ba*] variait avec la forme [*baiu*] pour l'expression de la même idée et dans les mêmes formules." This is also the case with *ka* and the plural *kau*.

the stars of heaven, able to gaze at the solar orb. If anything be spoken by the mouth in the cavern, it ascends into thine ears. Whatsoever is done in secret, thy eye seeth it. O Bacnra Meriamen, merciful Lord, creator of breath." Mr. Goodwin, whose version I have been quoting, judiciously observes:[1] "This is not the language of a courtier. It seems to be a genuine expression of the belief that the king was the living representative of Deity, and from this point of view is much more interesting and remarkable than if treated as a mere outpouring of empty flattery."

It must not be forgotten that the kings are frequently represented in the humblest postures of adoration before the gods. And they are also represented as worshipping and propitiating their own "genius."

The doctrine of the king's divinity was proclaimed by works of art even more eloquently than by words. Dean Stanley writes as follows:[2]

"What spires are to a modern city—what the towers of a cathedral are to its nave and choir—that the statues of the Pharaohs were to the streets and temples of Thebes. The ground is strewn with their fragments; there were avenues of them towering high above plain and houses. Three of gigantic size still remain. One was the granite statue of Rameses himself, who sat on

---

[1] "Records of the Past," Vol. IV. p. 102.
[2] "Sinai and Palestine," p. xxxv.

the right side of the entrance to his palace. By some extraordinary catastrophe, the statue has been thrown down, and the Arabs have scooped their millstones out of his face; but you can still see what he was—the largest statue in the world. Far and wide that enormous head must have been seen, eyes, mouth and ears. Far and wide you must have seen his vast hands resting on his elephantine knees. You sit on his breast and look at the Osiride statues which support the portico of the temple, and which anywhere else would put to shame even the statues of the cherubs in St. Peter's —and they seem pigmies before him. His arm is thicker than their whole bodies. The only part of the temple or palace at all in proportion to him must have been the gateway, which rose in pyramidal towers, now broken down, and rolling in a wide ruin down to the plain.

"Nothing which now exists in the world can give any notion of what the effect must have been when he was erect. . . . . No one who entered that building, whether it were temple or palace, could have thought of anything else but that stupendous being who thus had raised himself up above the whole world of gods and men.

"And when from the statue you descend to the palace, the same impression is kept up. . . . . Everywhere the king is conquering, worshipping, ruling. The palace is the Temple, the king is Priest. But everywhere the same colossal proportions are preserved. He and his horses are ten times the size of the rest of the army. Alike in battle and in worship, he is of the same stature as the gods themselves. Most striking is the familiar gentleness with which—one on each side—they take him by each hand, as one of their own order, and then in the next compartment introduce him to Ammon and the lion-headed goddess. Every distinction, except of degree, between divinity and royalty, is entirely levelled, and the royal majesty is always represented by making the king, not like Saul or Agamemnon, from the head and shoulders, but from the foot and ankle upwards, higher than the rest of the people.

"It carries one back to the days 'when there were giants on the earth.' It shows how the king, in that first monarchy, was the visible God upon earth. No pure Monotheism could for a moment have been compatible with such an intense exaltation of the conquering king."

THE RELIGIOUS BOOKS OF EGYPT.

THE hopes and fears of the Egyptians with reference to the world beyond the grave are revealed to us in various books or collections of writings which have been preserved to us by the tombs.

Most of the evidence upon which the preceding Lectures are based has been taken from inscriptions sculptured or painted upon monuments of stone. But from the very earliest times to which it is possible to go back, the Egyptians were acquainted with the use of the pen and of papyrus as a material for writing upon. Leather skins are also recorded to have been used for certain documents, and some of these have actually been preserved. But the durability and other qualities of the papyrus recommended it for ordinary use beyond all other writing materials. The age of some of the papyri now in our museums must necessarily seem fabulous to those whose experience has been limited to Greek or Latin manuscripts, which are considered as of most venerable antiquity if they were written in the fourth or fifth century after Christ, and, unless like the rolls of Herculaneum they can plead special reasons, are justly liable to suspicion if they lay claim to higher antiquity. There is probably not a Hebrew manuscript of the Old Testament which is a thousand years old. The oldest existing Sanskrit manuscripts were written only a few centuries ago. Some of our Egyptian papyri are not less than four thousand years old. You must bear in mind the difference of the conditions under which the oldest manuscripts of each country have been preserved. The climate and the insects of India are absolutely destructive of all organic substances. The Hebrew Biblical manuscripts of olden times have been intentionally destroyed, either out of reverence for a roll which was no longer in a condition suitable for use, or because the text of it, as being at variance with the Masoretic recension, was considered to be erroneous. The causes which have led to the destruction of Greek and Latin manuscripts, especially of the classical literature, are so obvious, that we can only wonder and be thankful that so much has been preserved. But the Egyptian manuscripts which we now possess—very few, alas! in comparison with the myriads which have perished—have been preserved by being kept from the air and damp in a perfectly dry climate, hermetically sealed in earthen or wooden vessels or under mummy coverings, sometimes at the depth of ninety feet within the living rock, and still further protected by a thick covering of the pure, dry sands of the desert.

The literature which has thus been preserved and recovered is naturally for the most part of a religious character.

It is perhaps necessary that I should apologize for using the term literature in speaking of compositions written in the hieroglyphic character. It is, I know, hard to make strangers to the writing understand that signs representing birds or beasts may be and are as purely alphabetic letters as our A, B, C. Such, however, is the fact, and *every* simple sound in the language, whether vowel or consonant, had its corresponding letter.[1] The language had no medial sounds, so that if a *g* or a *d* had to be transcribed from a foreign language, a *k* or a *t* had to be substituted. But it was from the alphabetic signs of the Egyptians that the Phœnicians derived their own, and from the Phœnician alphabet all those of Europe and Asia were derived: Greek, Etruscan, Roman, Hebrew, Syriac, Arabic, Sanskrit and Zend. The Egyptian writing, it is true, was not confined to alphabetic characters. Some signs are syllabic, but these might at will be exchanged for

---

[1] This is the case with the most ancient hieroglyphic writing known to us. If some scholars, like Dr. Hincks, have maintained that all the alphabetic signs were formerly syllabic, this is pure speculation, and may be true or false without interfering with the fact stated in the text.

the equivalent combination of alphabetic ones, just as the Greek abbreviations which are so puzzling to some persons, either in the manuscripts or in the Aldine and other old editions of the classics, give place at the present day to the simple letters. And just as some persons saw considerable advantage in the use of Greek abbreviations, every Egyptologist will tell you that, each syllabic character being necessarily confined to a limited number of words, he is able to detect at a glance over a page the presence of a word he is looking for. But syllabic signs were not used, any more than Greek abbreviations, in consequence of a want of signs to express purely alphabetic values. In this matter Egyptian orthography differs essentially from Chinese or Assyrian. It may, however, be objected that Egyptian writing admits a certain number of ideographic signs commonly called determinatives, which are not pronounced; a sign, for instance, representing two legs is placed after words signifying motion. But if we compare our own writing either with Sanskrit or with ancient Greek or Latin manuscripts, we shall find plenty of ideographic signs in it. What else are notes of exclamation or of interrogation? What are inverted commas and vacant spaces between the words? Capital letters are to this day determinatives of proper names in English and French, and of substantives in German orthography. Our ideography is undoubtedly much simpler than the Egyptian, but it is quite as real. An

English or French sentence written without it would be simply unintelligible to the ordinary English or French reader. I cannot therefore see what there is in the system of Egyptian writing which is to prevent the Maxims of Ptahhotep, written in the age of the Pyramids, or the tales in the Berlin papyri, written more than two thousand years before Christ, from being considered literature as truly as they would be if they were now written in English, French or Italian.

The Book of the Dead.

The majority of the manuscripts which have been recovered from the tombs contain chapters of the collection generally known under the title of the Book of the Dead. These chapters, though apparently handed down at first by tradition, were committed to writing at a very early period. The vignettes which are found on so many copies, and which represent the burial procession, suggested to Champollion the name of the "Funeral Ritual." Lepsius, however, pointed out the fact that the chapters are supposed to be recited by the deceased person himself in the nether world. M. de Rougé, though not objecting to the title "Book of the Dead," proposed by Lepsius as more appropriate, nevertheless defended the use of the term "Ritual" on the ground that many chapters contain prescriptions for parts of the funeral, and certain prayers are formally mentioned as intended to be recited during the burial. Although the prayers are as a rule put into the mouth of the departed, they were certainly recited for him by those present. On the first vignette of the book, a priest is seen reading the formulary out of a book which he holds in his hands. And rubrics at the end of several chapters attach important advantages in the next world to the accomplishment of what has been prescribed in the foregoing text.

It is not only in papyrus rolls that the Book of the Dead has been preserved. Many of the chapters are inscribed upon coffins, mummies, sepulchral wrappings, statues and the walls of tombs. Tombs of the time of the twenty-sixth dynasty, like those of Bekenrenef or Petamonemapt, may be said to contain entire recensions of the book. The chambers of the latter of these tombs occupy together nearly an acre and a quarter of ground excavated in the rock, and every square inch of their high walls is covered with beautifully sculptured inscriptions from the Book of the Dead and other religious texts.

The Egyptian title of the work is, "Book of the *peri em hru*," three very simple words, perfectly unambiguous when taken singly, but by no means easy of explanation when taken together without a context. *Peri* signifies "coming forth," *hru* is day, and *em* is the preposition signifying "from," but susceptible, like the same preposition in many other languages, of a great variety of uses. I will not take up your time with a discussion of the matter, but will simply tell you that *peri em hru* most probably means "coming forth by day," and that the sense of this expression can only be gathered from a study of the contents of the book so entitled.

It is a very curious fact that, out of the many manuscripts which are extant, no two contain exactly the same chapters or follow exactly the same arrangement. The papyrus of Turin, the facsimile of which is published by Lepsius, contains 165 chapters; and it is the longest known. A very considerable number of chapters, however, which are found in other manuscripts, are not included in it. None of the copies therefore contains the entire collection of chapters. The date of the Turin papyrus is not known, but it certainly is not anterior to the twenty-sixth dynasty. The more ancient manuscripts contain much fewer chapters, and their order is quite different. The antiquity of the chapters in the long recensions is not at all inferior to that of those in the shortest recensions, and the chapters omitted by the Turin manuscript are as old as any. The oldest chapters of all are omitted. There is a great uniformity in the style and the grammatical forms of the language as compared with other productions of Egyptian literature, especially those more recent than the twelfth dynasty. Nothing can exceed the simplicity and the brevity of the sentences.

And yet the difficulties which a translator has to overcome are very great.

In the first place, the text is extremely corrupt. This unsatisfactory condition of the text is owing to different causes. The reasons which writers on Hebrew, Greek or Latin palaeography have enumerated for the purpose of accounting for mistakes in manuscripts, apply with much greater force to the funereal manuscripts of the Egyptians; for as these were not intended to be seen by any mortal eye, but to remain for ever undisturbed in the tomb, the unconscientious scribe had no such check upon his carelessness as if his work were liable to be subjected to the constant inspection of the living. But the most conscientious scribe might easily admit numerous errors. Many of our finest manuscripts in hieroglyphic characters are evidently copied from texts written in the cursive or, as it is called, the hieratic character. Many of the errors of the manuscripts are to be traced to a confusion between signs which resemble each other in hieratic but not in hieroglyphic writing.

Besides the errors of copyists, there are different readings, the origin of which is to be traced to the period during which the chapters were handed down by word of mouth only. There are copies which bear evidence that a critical choice has been made between the different readings of a passage; but the common practice was to admit the inconsistent readings into the text itself, the first being followed by the words *ki t'et*, "otherwise said." This practice is of the most remote antiquity. The different readings of the seventeenth chapter according to the Turin text are already found in the text of that chapter which Sir Gardner Wilkinson copied from the sarcophagus of a queen of the eleventh dynasty.

Some of these variants have unquestionably arisen from the difficulty of understanding the ancient texts. I have no doubt whatever that some of the chapters of the Book of the Dead were as obscure to Egyptians living under the eleventh dynasty as they are to ourselves. The Book of the Dead is mythological throughout, and the true sense of a mythology dies away with the stage of culture which has produced it. A critical collation of a sufficient number of copies of each chapter will in time restore the text to as accurate a standard as could be attained in the most flourishing days of the Egyptian empire. This revision of the text, which, for want of the requisite leisure, I was sorrowfully compelled to decline when it was proposed to me by Dr. Lepsius at the Congress of Orientalists in 1874, is now being actively conducted by a most competent scholar, M. Naville, of Geneva. The most accurate knowledge of the Egyptian vocabulary and grammar will, however, not suffice to pierce the obscurity arising from what M. de Rougé called symbols or allegories, which are in fact simply mythological allusions. The difficulty is not in literally translating the text, but in understanding the meaning which lies concealed beneath familiar words. Dr. Birch's translation,[1] though made about thirty years ago, before some of the most important discoveries of the full meanings of words, may still be considered extremely exact as a rendering of the corrupt Turin text, and to an Englishman gives nearly as correct an impression of the original as the text itself would do to an Egyptian who had not been carefully taught the mysteries of his religion. Many parts of this translation, however, when most faithful to the original, must, in consequence of that very fidelity, be utterly unintelligible to an English reader.

The Book of the Dead, I repeat, is essentially mythological, and, like all other Egyptian books of the kind, it assumes the reader's thorough knowledge of the myths and legends. It is perhaps hopeless to expect that the legends will be recovered; the allusions to them will no doubt always remain obscure. But the mythical personages who are constantly mentioned are the very gods about whom I spoke in the last Lecture: Rā and his family and the dragon Apap, Seb and his family, Nut, Osiris, Isis, Horus, Set and Nephthys. Thoth is one of the most important names which occur. If the explanation which I gave of these personages is

---

[1] Published in the fifth volume of Bunsen's "Egypt's Place in Universal History."

borne in mind, one great difficulty in the interpretation of the Book of the Dead will be overcome. The subject always is the contest between Darkness and Light. Ptah, "the Opener," or "the Artist,"[1] and Chnemu, "the Builder,"[2] are only names of the Sun. Tmu,[3] "the Closer," whose name occurs more frequently, is also one of the principal designations of the Sun. The fifteenth chapter gives an instance of the very different mythological treatment which the same physical phenomenon may receive, according as it is looked at from different points of view. Osiris, Horus, and even Rā, suffer death or dismemberment; but Tmu is daily received into the arms of his mother Nut as he sinks into the west, and the arms of his father Tanen close

---

[1] The Egyptian *Ptah*, like the Hebrew פָּתַח [(*aperuit*, and in the Pihel terram *aperuit* aratro, *aravit* et (quod huic simile est) *sculpsit, insculpsit* tum ligno, tunc gemmis, etiam de ornandis lapidibus ad aedificandum. Gesenius], combines the sense of opening, or rather laying open, with that of artistic work. The primitive meaning is opening, and there are well-known instances of it in old Egyptian, but it no longer exists in Coptic, which has only retained the sense of *sculpere*. It was because the Sun was the Opener that he was considered the Artist, especially in Memphis, the seat of the arts, of which he was the chief divinity.

[2] The word is used as a common noun, and as the name of a profession. See Brugsch, "Bau u. Maasse des Tempels von Edfu," in the *Zeitschr.* 1872, p. 5.

[3] Otherwise written *Atmu*, the prosthetic vowel being prefixed as a support to the two consonants at the beginning of a word. For the meaning "shut," "close," of the word *tmu*, see Brugsch's Lexicon. It is preserved in Coptic.

over him. Neith, the great goddess of Sais, is rarely mentioned. She was the mother of the sun-god Rā, and is commonly supposed to represent Heaven; but some expressions[1] which are hardly applicable to Heaven render it more probable that she is one of the many names of the Dawn. The goddess Sechet is the raging heat of the Sun.[2]

The gods of Thebes are conspicuous by their absence from the Book of the Dead, or at least from almost every chapter. Amon, the great god of Thebes, is named once only, and that in a chapter where the text is extremely doubtful. Chonsu, the moon-god, is only once named. But even the frequent occurrence of these gods would not introduce a different series of conceptions.

Beatification of the Dead.

The Beatification of the Dead is, however, the main subject of every chapter. The everlasting life promised to the faithful may be considered in three of its aspects.

---

[1] For instance, the verb *uben*, expressive of an act of Neith (Todt. 114, 1, 2), is inapplicable to Heaven, and is never used except for the sunrise.

[2] [So it was generally thought. But I am now quite certain that Sechet also is one of the names of the Dawn.]

The renewed Existence "as upon Earth."

1. The blessed is represented as enjoying an existence similar to that which he had led upon earth. He has the use of all his limbs, he eats and drinks, and satisfies every one of his physical wants, exactly as in his former life. His bread is made of the corn of Pe, a famous town of Egypt, and the beer he drinks is made from the red corn of the Nile. The flesh of cattle and fowl is given to him, and refreshing waters are poured out to him under the boughs of sycamores which shade him from the heat. The cool breezes of the north wind breathe upon him. The gods themselves provide him with food: he eats from the table of Osiris at Ristat, and from the tables of the sun-god Rā. He is given to drink out of vessels of milk or wine; cakes and flesh are provided for him from the divine abode of Anubis. The gods of Heliopolis themselves bring the divine offerings. He eats the bread which the goddess Taït herself has cooked, and he breathes the sweet odour of flowers. He washes his feet in silver basins which the god Ptah of Memphis, the inventor of all arts, has himself sculptured. Fields also are allotted to him in the lands of Aarru and Hotep, and he cultivates them. It is characteristic of an industrious and agricultural population that part of the bliss of a future state should consist in such operations

as ploughing and hoeing, sowing and reaping, rowing on the canals and collecting the harvests daily. Warriors and kings who in the course of ages had risen to the head of a mighty empire, still looked forward towards these delights with the same religious faith which inspired them when, on the great panegyrical festival of the ithyphallic Amon, they received the iron sickle from the hands of a priestly ministrant, cut the ears of corn, and presented them as an offering to the god presiding over vegetation and increase.[1] We are told that the height of the corn in the fields of Aarru is seven cubits, and that that of the ears is two (in some readings, four) cubits. This blissful place is surrounded by a wall of steel, and it is from its gate that the sun comes forth in the eastern sky.

Transformation.

2. But the happy dead is not confined to this locality, or to the human form, or to an earthly mode of existence. He has the range of the entire universe in every shape and form that he desires. This is repeatedly stated in the Book of the Dead, and twelve of the chapters consist of formulas through which certain transformations are operated. The forms assumed, according to these chapters, are the turtle-dove, the

---

[1] There are two representations of this, one at the Memnonium (*Denkm.* iii. pl. 163, 164), and another at Medinet Abu (*Denkm.* iii. pl. 212, 213).

serpent Sata,[1] the bird called Bennu (which has generally, but, I think, upon insufficient grounds, been thought to have given rise to the story of the Phœnix), the crocodile Sebek, the god Ptah, a golden hawk, the chief of the principal gods, a soul, a lotus-flower and a heron. Brugsch has found a monument according to which these transformations correspond to the twelve successive hours of the day. There is, however, no evidence as to the date at which such a correspondence was first imagined, or of the general recognition of this correspondence. And the transformations to which these chapters refer are far from exhausting the list of possible ones. No limit whatever is imposed on the will of the departed.

The subject has often been misunderstood through a confusion between Egyptian notions and either Pythagorean or Hindu notions. The Pythagoreans held the notion of the metempsychosis, and the legendary history of their founder represented him as having travelled in the East, and as having been initiated by Egyptian priests into their mysteries. The Pythagorean doctrines about the destinies of the human soul have, in consequence of this unauthenticated history,

---

[1] The later texts show that Sata is Horus Sam-taui, who comes out of the lotus-flower in the middle of the solar bark. See picture in Mariette, *Dendera*, II. pl. 48, 49. In one of the crypts of Dendera he is called "the living soul of Atmu." Elsewhere, *Dendera*, III. pl. 45, he is called "the soul rising out of the lotus in the *Maat*," the morning boat of the sun.

been transferred to the Egyptians, even by scholars who might have known better. There is really no connection, either doctrinally or historically, between the two systems. Nothing in the Pythagorean system is foreign to previously existing Hellenic modes of thought, or which requires in any way to be accounted for by foreign influence, and its metempsychosis is essentially based upon the notions of expiation and purification. Men were supposed to be punished in various forms of a renewed life upon earth, for sins committed in a previous state of existence. There is not a trace of any such conception to be found in any Egyptian text which has yet been brought to light. The only transformations after death depend, we are expressly told, simply on the pleasure of the deceased or of his " genius."

Nor is there any trace to be found of the notion of an intermediate state of purification between death and final bliss. Certain operations have to be performed, certain regions have to be traversed, certain prayers to be recited, but there is no indication of anything of an expiatorial nature. If the judgment in the Hall of Law is favourable, the departed comes forth triumphantly as a god whom nothing can harm; he is identified with Osiris and with every other divinity. The nether world, and indeed the universe at large, is full of terrible and hostile forces; but through his identification with the great gods and his uttering words of power in their name, he passes unhurt in any direction that he pleases.

Identification with Osiris and other Gods.

3. The identification of the departed with Osiris is first found explicitly asserted on the wooden coffin (now in the British Museum) of king Menkaurā of the third pyramid. The inscription, which, with different names and other variations, occurs on a good many coffins, is as follows : " Osiris, king Men-kau-Rā, living eternally, born of Heaven, issue of the goddess Nut, heir of Seb! She stretches herself out, thy mother Nut, above thee in her name of Heavenly Mystery. She hath granted that thou shouldest become a god without an opponent, king Men-kau-Rā, living eternally !"

On two royal coffins of the eleventh dynasty, the goddesses Isis and Nephthys are quoted as addressing their brother Osiris.[1]

The rituals of this early period do not actually insert the name of Osiris before the name of the departed, but all later rituals do so, except in the more recent periods, when women were called Hathor instead of Osiris. And throughout the Book of the Dead in the earliest forms known to us, the identification with Osiris or assimilation to him is taken for granted, and

---

[1] See Birch, "On the Formulas of Three Royal Coffins," in the *Zeitschr.* 1869, p. 49.

all the deities of the family of Osiris, or whose acts have relation to Osiris, are supposed to perform for the deceased whatever the legend records as having been done for Osiris.

Thus in the eighteenth chapter (which, if we may judge from the innumerable copies of it, must have been considered one of the most important of all) the deceased is brought before a series of divinities in succession, the gods of Heliopolis, Abydos, Tattu and other localities, and at each station the litany begins: "O Tehuti, who causest Osiris to triumph against his opponents, cause the Osiris (such a one) to triumph against his opponents, even as thou hast made Osiris to triumph against his opponents." He then repeats the names of the divinities of the place, generally in conjunction with some allusion to the legendary history of Osiris. In the next chapter, which is another recension of the eighteenth, and is entitled the "Crown of Triumph," the deceased is declared triumphant for ever and ever, and all the gods in heaven and earth repeat this "in presence of Osiris, presiding in Amenti, Unnefer, the son of Nut, on the day that he triumphed over Set and his associates, before the great gods of Heliopolis on the night of the battle in which the rebels were overthrown, before the great gods of Abydos on the night wherein Osiris triumphed over his opponents, before the great gods of the western horizon on the day of the festival of 'Come thou to me.'" It ends: "Horus has repeated this declaration four times, and all his enemies fall prostrate before him annihilated. Horus, the son of Isis, repeats it millions of times, and all his enemies fall annihilated. They are carried off to the place of execution in the East; their heads are cut off, their necks are broken, their thighs are severed, and delivered up to the great destroyer who dwells in Aati; they shall not come forth from the custody of Seb for ever."

The term $ma\bar{a}$-χeru is always added to the name of the faithful departed, and used to be translated "the justified." The sense of "véridique," truthful of speech, veracious, has been defended by some French scholars; but the real sense is "triumphant;" literally, "one whose word is law," not merely truth.[1]

But, as I have said, it is not only to Osiris that the deceased is assimilated. In the forty-second chapter every limb is assimilated to a different deity: the hair to Nu, the face to Rā, the eyes to Hathor, the ears to Apuat, the nose to the god of Sechem, the lips to Anubis, the teeth to Selket, and so on, the catalogue ending with the words, "There is not a limb in him without a god, and Tehuti is a safeguard to all his members." Later on, it is said, "Not men, nor gods, not the ghosts of

---

[1] The sense "triumphant" is manifest from a multitude of passages, and is not denied; but it cannot be etymologically derived when $ma\bar{a}t$ is taken for Truth, and the whole compound is translated "véridique."

the departed, nor the damned, not past, present or future men, whoever they be, can do him hurt. He it is who cometh forth in safety; 'Whom men know not' is his name. The 'Yesterday which sees endless years' is his name, passing in triumph by the roads of heaven. The deceased is the Lord of eternity; he is reckoned even as Chepera; he is the master of the kingly crown." And as Osiris himself is identified with many other gods, so the deceased person is perpetually introduced speaking of himself in the person of Rā, Tmu, Chnemu, Seb, Horus and many others. The allusions are often simple enough, as when it is said, "I am Horus, and I am come to see my father Osiris;" or even, "I am he who resides in the middle of the eye;" for in all mythologies the Sun is spoken of as the eye, either of heaven[1] or of some deity. But a

---

[1] "Heaven's eye" is a frequent expression in Shakespeare, and the Friar in "Romeo and Juliet" says :
 "Now ere the Sun advance his burning eye."
The following expressions of the Greek poets will be familiar to all:
 Τον πανόπτην κύκλον ἡλίου.   Æsch. Prom. 92.
 Ὦ χρυσέας ἀμέρας βλέφαρον.   Soph. Antig. 103.
 Ἅλιον, Ἅλιον αἰτῶ τοῦτο . . .
 ὦ κρατιστεύων κατ' ὄμμα.   Trach. 96.
 Ἀλλὰ σὺ γὰρ δὴ πᾶσαν ἐπὶ χθόνα καὶ κατὰ πόντον
 αἰθέρος ἐκ δίης καταδέρκεαι ἀκτίνεσσι.
                         Homer, Hymn. in Dem. 69.
From the Latin poets I will only quote Ovid's
 Omnia qui video, per quem videt omnia tellus,
 Mundi oculus.   Met. iv. 227.

god is sometimes named who is never mentioned elsewhere, and whose name was so little familiar to the copyists of the book that they write it in very different ways. Our ignorance here is of very trifling importance.

The preliminaries to the beatification of the dead consisted in the removal of all physical or moral obstacles originating either in himself or in others. Those things of which death had deprived him are restored to him. His soul, his *ka* and his shadow are given back to him. There is a chapter, with a vignette, representing the soul uniting itself to the body, and the text promises that they shall never again be separated. The use of his mouth, hands and other limbs is given to him. There is a series of chapters relating to the restoration and protection of the heart, two forms of which, the *ab* and the *hāti*, are distinctly and repeatedly mentioned. The next eleven chapters have reference to combats which the deceased has to encounter with strange animals—crocodiles, serpents, tortoises—and to the sacred words in virtue of which he may confidently rely upon success. The chapter for repelling all reptiles is a short one. "O serpent Rerek! advance not! the gods Seb and Shu are my protection; stop! thou who hast eaten the rat which the sun-god abhors, and hast chewed the bones of a rotten cat."

Another series of eleven chapters is intended to

secure the Osiris against other dangers in the nether world, such as having his head cut off, dying the second death, suffering corruption, being turned away from one's house, going to the Nemmat, an infernal block for the execution of the wicked, going headlong in the *cherti-nutar*, eating or drinking filth. The next series of chapters in the Turin manuscript gives the deceased power over air and water, and some chapters are but different recensions of one text, the well-known vignette of which represents the Osiris receiving the water poured out to him by a hand coming out of a tree. The chapter begins, "O sycamore of the goddess Nut! let there be given to me the water that is in thee."

The 149th chapter gives an account of the terrible nature of certain divinities and localities which the deceased must encounter — gigantic and venomous serpents, gods with names significant of death and destruction, waters and atmospheres of flames. But none of these prevail over the Osiris; he passes through all things without harm; unhurt he breathes the fiery atmosphere and drinks the waters of flame; and he lives in peace with the fearful gods who preside over these abodes. Some of these gods remind one of the demons in the Inferno of Dante. But though ministers or angels of divine justice, their nature is not evil. Some of the invocations contained in the seventeenth chapter will give some idea of the terrors of the Egyptian nether world.

"O Rā, in thine egg, radiant in thy disk shining forth from the horizon, swimming over the steel firmament, sailing over the pillars of Shu, thou who hast no second among the gods, who producest the winds by the flames of thy mouth, and who enlightenest the worlds with thy splendours, save the departed from that god whose nature is a mystery and whose eyebrows are as the arms of the balance on the night when Aauit was weighed."

"O Lord of the great dwelling,[1] supreme king of the gods, save the Osiris from that god who has the face of a hound and the eyebrows of a man, who feeds upon the accursed."

"O Lord of victory in the two worlds, . . . save the Osiris from that god who seizes upon souls, devours hearts and feeds upon carcases."

"O Scarabaeus god in thy bark, whose substance is self-originated, save the Osiris from those watchers to whom the Lord of spirits has entrusted the observation of his enemies, and from whose observation none can escape. Let me not fall under their swords nor go to their block of execution, let me not remain in their abodes, let me not rest upon their beds [of torment], let me not fall into their nets. Let nought befal me which the gods abhor."

---

[1] "The great dwelling" is the universe, as the Hall (*usex̌et*) of Seb is the earth, the Hall of Nut is the heaven, and the Hall of the two-fold Maāt is the nether world.

These trials which the departed undergo, and which are triumphantly overcome by the Osiris, sufficiently show the fate which the wicked must expect. This fate is called "the second death."

The faithful dead expect to be protected from the dangers of their new existence, partly indeed by the virtue of amulets and talismans to which the gods have given power, partly also by the knowledge of religious formulas (such as the chapters of the Book of the Dead) or of divine names, but chiefly by the conformity of their conduct with the standard of law by which they are judged by Osiris in the Amenti.

Amulets.

The use of amulets was certainly carried to the most extravagant excess, and the Book of the Dead even in its earliest form shows the importance attached to such things. In the thirty-second chapter, the deceased drives off the infernal crocodiles by pointing to the potent talismans upon his person. "Back! Crocodile of the West!" he says, "who livest upon the Achemu who are at rest; what thou abhorrest is upon me; I have eaten the head of Osiris; I am Set. Back! Crocodile of the West! there is an asp upon me; I shall not be given to thee; dart not thy flame upon me. Back! Crocodile of the East! who feedest upon impurities; what thou abhorrest is upon me; I have passed; I am Osiris;" and so on. Directions are given in the rubrics of certain chapters for the construction of these talismans, such as the Tat of gold (ch. 155), emblematic of the vertibræ of Osiris; the buckle of red quartz (ch. 156), which the text connects with the blood of Isis and the magic words of Osiris; and the golden vulture (ch. 157), which has reference to some parts of the history of Isis and Horus. The most important probably of these talismans was the scarabaeus which had the thirtieth chapter inscribed upon it. The rubric directs it to be placed upon the heart of the deceased person. An immense number of these scarabaci have been found with the chapter inscribed upon them; there is probably no chapter of which the text can be restored with greater difficulty. Its antiquity is extreme, and the different readings already abounded at the time of the eleventh dynasty.

Words of Power.

The belief in the magic power of sacred words, whether religious formulas or the names of gods, was also acknowledged, and was the source of a frightful amount of superstition. The rubric at the end of the first chapter is a specimen of what occurs in others. "If this chapter be known upon earth, or if it be written upon his coffin, he will come forth every day that he pleases, and enter his house without being prevented;

there shall be given to him bread and beer, and flesh upon the tables of Rā; he will work in the fields of Aarru, and there shall be given to him the wheat and barley which are there, for he shall flourish as though he were upon earth." Another rubric says: "If this hapter be recited over him, he will go forth over the earth, and he will pass through every kind of fire, no evil thing being able to hurt him."

The power of the book of Tehuti (that is, of the Book of the Dead), it is said in one place, is the cause of the triumph of Osiris over his ghostly enemies. And in very many places the Osiris bases his claims on the simple fact of knowing the names of the gods whom he addresses, or of the localities in the divine world which he inhabits.

The superstitious repetition of names (many of which perhaps never had any meaning at all) is particularly conspicuous in numerous documents much more recent than the Book of the Dead; from the time, in fact, of the eighteenth dynasty down to Christian times. But the last chapters of the Turin copy of the Book of the Dead, which, though really no portion of it, are probably very ancient, already indulge in this gross superstition. "Iruka is thy name, Markata is thy name, Ruta is thy name, Nasakaba is thy name, Tanasatanasa is thy name, Sharusatakata is thy name."

Moral Doctrine.

From rubbish like this, which is only worthy of the spells of vulgar conjurors, it is pleasant to pass to the moral doctrines of the Book of the Dead, which are the same which were recognized in the earliest times. No one could pass to the blissful dwellings of the dead who had failed at the judgment passed in presence of Osiris. No portion of the Book of the Dead is so generally known as the picture which represents the deceased person standing in the presence of the goddess Maāt, who is distinguished by the ostrich-feather upon her head; she holds a sceptre in one hand and the symbol of life[1] in the other. The man's heart, which represents his entire moral nature, is being weighed in the balance in presence of Osiris, seated upon his throne as judge of the dead. The second scale contains the image of Maāt. Horus is watching the indicator of the balance, and Tehuti, the god of letters, is writing down the result. Forty-two divinities are represented in a line above the balance. These gods correspond to the same number of sins which it is their office to punish. It is with reference to these sins and the

---

[1] Let me protest in this place against the stupid and utterly unfounded identification of this symbol of life with phallic emblems. When the Egyptians meant to represent anything phallic, they did so in such a way as to leave no doubt as to their meaning.

virtues to which they are opposed that the examination of the deceased chiefly consists.

The hundred and twenty-fifth chapter is entitled, "Book of entering into the Hall of the Two-fold Maāt:[1] the person parts from his sins that he may see the divine faces." The deceased begins: "Hail to you, ye lords of the Two-fold Maāt, and hail to thee, great god, lord of the Two-fold Maāt! I have come to thee, my lord, I have brought myself to see thy glories.... I know thy name, and I know the names of thy forty-two gods who are with thee in the Hall of the Two-fold Maāt, who live by the punishment of the wicked, and devour their blood on that day of weighing the words in presence of Unnefer, the triumphant." A good deal which follows in the Turin copy is not contained in all the manuscripts. But the following extracts deserve mention. "I have brought you Law,[2] and subdued for you iniquity. I am not a doer of fraud and iniquity against men. I am not a doer of that which is crooked

---

[1] *Maāt* is here and elsewhere put in the dual. The reason of this is not quite clear. The word used to be translated "the two Truths;" according to M. de Rougé, "la double Justice." Dr. Ludwig Stern argues from the analogy of other Eastern expressions that the dual form here signifies "Right and Wrong." I rather adhere to M. Grébaut's view, that the realm of Maāt, being traversed by the sun, is thereby divided, like heaven and earth, into two parts.

[2] The kings of Egypt are constantly represented with the image or emblem of Maāt in their hands as a religious offering.

in place of that which is right. I am not cognizant of iniquity; I am not a doer of evil. I do not force a labouring man to do more than his daily task. . . . I do not calumniate a servant to his master; I do not cause hunger; I do not cause weeping; I am not a murderer; I do not give order to murder privily; I am not guilty of fraud against any one; I am not a falsifier of the measures in the temples. . . . . I do not add to the weight of the scale; I do not falsify the indicator of the balance; I do not withhold milk from the mouth of the suckling." The catalogue of the forty-two sins, each of which has an avenging deity, includes some of those I have quoted and omits others. The sins are not catalogued according to any scientific arrangement. Besides the crimes of violence and theft, different sins against chastity are mentioned; not only evil-speaking and lying, but exaggeration, chattering and idle words are condemned; he who reviles the king, his father or his god, the evil listener and he who turns a deaf ear to the words of truth or justice, he who causes pain of mind to another, or who in his heart thinks meanly of God—all these fail to satisfy the conditions of admission into the ranks of the triumphant dead.

The 125th chapter of the Book of the Dead certainly contains the oldest known code of private and public morality. The fifteenth chapter, which is a hymn to the rising and to the setting Sun, is the most ancient piece of poetry in the literature of the world.[1] The seventeenth chapter is not less remarkable. It consists, as Bunsen says,[2] "of short and obscure ejaculations, and of glosses and commentaries upon this text;" "of an original sacred hymn, interspersed with such glosses or scholia as must have been collected by a vast number of interpreters. This is identical with saying that the record was at that time no longer intelligible. Yet the text of the whole chapter is written, not only in the Turin papyrus, but on the coffin of the eleventh dynasty. Add to this that the text thus confounded in every verse with its glosses is written so confusedly, both on the coffin and in the papyrus, that the scholia are jumbled into wrong spaces. . . . . Suppose a psalm of the Hebrew text to have been copied on a royal monument with a whole catena of commentaries and glossaries, but copied *uno tenore*, without distinction of text and notes. Such exactly is the state of the Egyptian record." Since Bunsen wrote, considerable light has been thrown upon the chapter. M. de Rougé has translated the chapter, after having carefully collated all the manuscripts accessible to him, and has learnedly commented upon both the original texts and the glosses.[3] Lepsius has

---

[1] M. Léfébure has published a critical edition, with a translation and commentary.

[2] "Egypt's Place in Universal History," Vol. V. pp. 89, 90.

[3] "Etudes sur la Rituel Funéraire des anciens Egyptiens," 1860.

greatly added to our knowledge by publishing two texts of the chapter copied from coffins of the ancient empire, with his learned annotations.[1] The whole of the chapter is important, but the most interesting portion is the beginning of it, which may be thus translated: "I am Tmu, who have made heaven, and have created all the things which are; and I exist alone, rising out of Nu. I am Rā with his diadem, when he began the kingdom which he made." The gloss asks, "What is this?" and the answer is, that "Rā began to exercise his sovereignty when as yet there was no firmament, and when he was on the height of Am-chemun, for then he established the children of inertness[2] upon the height of Am-chemun." The meaning of this is, that there was a time of chaos when no distinction as yet existed between earth and sky. But the kingdom of Rā was already established, and in his reign the firmament was raised, and certain personages, called the children of inertness, were established (as gods, according to one reading) on the height of Am-chemun, where Rā himself had resided before.

---

[1] "Aelteste Texte des Todtenbuchs," 1867.

[2] "Fils de la révolte," according to M. de Rougé. There are two words which are sometimes confounded, even in Egyptian texts, *beshet* and *betesh*. They may be etymologically connected by metathesis (the first is even sometimes written *shebet*), for both mean "stretch out;" the former, however, in active opposition, the second in helplessness. *Betesh* has some of the meanings of the Hebrew שבת, cessavit, desiit; hence desidia, interpellatio operis.

Chemun is the Egyptian name of Hermopolis, but it also signifies the number Eight. The "children of inertness" are the *elementary* forces of nature, which according to Egyptian ideas were eight in number. These elements, born out of chaos or inertness, henceforth became active, and were made to rule the world under Rā as the demiurgus.[1]

The text proceeds—"I am the great God, self-existent;" but a longer recension adds, "that is to say the Water, that is to say Nu, the father of the gods." According to a gloss, the self-existent god is Rā Nu, the father of the gods, and other glosses speak of Rā as "creating his name as lord of all the gods, or as producing his limbs, which become the gods who are in his company." Besides this cosmology, the chapter contains a number of interesting details on the mythology and on the symbolism which is connected with it; as, for instance, that the ithyphallic god Amesi is Horus, the avenger of his father, and that the two feathers upon his head are the twin sisters Isis and Nephthys.[2]

The sixty-fourth chapter is scarcely less interesting; but in spite of the excellent labours of M. Guyesse, who has carefully edited and translated several recensions of it, much remains to be done before it can be

---

[1] See the excellent article of M. Naville in the *Zeitschrift*, 1874, p. 57.

[2] There are other glosses at variance with this interpretation.

made thoroughly intelligible, not only to the public at large, but to professional scholars. Tradition, as represented by the rubrics of the chapter, assigned the discovery of this document either to the time of king Menkaurā, according to some manuscripts, or to that of king Septi of the first dynasty. The chapter is twice copied on the sarcophagus of the queen of the eleventh dynasty, and in one of the copies king Septi's name is given; the other copy follows the tradition in favour of king Menkaurā, though the scribe has blundered about the name, and inserted that of Mentuhotep, which is the royal name to which the coffin itself belongs. The 130th chapter is also said to have been found in the palace of king Septi. It is very doubtful whether these traditions rest upon any authentic basis.

Other Sacred Books.

As the Book of the Dead is the most ancient, so it is undoubtedly the most important of the sacred books of the Egyptians. Other works are interesting to the archaeologist, and require to be studied by those who desire to have minute and accurate knowledge of the entire mythology, but they are extremely wearisome and repulsive to all whose aim extends beyond mere erudition. I am not now referring to hymns and other private compositions (found in papyri or on the walls of tombs and temples), some of which I shall have occasion to speak of in the next Lecture, but to the books which were evidently recognized as having public and, if I may say so, canonical authority. Those which are best known have reference to the passage of the sun through the twelve hours of the night. That part of the world which is below the earth and visited by the sun after his setting, is called the Tuat. The bark of the sun is represented as proceeding over a river called the Uranes, through fields cultivated by the departed. The whole space is divided into twelve parts, separated by gates. The "Book of that which is in the Tuat" contains a short description of these twelve divisions, their names, the names of the hours of the night, of the gates and of the gods belonging to each locality, and it states the advantages to be derived from a knowledge of these names, and also from the due observance upon earth by the living of the rites due to the departed. It is said, for instance, that if these rites are conducted *em shes maāt*, "with the strict accuracy of Law," the honours paid to him on earth are transmitted to him in the lower world. If he knows the names of the gods he encounters, no harm will come to him. The papyri which contain this composition are always illustrated; the text is indeed in great part simply descriptive of the picture to which it refers.

Very similar in its nature is the composition which covers the beautiful alabaster sarcophagus of Seti I.

now in the Soane Museum. Other copies of it are known to us. Perhaps the most interesting part of this text is the scene which recognizes men of foreign and hostile races, the Tamehu, the Aamu, and the Negroes, men of the Red land (*Tesheret*) as well as those of the Black land (*Kamit*, Egypt), as created and protected by the gods of Egypt. M. Léfébure has translated this text, and part of his translation has already appeared in the "Records of the Past."[1]

---

[1] See also his paper on "Les quatre races au Jugement Dernier," in the fourth volume of the *Transactions of the Society of Biblical Literature*.

RELIGIOUS BOOKS AND HYMNS:

HENOTHEISM, PANTHEISM AND MATERIALISM.

Lamentations of Isis and Nephthys.

THE Lamentations of Isis and Nephthys are a poetical composition supposed to be recited by the two sisters of Osiris for the purpose of effecting his resurrection, but intended to be repeated by two priestly personages over the dead. It has been completely translated for the first time by M. de Horrack. The first section begins with the cries of Isis:

"Come to thine abode, come to thine abode! God An, come to thine abode! Thine enemies are no more. O gracious Sovereign, come to thine abode! Look at me: I am thy sister who loveth thee. Do not remain far from me, O beautiful youth! Come to thine abode, quickly! quickly! I see thee no more. My heart is full of sorrow because of thee. Mine eyes seek after thee. I seek to behold thee: will it be long ere I see thee? will it be long ere I see thee? Beholding thee is happiness (*bis*); O god An, beholding thee is happiness. O Unnefer the triumphant, come to thy sister, come to thy wife (*bis*). O thou whose heart is motionless, come to thy spouse. I am thy sister by thy mother; do not separate from me. Gods and men turn their faces towards thee, weeping together for thee, whenever they behold me. I call thee in my lamentations even to the heights of heaven, and thou hearest not my voice. I am thy sister who loveth thee upon earth; no one else hath loved thee more than I, thy sister, thy sister!"

Then Nephthys takes up the strain:

"O gracious Sovereign, come to thine abode! Rejoice; all thine enemies are annihilated. Thy two sisters are near thee, protecting thy funeral bed; calling thee in weeping, thee who art prostrate on thy funeral bed. Speak to us, supreme Ruler, our Lord. Chase all the anguish which is in our hearts," &c.

In the invocations of which this book chiefly consists, protection is said to be afforded to the body of Osiris, that is, of the deceased person, by various gods in succession: by Isis, Nephthys, Tehuti, Neith, the divine mother of Osiris, and the children of Horus.

The last invocation is as follows: "Come and behold thy son Horus as supreme ruler of gods and men. He hath taken possession of the cities and the districts by the greatness of the respect he inspires. Heaven and earth are in awe of him; the barbarians are in fear of him. Thy companions who are gods and men have become his.... Thy two sisters are near to thee, offering libations to thy *ka;* thy son Horus accomplished for thee the funeral offering of bread, of beverages, of oxen and of geese. Tchuti chanteth thy festival songs, invoking thee by his beneficial formulae. The children of Horus are the protection of thy members, benefiting thy soul each day. Thy son Horus saluteth thy name in thy mysterious abode; the gods hold vases in their hands to make libations to thee. Come to thy companions, supreme Ruler, our Lord! Do not separate thyself from them."

The rubric prescribes that whilst this is recited, two beautiful women are to sit upon the ground, with the names Isis and Nephthys inscribed upon their shoulders. Crystal vases of water are to be placed in their right hands, and loaves of bread made in Memphis in their left hands.

Book of glorifying Osiris.

Very similar to these Lamentations is the "Book of glorifying Osiris in Aqerti," contained in a papyrus of the Louvre, which has been published and translated by M. Pierret. It is also supposed to be recited by Isis and Nephthys, and it begins:

"Come to thine abode, O come to thine abode, god An, come to thine abode; good bull, the Lord of all men who love thee and all women; god of the beautiful countenance, who residest in Aqerti. Ancient one among those of the sacred West. Are not all hearts swelling with love of thee, O Unnefer! . . . . Gods and men raise their hands in search of thee, as a son seeketh his mother. Come to them whose hearts are sick, grant to them to come forth in gladness, that the bands of Horus may exult, and the abodes of Set may fall in fear of thee. Ho! Osiris, who dwellest among those in Amenti; I am thy sister Isis; neither god nor goddess hath done what I have done for thee. I who am a female have done a man's part to give life to thy name upon earth. Thy potent seed within my womb I have set down upon the earth to avenge thee. . . . . Set yields to his wounds, the partizans of Set rejoin him, but the throne of Seb is for thee who art his beloved son." The book continues to speak of the war energetically conducted with the aid of Nephthys and Horus against all the enemies of Osiris.

The departed, considered as Osiris, is directly identified with the first cause of all things.

"O Osiris . . . . thou art the Youth at the horizon of heaven daily, and thine old age is the beginning of all seasons. The Nile cometh at the bidding of thy mouth, giving life to men by the emanations which proceed from thy limbs, who by thy coming causest all plants to grow up. . . . . O Osiris, thou art the Lord of millions, raising up all wild animals and all cattle; the creation of all that is proceedeth from thee. To thee belongeth all that is upon earth; to thee all that is in heaven; to thee all that is in the waters; to thee belongeth all that is in life or in death; to thee all that is male or female. Thou art the sovereign king of the gods, the prince amid the company of the gods."

The text concludes with enumerating a multitude of localities in which Osiris is adored, and is more interesting from a geographical than from a religious point of view. In this composition (the manuscript of which belongs to the time of the twenty-sixth dynasty) the only passages which imply any ethical sympathy are these: "Thou art the lord of Maāt (here signifying Righteousness), hating iniquity. . . . . The goddess Maāt is with thee, and the whole day she never withdraweth herself from thee. Iniquity approacheth thee not wherever thou art."

Book of the Breaths of Life.

In the later periods, instead of the Book of the Dead, another work, more systematically composed and partly abridged from it, was buried with the dead and placed under the left arm near the heart. This book was called the *Shāit en sensen*, "Book of the Breaths of Life, made by Isis for her brother Osiris, for giving new life to his soul and body and renewing all his limbs, that he may reach the horizon with his father the Sun, that his soul may rise to heaven in the disk of the Moon, that his body may shine in the stars of the constellation Orion, on the bosom of Nut." It might be called a Breviary of the Book of the Dead, all the ideas in it being borrowed from that older collection, but the obscurities both in form and in matter are studiously avoided.

It was first published in the plates to the Travels of Vivant-Denon; then Brugsch, in an early publication of his, translated it into Latin, calling it the Book of the Metempsychosis of the Ancient Egyptians; and finally, a critical edition has been given of it, with a French translation, by M. de Horrack.

Of the many other compendiums, paraphrases and imitations of the Book of the Dead, I shall only mention one, and that for the sake of a sort of definition which it gives of the gods. The English language is less suited than Greek or German for the translation of *cheper chenti chep chet neb em-chet cheper-sen*, which is literally, "the Becoming which is in the Becoming of all things when they become." Under this play of words the writer wishes to describe "the *cause* of change in everything that changes," and he adds: "the mighty ones, the powerful ones, the beneficent, the *nutriu*, who test by their level the words of men, the Lords of Law (Maāt), Hail to you, ye gods, ye associate gods, *who are without body*, who rule that which is born from the earth and that which is produced in the house of your cradles [in heaven]. . . . .

RELIGIOUS BOOKS AND HYMNS. 209

Ye prototypes of the image of all that exists, ye fathers and mothers of the solar orb, ye forms, ye great ones (*uru*), ye mighty ones (*āaiu*), ye strong ones (*nutriu*), first company of the gods of Atmu, who generated men and shaped the form of every form, ye lords of all things: hail to you, ye lords of eternity and everlasting!"

The author of this composition, the text of which has only been published quite recently,[1] and was quite unknown to me when I delivered my third Lecture, has evidently the same conception of the gods of Egypt as that which I inferred from the scattered utterances we come across in the course of the national literature. The gods of Egypt are the "mighty ones," the forces acting throughout the universe, in heaven and on earth, according to fixed and unchangeable law, for ever and ever.

Rhind Papyri.

A still more recent book is one which was discovered by Mr. Rhind at Thebes. The papyri are of the Roman period, and they are bilingual. The upper portion of each page is in the ancient language, written in hieratic characters; the lower contains a

---

[1] Wiedemann, *Hieratische Texte aus den Museen zu Berlin und Paris;* Leipzig, 1879, Taf. 1. This text is from the Louvre papyrus 3283, of which a notice is found in Devéria's "Catalogue des Manuscrits Egyptiens," p. 143.

translation into the vernacular language of Egypt in the time of Augustus, and this is written in demotic characters. The form of this work is quite unlike that of the Book of the Dead, but the ideas remain unchanged. The same view of the world beyond the grave, and of the gods who influence the destiny of the departed, prevails to the last. The actual deification of the departed is not perpetually dwelt upon, but it is distinctly recognized. "Thou art the eldest brother among the five gods to whom thou art going" (Osiris is called in the Book of the Dead the eldest of the five gods of the family of Seb). "O thou august child of the gods and goddesses, O thou king of the gods and men, who art king of the Tuat," that is, of the nether world. And there is the same disregard of consistency as in the older times, for the departed is spoken of, almost in the same sentence, as one of those who are in the service of Osiris, whom he addresses, "O my lord and father Osiris!"

Magical Literature.[1]

One of the chief differences between the earlier and the more recent formularies is, that the latter are simply

---

[1] The authorities to be consulted on this subject are:

Chabas, "Papyrus Magique Harris."

Birch, "Egyptian Magical Text," in "Records of the Past," Vol. VI. p. 113.

Pleyte, "Etudes Egyptologiques," and "Papyrus de Turin."

said over the deceased, instead of being intended to be said by him. Hence the absence of the constant personification of the gods by the dead, and the utterance in their names of words of power. This assimilation to divinity, which appears to be the most potent means of overcoming all dangers and disasters after death, was equally resorted to for the purpose of triumphing over all the dangers and disasters of the present life. The metaphysical axiom, that every effect has its cause, the Egyptians conceived in another way; namely, that everything that happened was owing to the action of some divinity. They believed therefore in the incessant intervention of the gods; and their magical literature is based on the notion of frightening one god by the terrors of a more powerful divinity, either by prayer placing a person under the protection of this divinity, or by the person actually assuming its name and authority. Disease and pain being caused by the intervention of some god, the efficacy of the medicines which are taken is owing chiefly to the prayers or incantations

---

Ebers, "Papyros Ebers, das Hermetische Buch über die Arzneimittel der alten Aegypten."

Goodwin, "Graeco-Egyptian Fragment on Magic," in the *Publications of the Cambridge Antiquarian Society.*

A good many extracts from magical works will be found in Brugsch's "Grammaire Démotique," and some entire compositions are translated by M. Maspero in his "Etudes Démotiques," published in the *Recueil de travaux rélatifs à la philologie et à l'archéologie égyptiennes et assyriennes.*

which are said over them. Isis is the great enchantress, and she delivers the sick and suffering from the gods and goddesses who afflict them, even as she delivered her son Horus from his wounds received in his battle with Set. The sun-god Rā had himself been ill, and the gods Shu, Tefnut, Seb, Nut and Isis, had prepared medicine for him. Even when no medicines are taken, palm-sprigs may serve as a charm, if a formula be pronounced relative to the palm-branch with which Horus defended himself against Set, and if Isis, the mother of Horus, be invoked. But sometimes the speaker boldly says, "I am Anubis, the son of Nephthys; I am Anubis, the son of Rā; I am Horus, I am Amon, I am Mentu, I am Set." Sometimes threats are uttered. The person using the spell relies upon his knowledge, and consequently on his power of revealing mysterious secrets. "N., son of N., is the messenger of Rā. . . . He is the messenger of every god and every goddess, and he utters the proclamation of Tehuti. N., son of N., knows the mysterious chest which is in Heliopolis, and all the hidden things of Heliopolis." "If he who is in the waters opens his mouth, . . . I will cause the earth to fall into the sea, the south to be changed into the north, and the whole world to be overturned." There is a terrible spell in behalf of a lady in childbirth. The lady is first identified with Isis, and the gods are invoked to prepare a place for her delivery. They are told that, in case of their not doing so, "You shall be undone, you cycle of the gods; there shall no longer be any earth; there shall no longer be the five supplementary days of the year; there shall be no more any offerings to the gods, lords of Heliopolis. There shall be a sinking of the southern sky, and disasters shall come from the sky of the north; there shall be cries from the tomb; the midday sun shall no longer shine; the Nile shall not furnish its waters at its wonted time. It is not I who say this; it is not I who repeat it; it is Isis who speaketh; she it is who repeateth it."

The very same kind of threats are spoken of by Porphyry, about 270 A.D., as mentioned by Chaeremon, a sacerdotal scribe in the first century, and affirmed by him to be of potent efficacy. "What a height of madness," says Porphyry, "does it not imply in the man who thus threatens what he neither understands nor is able to perform, and what baseness does it not attribute to the beings who are supposed to be frightened by these vain bugbears and figments, like silly children!" An Egyptian priest of the name of Abammon is introduced in the work of Jamblichos as replying to the objections of Porphyry. He distinguishes between the gods, properly speaking, and the δαίμονες, who are subordinate ministers, and he says that it is to the latter alone that threats are used. And the authority of the theurgist he derives from identification with the divinity. But the days of the Egyptian religion were already numbered when the book of Jamblichos was written. Constantine was reigning, and the gods of Egypt were already being deserted by their worshippers, who transferred their devotion to Christianity in one of its austerest forms. A very few years after the work of Jamblichos was written, the emperor Valens issued an edict against the monks of Egypt, and a detachment of cavalry and infantry, consisting of three thousand men, was sent into the desert of Nitria to compel the able-bodied ascetics who had retired thither to enlist in the imperial armies. In the next generation, Gibbon tells us, "The stately and popular city of Oxyrinchus, the seat of Christian orthodoxy, had devoted the temples, the public edifices and even the ramparts, to pious and charitable uses; and the bishop who might preach in twelve churches computed 10,000 females and 20,000 males of the monastic profession. The Egyptians, who gloried in this marvellous revolution, were disposed to hope and to believe that the number of monks was equal to the remainder of the people."

We have unfortunately no history of the gradual conversion of the Egyptians to Christianity. But when we compare the notions of the Divinity as contained in the authorized books of Egyptian theology with those which we ourselves hold, we cannot but ask whether so intelligent a people never came nearer to the truth than their most recent books would appear to show.

What, then, do we mean by God? I will not venture to use my own words, but will use those of one of the greatest masters of the English language.

True Notion of God.

"I mean, then, by the Supreme Being, one who is simply self-dependent, and the only Being who is such; moreover, that he is without beginning, or eternal; that in consequence he has lived a whole eternity by himself; and hence that he is all-sufficient, sufficient for his own blessedness, and all-blessed, and ever-blessed. Further, I mean a Being who, having these prerogatives, has the supreme Good, or rather is the supreme Good, or has all the attributes of Good in infinite intenseness; all wisdom, all truth, all justice, all love, all holiness, all beautifulness; who is omnipotent, omniscient, omnipresent; ineffably one, absolutely perfect; and such that what we do not know, and cannot even imagine of him, is far more wonderful than what we do and can. I mean, moreover, that he created all things out of nothing, and preserves them every moment, and could destroy them as easily as he made them; and that in consequence he is separated from them by an abyss, and is incommunicable in all his attributes. And farther, he has stamped upon all things, in the hour of their creation, their respective nature, and has given them their work and mission, and their length of days, greater or less, in their appointed place. I mean, too, that he is ever present with his works, one by one, and confronts everything he has made by his particular and most loving Providence, and manifests himself to each according to its needs; and has on rational beings imprinted the moral law, and given them power to obey it, imposing on them the duty of worship and service, searching and scanning them through and through with his omniscient eye, and putting before them a present trial and a judgment to come."

Now, as I carefully examine each paragraph of this beautiful passage (in which many will at once recognize the language of John Henry Newman),[1] I am obliged to acknowledge that single parallel passages to match can be quoted from Egyptian far more easily than either from Greek or from Roman religious literature. I am not speaking of philosophy, which both in Greece and Rome was generally subversive of the popular religion. Where shall we find a heathen Greek or Latin saying like that of a papyrus on the staircase of the British Museum: "The great God, Lord of heaven and of earth, who made all things which are"? Or where shall we find such a prayer in heathen Greek or Roman times as this: "O my God and Lord, who hast made me, and formed me, give me an eye to see and an ear to hear thy glories"? On the other hand,

---

[1] "Idea of a University," p. 60 and following.

passages like these are constantly accompanied by others in which the old polytheistic language is used without hesitation. Some phrases, again, are ambiguous, and if their true sense be a good one, the popular interpretation may be a bad one. No words can more distinctly express the notion of "self-existent Being" than *chepera cheper t'esef*, words which very frequently occur in Egyptian religious texts. But the word *chepera* signifies *scarabaeus* as well as *being*, and the scarabaeus was in fact an object of worship, as a symbol of divinity. How many Egyptians accepted the words in a sense which we ourselves should admit to be correct? Was there really, as is frequently asserted, an esoteric doctrine known to the scribes and priests alone, as distinct from the popular belief? No evidence has yet been produced in favour of this hypothesis.

Henotheism.

The nature of Henotheism as distinct from Monotheism was explained in last year's Lectures as a phase of religious thought in which the individual gods invoked are not conceived as limited by the power of others. "Each god is to the mind of the suppliant as good as all the gods. He is felt at the time as a real divinity, as supreme and absolute, in spite of the necessary limitations which to our mind a plurality of gods must entail on every single god. All the rest disappear from the vision, ... and he only who is to fulfil their desires stands in full light before the eyes of the worshippers."[1]

This phase of religious thought is chiefly presented to us in a large number of hymns, beginning with the earliest days of the eighteenth dynasty. It is certainly much more ancient, but the literature, properly speaking, of the older period is very small. None of the hymns of that time have come down to us.

One of the most interesting hymns to Osiris is engraved on a funereal tablet now in the Bibliothèque Nationale in Paris, and was published and translated in 1857 by M. Chabas. The ancient date of it is marked by the hammering out of it of the name Amon, during the period of the sun-disk worshippers. It probably belongs to the time of Tchutimes III.

Osiris is called "Lord of eternity, king of the gods, of many names, of holy transformations, of mysterious forms in the temples. . . . . He is the substance of the world, Atmu, feeder of beings among the gods, beneficent spirit in the abode of spirits. From him the (celestial ocean) Nu derives its waters, from him comes the wind, and respirable air is in his nostrils for his satisfaction and the taste of his heart. For him the ground brings forth its abundance; in obedience to

---

[1] Max Müller, "Lectures on the Origin and Growth of Religion, as illustrated by the Religions of India," p. 285.

him is the upper heaven and its stars, and he opens the great gates. He is the master of invocations in the southern heavens, and of adorations in the northern heavens; the ever-moving stars are under obedience to him, and so are the stars which set..... He is the excellent master of the gods, fair and beloved by all who see him..... He is the eldest, the first of his brothers, the chief of the gods; he it is who maintains law in the universe, and places the son in the seat of his father..... He has made this world with his hands; its waters, its atmosphere, its vegetation, all its flocks, all its flying things, all its fish, all its reptiles and quadrupeds.... His diadem predominates at the zenith of heaven and accompanies the stars; he is the guide of all the gods. He is beneficent in will and words; he is the praise of the great gods, and the love of the inferior gods."

What follows is textually applied to Horus, but it is to Horus considered as Osiris born again, and as the son of the widowed Isis.

"The gods recognize the universal Lord..... He takes the royalty of the double world; the crown of the south is fixed upon his head. He judges the world according to his will; heaven and earth are in subjection to him; he giveth his commands to men, to the generations present, past and future, to Egyptians and to strangers. The circuit of the solar orb is under his direction; the winds, the waters, the wood of the plants and all vegetables. A god of seeds, he giveth all herbs and the abundance of the soil. He affordeth plentifulness, and giveth it to all the earth. All men are in ecstacy, all hearts in sweetness, all bosoms in joy, every one in adoration. Every one glorifieth his goodness; his tenderness encircles our hearts; great is his love in all bosoms."[1]

An ancient text now in the British Museum is in so mutilated a condition that it is in many places quite illegible. There is one passage in it which refers either to Tehuti or to Ptah. Of this god it is said that "he gave birth to the gods, he made towns and organized provinces.... All things proceed from him. The divine word is made for those who love and for those who hate it; it gives life to the righteous, and it gives death to the unjust. To him is due the work of the hands, the walking of the feet, the sight of the eyes, the hearing of the ears, the breathing of the nostrils, the fortitude of heart, the vigour of hand, activity in body and in mouth of all the gods and men and of all living animals, intelligence and speech; whatever is in the heart and whatever is on the tongue."

"Hail to thee, Tehuti," says the tablet of Hor-em-

---

[1] The "Records of the Past" give the translation of this hymn, and of some of the others which are here quoted. I have in these Lectures availed myself freely of the existing translations, but have not scrupled to introduce important alterations, for which no one but myself is responsible.

heb in the British Museum, "Lord of Hermopolis, self-existent, without birth, sole God, who regulatest the nether world and givest laws to those who are in the Amenti, and to those who are in the service of Rā."

"Hail to thee," we read in another hymn, "Rā-Tmu-Horus of the double horizon, the one God, living by Maāt, who makest all things which are, who createst all that exists of beasts and men proceeding from thine eyes. Lord of heaven, Lord of earth, who makest those who are below and those who are above, Lord of all..... King of heaven, Lord of all gods. O supreme King, amid the society of the gods, almighty God, self-existent, two-fold substance, existing from the beginning."

In a papyrus at Turin, the following words are put into the mouth of "the almighty God, the self-existent, who made heaven and earth, the waters, the breaths of life, fire, the gods, men, animals, cattle, reptiles, birds, fishes, kings, men and gods" [in accordance with one single thought]..... "I am the maker of heaven and of the earth. I raise its mountains and the creatures which are upon it; I make the waters, and the Mehura comes into being..... I am the maker of heaven, and of the mysteries of the two-fold horizon. It is I who have given to all the gods the soul which is within them. When I open my eyes, there is light; when I close them, there is darkness..... I make the hours, and the hours come into existence. I am

Chepera in the morning, Rā at noon, Tmu in the evening."

Another text says, "I am yesterday, I am to-day, I am to-morrow."

"Hail to thee, O Ptah-tanen, great god who concealeth his form, ... thou art watching when at rest; the father of all fathers and of all gods. . . . . Watcher, who traversest the endless ages of eternity. The heaven was yet uncreated, uncreated was the earth, the water flowed not; thou hast put together the earth, thou hast united thy limbs, thou hast reckoned thy members; what thou hast found apart, thou hast put into its place; O God, architect of the world, thou art without a father, begotten by thine own becoming; thou art without a mother, being born through repetition of thyself. Thou drivest away the darkness by the beams of thine eyes. Thou ascendest into the zenith of heaven, and thou comest down even as thou hast risen. When thou art a dweller in the infernal world, thy knees are above the earth, and thine head is in the upper sky. Thou sustainest the substances which thou hast made. It is by thine own strength that thou movest; thou art raised up by the might of thine own arms. Thou weighest upon thyself, kept firm by the mystery which is in thee. The roaring of thy voice is in the cloud; thy breath is on the mountain-tops; the waters of the inundation cover the lofty trees of every region. . . . . Heaven and earth obey the commands which thou hast given; they travel by the road which thou hast laid down for them; they transgress not the path which thou hast prescribed to them, and which thou hast opened to them. .... Thou restest, and it is night; when thine eyes shine forth, we are illuminated. .... O let us give glory to the God who hath raised up the sky, and who causeth his disk to float over the bosom of Nut, who hath made the gods and men and all their generations, who hath made all lands and countries, and the great sea, in his name of 'Let-the-earth-be!' .... The babe who is brought forth daily, the ancient one who has reached the limits of time, the immovable one who traverses every path, the height which cannot be attained."

A beautiful hymn (written, it is expressly stated, for the harp), preserved in two MSS. now in the British Museum, identifies the Nile with Rā, Amon, Ptah and other gods, and even with the maker and creator of all things.

"Bringer of food! great lord of provisions, creator of all good things. Lord of terrors and of chiefest joys! all are combined in him. He produceth grass for the oxen; providing victims for every god. .... He filleth the granaries, enricheth the storehouses; he careth for the state of the poor. He causeth growth to fulfil all desires—he never wearies of it. He maketh his might a buckler. He is not graven in marble as an image bearing the double crown. He is not beheld;

he hath neither ministrant nor offerings; he is not adored in sanctuaries; his abode is not known; no shrine [of his] is found with painted figures. There is no building that can contain him..... Unknown is his name in heaven; he doth not manifest his forms! Vain are all representations." Yet the last of these passages, which would seem to have reference to the purest worship of one God, is preceded by lines which speak simply of the Nile inundation and of the offerings made to it, oxen slain and great festivals celebrated.

But it is chiefly in honour of Amon[1] that we find hymns full of expressions closely approaching the language of Monotheism. This pre-eminence which Amon enjoys in the literature we have recovered, arises no doubt chiefly from the fact of his being the principal divinity at Thebes, and consequently of the great capital of Egypt during its most splendid period. Amon himself, according to the popular mythology, was not without a beginning. His legend relates that every year he left his temple at Karnak, and paid a visit to the valley of the dead, and poured a libation of lustral water upon a table of propitiation to his father and mother. Yet he is identified with the supreme and uncreated Being in hymns such as that (now in the

---

[1] He is called in the temple of Seti at Qurnah "the Lord of lords, King of the gods, the father of fathers, the powerful of the powerful, the substance which was from the beginning." *Denkm.* iii. 150.

Museum at Bulaq) from which the following extracts are made.

"Hail to thee, Amon Rā, Lord of the thrones of the earth, ... the ancient of heaven, the oldest of the earth, Lord of all existences, the support of things, the support of all things. The ONE in his works, single among the gods; the beautiful bull of the cycle of the gods; chief of all the gods; Lord of truth, father of the gods; maker of men, creator of beasts, maker of herbs, feeder of cattle, good power begotten of Ptah, ... to whom the gods give honour. Maker of things below and above, enlightener of the earth, sailing in heaven in tranquillity; king Rā, triumphant one, chief of the earth. Most glorious one, Lord of terror, chief maker of the earth after his image, how great are his thoughts above every god! Hail to thee, Rā, Lord of law, whose shrine is hidden, Lord of the gods; Chepra in his boat, at whose command the gods were made. Atmu, maker of men, . . . giving them life, . . . listening to the poor who is in distress, gentle of heart when one cries to him. Deliverer of the timid man from the violent, judging the poor, the poor and the oppressed. Lord of wisdom, whose precepts are wise; at whose pleasure the Nile overflows: Lord of mercy, most loving, at whose coming men live: opener of every eye, proceeding from the firmament, causer of pleasure and light; at whose goodness the gods rejoice; their hearts revive when they see him. O Rā, adored in Thebes, high crowned in the house of the obelisk (Heliopolis), sovereign of life, health and strength, sovereign Lord of all the gods; who art visible in the midst of the horizon, ruler of the past generations and the nether world; whose name is hidden from his creatures; in his name, which is Amon. . . . .

"The ONE, maker of all that is; the one, the only one, the maker of existences; from whose eyes mankind proceeded, from whose mouth are the gods; maker of grass for the cattle (oxen, goats, asses, swine and sheep); of fruitful trees for men of future generations; causing the fish to live in the river, the birds to fill the air; giving breath to those in the egg; feeding the bird that flies; giving food to the bird that perches, to the creeping thing and the flying thing alike; providing food for the rats in their holes; feeding the flying things in every tree.

"Hail to thee for all these things—the *one*, alone with many hands, lying awake while all men sleep, to seek out the good of his creatures, Amon, sustainer of all things: Tmu and Horus of the horizon pay homage to thee in all their words; salutation to thee because thou abidest in us, adoration to thee because thou hast created us.

"Hail to thee, say all creatures: salutation to thee from every land; to the height of heaven, to the breadth of the earth, to the depth of the sea; the gods adore thy majesty, the spirits thou hast created exalt thee, rejoicing before the feet of their begetter; they cry out, Welcome to thee, father of the fathers of all the gods, who raises the heavens, who fixes the earth. Maker of beings, creator of existences, sovereign of life, health and strength, chief of the gods, we worship thy spirit who alone hast made us; we whom thou hast made (thank thee) that thou hast given us birth; we give to thee praises on account of thy abiding in us.

"Hail to thee, maker of all beings, Lord of law, father of the gods; maker of men, creator of beasts; Lord of grains, making food for the beast of the field..... The One alone without a second..... King alone, single among the gods; of many names, unknown is their number."

Another hymn begins: "I come to thee, O Lord of the gods, who hast existed from the beginning, eternal God who hast made all things that are. Thy name be my protection; prolong my term of life to a good age; may my son be in my place (after me); may my dignity remain with him (and his) for ever, as is done to the righteous, who is glorious in the house of his Lord."

And it is with reference to Amon that we most frequently find evidence of the devotion of the people. Thus the prayer of Rameses II. when in danger:

"Who then art thou, O my father Amon? Doth a father forget his son? Surely a wretched lot awaiteth him who opposes thy will; but blessed is he who knoweth thee, for thy deeds proceed from a heart full of love. I call upon thee, O my father Amon! behold me in the midst of many peoples, unknown to me; all nations are united against me, and I am alone; no other is with me. My many soldiers have abandoned me, none of my horsemen hath looked towards me; and when I called them, none hath listened to my voice. But I believe that Amon is worth more to me than a million of soldiers, than a hundred thousand horsemen and ten thousands of brothers and sons, even were they all gathered together. The work of many men is nought; Amon will prevail over them."

The same confidence is expressed by humbler men in poems contained in papyri of the British Museum.

"Oh! Amon, lend thine ear to him who is alone before the tribunal; he is poor (and not) rich. The court oppresses him; silver and gold for the clerks of the books, garments for the servants. There is no other Amon, acting as a judge to deliver one from his misery when the poor man is before the tribunal."

"I cry, the beginning of wisdom is the cry of Amon, the rudder of (truth). Thou art he that giveth bread to him who has none, that sustaineth the servant of his house. Let no prince be my defender in all my troubles. Let not my memorial be placed under the power of any man who is in the house. . . . . My Lord is my defender. I know his power, to wit (he is) a strong defender. There is none mighty except him alone. Strong is Amon, knowing how to answer, fulfilling the desire of him who cries to him."

Another hymn says: "Come to me, O thou Sun; Horus of the horizon, give me (help); thou art he that giveth (help); there is no help without thee, except thou givest it. . . . . Let my desires be fulfilled, let my heart be joyful, my inmost heart in gladness. Hear my vows, my humble supplications every day, my adorations by night. . . . . O Horus of the horizon, there is no other besides like him, protector of millions, deliverer of hundreds of thousands, the defender of him that calls to him. . . . . Reproach me not with my many sins."

It is remarkable that a religious reformation at the end of the 18th dynasty in behalf of one god, spent its special wrath upon the name of Amon. The king, whose title would under ordinary circumstances have been Amenhotep IV., set up the worship of a single god whose symbol was the sun-disk; he caused the names of other gods, particularly that of Amon, to be hammered out of inscriptions even when it only occurred in proper names, as in his own, which he changed into *Chut en Aten,* "Glory of the Sun-disk." And as Thebes was the great seat of the worship of Amon, he abandoned it and tried to set up another capital. His reformation lasted but a short time, his own immediate family having abandoned it after his death. All his monuments were destroyed by his successors, yet several hymns belonging to this short-lived phase of religion have escaped destruction. One of them says:

"The whole land of Egypt and all people repeat all thy names at thy rising, to magnify thy rising in like manner as thy setting. Thou, O God, who in truth art the living one, standest before the Two Eyes. Thou art he which createst what never was, which formest everything, which art in all things: we also have come into being through the word of thy mouth."

Another says: "Thou living God! there is none other beside thee! Thou givest health to the eyes by thy beams. Creator of all beings. Thou goest up on the eastern horizon of heaven to dispense life to all that thou hast created: to man, to four-footed beasts, birds, and all manner of creeping things on the earth where they live. . . . . Grant to thy son who loves thee, life in truth . . . . that he may live united with thee in eternity."

The language of these hymns and prayers is exactly similar to that of ordinary Egyptian orthodoxy, and there is nothing heterodox in the symbol itself; the heresy consisted in refusing worship to all the other gods.

Pantheism.

But the magnificent predicates of the one and only God, however recognized by Egyptian orthodoxy, never in fact led to actual Monotheism. They stopped short in Pantheism—namely, in the doctrine that "all individual things are nothing but modifications, affections, of the One and All, the eternal and infinite God-world; that there is but one universal force in nature in different forms, in itself eternal and unchangeable."

This doctrine is perhaps most clearly expressed in a hymn upon the walls of the temple in the oasis of El-Khargeh:

"The gods salute his royal majesty as their Lord, who revealeth himself in all that is, and hath names in everything, from mountain to stream. That which persisteth in all things is Amon. This lordly god was from the very beginning. He is Ptah, the greatest of the gods. . . . . Thy secret is in the depths of the secret waters and unknown. Thou hast come on the road, thou hast given light in the path, thou hast overcome all difficulties in thy mysterious form. Each god has assumed thy aspect; without shape is their type compared to thy form. To thee, all things that are give praise when thou returnest to the nether world at even. Thou raisest up Osiris by the radiance of thy beams. To thee, those give praise who lie in their tombs, ... and the damned rise up in their abodes. . . . . Thou art the King, thine is the kingdom of heaven, and the earth is at thy will. The gods are in thine hand, and men are at thy feet. What god is like to thee? Thou hast made the double world, as Ptah. Thou hast placed thy throne in the life of the double world, as Amon. Thy soul is the pillar and the ark of the two heavens. Thy form emanated at first whilst thou shinest as Amon, Rā and Ptah. .... Shu, Tefnut, Nut and Chonsu are thy form, dwelling in thy shrine under the types of the ithyphallic god, raising his tall plumes, king of the gods. .... Thou art Mentu Rā. Thou art Sekar; thy transformations are into the Nile. Thou art Youth and Age. Thou givest life to the earth by thy stream. Thou art heaven, thou art earth, thou art fire, thou art water, thou art air, and whatever is in the midst of them."

This very remarkable hymn is put in the mouth of the gods of the elements, eight in number, four male and four female. What these elements are is not perfectly clear. They used to be thought peculiar to the Ptolemaic period, and were then supposed to have been borrowed from the four Greek elements, Earth, Air, Fire and Water, but they have been recognized in much earlier texts. They are, in fact, the eight gods mentioned in the seventeenth chapter of the Book of the Dead, and belong to the oldest cosmogonical part of the religion. This chapter, as we have already seen, speaks of a time when as yet there was no firmament, and when these eight divinities were set up as the gods of Hermopolis; in other words, when chaos disappeared, and the elements began to rule with fixed and unchangeable laws.

Another hymn, copied by Brugsch at the same temple, sings "the mysterious names of the God who is *immanent in all things (men em χet neb)*, the soul of Shu (breath) to all the gods. He is the body of the living man, the creator of the fruit-bearing tree, the author of the inundation; without him nothing liveth within the circuit of the earth, whether north or south, under his name of Osiris, the giver of light: he is the Horus of the living souls, the living god of the generations yet to come. He is the creator of every animal under his names of Ram of the sheep, god of the goats, Bull of the cows. .... He loves the scorpion in his hole; he is the god of the crocodiles who plunge in the water .... he is the god of those who rest in their graves. Amon is an image, Atmu is an image, Chepera is an image, Rā is an image; he alone maketh himself in millions of ways. He is a great architect, who was from the beginning, who fashioned his body with his own hands, in all forms according to his will. .... Permanent and enduring, he never passeth away. Through millions upon millions of endless years he traverseth the heavens, he compasseth the nether world each day. .... He is the moon in the night and king of the stars, who maketh the division of seasons, months and years; he cometh living everlastingly both in his rising and in his setting. There is no other like him; his voice is heard, but he remains unseen to every creature that breathes. He strengthens the heart of the woman in travail, and gives life to those who are born from her. . . . . He travels in the cloud to separate heaven and earth, and again to re-unite them, permanently abiding in all things, the Living One in whom all things live everlastingly."

But the Litanies of Rā which M. Naville copied from the royal tombs of the 19th dynasty are already pantheistic. All things are represented as mere emanations from Rā. The learned editor of these Litanies has not failed to remark that the pantheistic influence of the doctrine has told upon the ethical system, which can hardly be said to exist at all; whereas the notions of right and wrong, iniquity and sin, are perpetually occurring in the Book of the Dead and in all the ancient inscriptions.[1] It is only out of condescension to popular language that pantheistic systems can recognize these notions. If everything really emanates from God, there can be no such thing as sin. And the ablest philosophers who have been led to pantheistic views have vainly endeavoured to harmonize these views with what we understand by the notion of sin or moral evil. The great systematic work of Spinoza is entitled "Ethica," but for real ethics we might as profitably consult the Elements of Euclid.

---

[1] "Puisque toute chose bonne ou mauvaise émane également du Grand Tout, il est clair que la valeur morale du bien est nécessairement fort affaiblie. Nous ne trouvons rien dans ces textes qui rappelle la morale si élevée qu'enseigne le chapitre 125 du Livre des Morts, rien même qui nous parle de la responsabilité."—*La Litanie du Soleil*, p. 128.

I believe, therefore, that, after closely approaching the point at which polytheism might have turned into monotheism, the religious thought of Egypt turned aside into a wrong track. And this was followed by a decided and hopeless course of retrogression. Those elements of the Egyptian religion which the Greeks and the Jewish and Christian writers looked upon with such disgust, had existed from the first, but in a very subordinate position; they now became nearly predominant.

There can be no doubt that, from the earliest days, symbolism had played a great part in the religion of Egypt. We are ourselves so familiar with certain symbols in Hebrew or Christian writings, or with the poetic figures which classical literature has brought home to us, that when we meet with symbols of another kind, we are far more shocked than we really have a right to be. We think it natural enough to speak of a hero we venerate as a lion or an eagle, while quite other associations are connected with a fox or a dog. Christians have other associations with the lamb or the dove. But the Egyptians, as far back as we know them, seem to have studied the animal creation with a minute accuracy which only the natural history of our own times can rival. Their symbolism is not necessarily the same as ours. Certain characteristics of animals have in the course of ages fixed themselves in our minds, but in this we are simply following a tradition.

Other characteristics of the same animals had impressed the minds of the Egyptians, and their symbolism is based on the peculiar observations made by them. Some of the inscriptions enable us to understand parts of the symbolism. Who of us would like to be called a crocodile, a jackal, or even a young bull? Yet the Egyptian poet gives these names to Tehutimes III. in a song of triumph, and he at the same time enlightens us as to the meaning of these words: the crocodile is terrible in the waters, and not to be encountered without disaster; the young bull whets his horns, and is not to be attacked without peril; and so on. The " bull" is a favourite name for a king or a god. However foreign the symbol may be to our own poetical conceptions, we can easily understand how an ancient agricultural people was impressed by certain qualities of the animal, his might, his courage, the terror he inspires when angry, the protection he affords to the herd, and his marital or paternal relations to it. The rays of the sun and the moon's crescent have at all times suggested the notion of horns. The cow in Egypt, as well as in India, represents the Sky,[1] the Dawn and other powers. The hawk was among birds what the bull was among quadrupeds, and they admired his rapid, lofty and unerring flight, the piercing sight

---

[1] See *Transactions of the Society of Biblical Archaeology*, Vol. IV. pl. 1, where the cow has the stars upon its belly.

which nothing can escape, and the irresistible grasp of his talons. All this with us is mere poetry, but all early language is poetry. There is nothing more certainly established by the science of language than "the fact that all words expressive of immaterial conceptions are derived by metaphor from words expressive of sensible ideas." But besides such metaphors as those of which I have just been speaking, and which are intelligible even when translated, there are others which are necessarily peculiar to the language in which they originated. The names of Seb and of Tehuti, as we have seen, were to the Egyptians connected with the names of the goose and the ibis. Anpu (Anubis) "is apparently," as Mr. Goodwin says, "the ancient Egyptian name for a jackal." Sebek, one of the names of the Sun-god, is also the name of a kind of crocodile. It is not improbable that the cat, in Egyptian *mäu*, became the symbol of the Sun-god, or Day, because the word *mäu* also means light. It is, I think, quite easy to see how the mythological symbolism arose through these varieties of metaphorical language. And this metaphorical language reacted upon thought, and, as in other religions, obtained the mastery.

The triumph of the symbol over the thought is most sensibly visible in the development of the worship of the Apis Bull. This worship is indeed as old as the age of the Pyramids, but an inspection of the tombs of the bulls in the Serapeum discovered by M. Mariette under the sands of Saqāra, shows how immeasurably greater the devotion to the sacred animals was in the later times than in the former. Dean Stanley[1] has described these

"Long galleries, hewn in the rock and opening from time to time—say every fifty yards—into high-arched vaults, under each of which reposes the most magnificent black marble sarcophagus that can be conceived —a chamber rather than a coffin[2]—smooth and sculptured within and without; grander by far than even the granite sarcophagi of the Theban king,—how much grander than any human sepulchres anywhere else! And all for the successive corpses of the bull Apis! These galleries formed part of the great temple of Serapis, in which the Apis mummies were deposited; and here they lay, not in royal, but in divine state. The walls of the entrances are covered with ex-votos. In one porch there is a painting at full length, black and white, of the Bull himself as he was in life."

No one who has seen the tombs of these strange gods can doubt the accounts given by the classical writers as to the extravagant expenses incurred at a single funeral. But if one of the funerals of an Apis cost fifty talents, not less than a hundred talents are said to have been expended by curators of other sacred

---

[1] "Sinai and Palestine," p. lii.
[2] A breakfast-party has been held in one of these coffins.

animals. The Apis was called "the second life of Ptah," the god of Memphis. The sacred Ram of Mendes was called "the life of Rā." Three other sacred Rams are mentioned, " the soul of Osiris," " the soul of Shu," and "the soul of Chepra."[1] They were also conceived as united in one, who is represented with four heads, and bears the name of *Shefthāt*, Primeval Force. This name I believe to be comparatively modern, and to bear the impress of pantheistic speculation rather than of mythology; but the word *Ba*, which means a ram, also means soul; so that here again there is every probability that the god originated, like so many others, in homonymous metaphor. The encouragement given to his worship by the Ptolemies is circumstantially exhibited in the great tablet of Mendes, published by M. Mariette,[2] and translated by Brugsch-Bey.[3]

Materialism.

If Pantheism strongly contributed to the development of this animal worship and to all the superstition therewith connected, it also led to simple Materialism. The hymns at Dendera in honour of the goddess Hathor irresistibly remind one of the opening of the poem of

---

[1] Or, according to another text, "of Seb."

[2] *Monuments divers*, pl. 43, 44.

[3] *Zeitschrift*, 1875, p. 33. An English version has been published in the "Records of the Past."

Lucretius. Hathor, like the mother of the Aeneadae, is "sole mistress of the nature of things, and without her nothing rises up into the divine borders of light, nothing grows to be glad or lovely;" "through her every kind of living thing is conceived, rises up and beholds the light of the sun."[1] But we know the Roman poet's apology[2] for these poetical conceptions, "however well and beautifully they may be set forth." "If any one thinks proper to call the sea Neptune, and corn Ceres, and chooses rather to misuse the name of Bacchus than to utter the term that belongs to that

---

[1] Per te genus omne animantum
Concipitur visitque exortum lumina solis;
Te dea, te fugiunt venti, te nubila caeli
Adventumque tuum, tibi suavis daedala tellus
Summittit flores tibi rident aequora ponti
Placatumque nitet diffuso lumine caelum. . . . .
Quae quoniam rerum naturam sola gubernas
Nec sine te quicquam dias in luminis oras
Exoritur neque fit laetum neque amabile quicquam, &c.
De Rerum Natura, i. 4—9, 21—24 : Munro.

I do not quote these lines to prove that the hymns of Dendera are atheistic or epicurean, but that they are not inconsistent with an entire disbelief in religion. All these hymns are absolutely epicurean.

[2] Hic siquis mare Neptunum Cereremque vocare
Constituit fruges et Bacchi nomine abuti
Mavolt quam laticis proprium proferre vocamen,
Concedamus ut hic terrarum dictitet orbem
Esse deum matrem, dum vera re tamen ipse
Religione animum turpi contingere parcat.
Ib. ii. 652—657.

liquor, let us allow him to declare that the earth is mother of the gods, if he only forbear in earnest to stain his mind with foul religion." Man had formerly been led to associate the earth and sun and sky with the notion of infinite power behind those phenomena; he now retraced his steps and recognized in the universe nothing but the mere phenomena. The heathen Plutarch and the Christian Origen equally give evidence of this atheistical interpretation put upon the myths of Osiris and Isis. Plutarch protests against the habit of explaining away the very nature of the gods by resolving it, as it were, into mere blasts of wind, or streams of rivers, and the like, such as making Dionysos to be wine and Hephaistos fire. We might suppose that Plutarch is simply alluding to Greek speculation, but it is certain that the Egyptian texts of the late period are in the habit of substituting the name of a god for a physical object, such as Seb for the earth, Shu for the air, and so on. Origen, as a Christian apologist, sees no advantage to be gained by his adversaries in giving an allegorical interpretation to Osiris and Isis, "for they will nevertheless teach us to offer divine worship to cold water and the earth, which is subject to men and all the animal creation."

The transformation of the Egyptian religion is nowhere more apparent than in the view of the life beyond the grave which is exhibited on a tablet which has already been referred to, that of the wife of

Pasherenptah. This lady thus addresses her husband from the grave:[1]

"Oh my brother, my spouse, cease not to drink and to eat, to drain the cup of joy, to enjoy the love of woman, and to make holiday: follow thy desires each day, and let not care enter into thy heart, as long as thou livest upon earth. For as to Amenti, it is the land of heavy slumber and of darkness, an abode of sorrow for those who dwell there. They sleep in their forms; they wake not any more to see their brethren; they recognize not their father and their mother; their heart is indifferent to their wife and children. Every one [on earth] enjoys the water of life, but thirst is by me. The water cometh to him who remaineth on earth, but I thirst for the water which is by me. I know not where I am since I came into this spot; I weep for the water which passes by me. I weep for the breeze on the brink of the stream, that through it my heart may be refreshed in its sorrow. For as to the god who is here, 'Death-Absolute' is his name.[2] He calleth on all, and all men come to obey him, trembling with fear before him. With him there is no respect for gods or men; by him great ones are as little ones. One feareth to pray to him, for he listeneth

---

[1] Sharpe, *Egyptian Inscriptions*, i. pl. 4.

[2] Τὸν πανώλεθρον θεόν . . . .
"Ὅς οὐδ' ἐν "Ἀιδου τὸν θανόντ' ἐλευθεροῖ.
Aesch. Suppl. 414.

not.[1] No one comes to invoke him, for he is not kind to those who adore him; he has no respect to any offering which is made to him." There is something of this undoubtedly in the song of King Antuf and in the Lay of the Harper, but the moral which the harper taught has utterly disappeared: "Mind thee of the day when thou too shalt start for that land." There is no allusion to the necessity of a good life; no recommendation to be just and hate iniquity; no assurance that he who loveth what is just shall triumph. The tablet on which this strange inscription is found has upon it the figures of several of the Egyptian gods, in whom it professes faith, but the religion must have been already at its end when such a text could be inscribed on a funereal tablet.

Influence of Egyptian upon Foreign Thought.

The short time which is now left will not allow me to enter at length into a discussion of certain questions which have naturally arisen as to the influence of Egyptian upon foreign thought, as, for instance, on the Hebrew or Greek religions and philosophies. It may be confidently asserted that neither Hebrews nor Greeks borrowed any of their ideas from Egypt. It ought, I

---

[1] La Mort a des rigueurs à nulle autre pareilles,
  On a beau la prier;
La cruelle qu'elle est se bouche les oreilles,
  Et nous laisse crier.

think, to be a matter of wonder that, after a long time of bondage, the Israelites left Egypt without having even learnt the length of the year. The Hebrew year consisted of twelve lunar months, each of them empirically determined by actual inspection of the new moon, and an entire month was intercalated whenever it was found that the year ended before the natural season. The most remarkable point of contact between Hebrew and Egyptian religion is the identity of meaning between "*El Shaddai*" and *nutar nutra;* but the notion which is expressed by these words is common to all religion, and is only alluded to as characterizing the religion of the patriarchs in contrast to the new revelation made to Moses. But even this revelation is said to have been borrowed from Egypt. I have repeatedly seen it asserted that Moses borrowed his concept of God, and the sublime words, *ehyeh asher ehyeh* ("I am that I am," in the Authorized Version), from the Egyptian *nuk pu nuk*. I am afraid that some Egyptologist has to bear the responsiblity of this illusion. It is quite true that in several places of the Book of the Dead the three words *nuk pu nuk* are to be found; it is true that *nuk* is the pronoun I, and that the demonstrative *pu* often serves to connect the subject and predicate of a sentence. But the context of the words requires to be examined before we can be sure that we have just an entire sentence before us, especially as *pu* generally comes at the end of a sentence. Now if we look at the passages of the Book of the Dead where these words occur, we shall see at once that they do not contain any mysterious doctrine about the Divine nature. In one of these passages[1] the deceased says, "It is I who know the ways of Nu." In another place[2] he says, "I am the Ancient One in the country [or fields];[3] it is I who am Osiris, who shut up his father Seb and his mother Nut on that day of the great slaughter." "It is I who am Osiris, the Ancient One." In another recension of the same text, contained in the 96th chapter, the words *nuk pu nuk* disappear, because the narrative is in the third person. "He is the Bull in the fields, he is Osiris who shut up his father," and so forth. I have looked through a number of works professing to discover Egyptian influences in Hebrew institutions, but have not even found anything worth controverting. Purely external resemblances may no doubt be discovered in abundance, but evidence of the transmission of ideas will be sought in vain. I cannot find that any of the idolatries or superstitions of the Israelites are derived from Egyptian sources. The golden calf has been supposed, but on no sufficient grounds, to represent Apis or Mnevis.

---

[1] Todt. 78, 21. See an excellent article of Dr. Pietschmann in the *Zeitsch. f. ägypt. Spr.* 1879, p. 67.

[2] Ib. 31, 4.

[3] Two of the many names of Horus are "the Youth in Town" and "the Lad in the Country." Todt. 85, 8, 9.

The worship of oxen, as symbols of a Divine power, is not peculiar to Egypt, but is met with in all the ancient religions. The chariot and horses of the sun which the kings of Judah had set up "at the entering in of the house of the Lord," and which Joash burnt with fire, show that the Israelites had an independent mythology of their own.

The existence of Egyptian elements in Hellenic religion and philosophy has long since been disproved. The supposed travels of Pythagoras and other ancient philosophers to Eastern climes, Chaldaea, Persia, India and Egypt, are fabulous inventions, the historical evidence of which does not begin till at least two centuries after the death of the philosopher, but continues increasing after this time. Internal evidence tells the same tale as the external. Every step in the history of Greek philosophy can be accounted for and explained from native sources, and it is not merely unnecessary, but impossible (to the historian of philosophy, ridiculously impossible), to imagine a foreign teacher, to whom the Greeks would never have listened, as being the author of doctrines which without his help the Greeks would themselves certainly have discovered, and at the very time that they did so.

The importance of Alexandria as a medium of interchange of ideas between the Eastern and Western worlds must also be considered as exploded. Nothing was more common, about forty or fifty years ago, than to hear learned men account for the presence of Oriental ideas in Europe, by the transmission of these ideas through the channel of Alexandria. Alexandria was supposed to be the seat of Oriental philosophy, and Philo, Origen, Porphyry, Plotinos and other great names, were imagined to be the representatives of the alliance between Greek and Oriental thought. All this is now considered as unhistorical as the reign of Jupiter in Crete. It was a mere *a priori* fancy, which has not been verified by facts. The most accurate analysis of the Alexandrian philosophy has not succeeded in discovering a single element in it which requires to be referred to an Oriental source. All attempts to refer Alexandrian opinions to Eastern sources have proved abortive. And long before the great work of Zeller on Greek Philosophy had dealt with the problem in detail, M. Ampère had shown how extremely improbable the received hypothesis was. Alexandria was a commercial Greek town, inhabited by a population which cared not the least for Eastern ideas. The learned men in it were Greeks who had the utmost contempt for barbarians and their opinions. Of the Egyptian language and literature, they were profoundly ignorant. "It is incredible," he says, "to what an extent the Greeks of Alexandria remained strangers to the knowledge of the Egyptian language and writing; one could not understand it if there were not other instances of the contemptuous aversion of the

Greeks and Romans to the study of the barbarous languages." The greatest part of the information they give us is utterly erroneous, and even when it has been derived from an authentic source, it never fails to be completely hellenized in passing through a Greek channel. The Oriental works, like those attributed to Zoroaster, said to have been preserved in the Library at Alexandria, were Greek forgeries. "En somme," M. Ampère says, "Alexandrie fut très grecque, assez juive et presque point égyptienne."[1] And if Alexandria was not the means of communicating Egyptian ideas to the Western world, still less was it the channel of learning from the farther East. It is an error to suppose that Alexandria was on the chief line of traffic between Europe and Asia. During the whole period which followed the foundation of Alexandria down to the Roman times, there was no direct communication between this city and the distant East. Indian traffic was in the hands of the seafaring Arabs of the Persian Gulf, the Gulf of Oman, and the Gulf of Akaba. It came to the shores of the Mediterranean through Seleucia, Antioch and Palmyra, or through Gaza and Petra, the chief town of the Nabataeans.[2]

---

[1] *Revue des Deux Mondes*, Sept. 1846, p. 735. Ampère refutes the opinions of Matter and of Jules Simon as expressed in their Histories of the Alexandrian School.

[2] "Presque tout le temps que les Ptolémées regnèrent en Egypte, les navires qui partaient des côtes égyptiennes ne dépassaient pas la

Conclusion.

The interest which the history of Egyptian religion inspires must be derived solely from itself, not from any hypothetical connection with other systems.

We have seen Egypt a powerful and highly civilized kingdom not less than two thousand years before the birth of Moses, with religious beliefs and institutions at least externally identical with those which it possessed till the last years of its existence.

This religion, however, was not from the first that mere worship of brutes which strangers imagined in the days of its decline.

The worship of the sacred animals was not a principle, but a consequence; it presupposes the rest of the religion as its foundation, and it acquired its full development and extension only in the declining periods of the Egyptian history.

It is based upon symbols derived from the mythology.

---

côte méridionale de l'Arabie. Ils relâchaient soit dans un port situé en terre ferme, notamment Aden, ou bien dans quelqu' île, telle que Socotora. Là arrivaient les navires arabes, indiens et malais, avec les produits destinés à l'occident."—Reinaud, " Sur le royaume de la Mésène et de la Kharasène," in the *Mem. de l'Acad. des Inscr.* t. xxiv. pt. 2, p. 215. See also the chapter vi. (Du Commerce) of Lumbroso, " Recherches sur l'économie politique de l'Egypte sous les Lagides." M. Reinaud has also shown that the Periplus of the Erythraean Sea, which displays an accuracy of information quite unknown to Strabo, Pliny or Ptolemy, was not written before the middle of the third century after Christ.

The mythology has exactly the same origin as the mythology of our own Aryan ancestors. The early language had no words to express abstract conceptions, and the operations of nature were spoken of in terms which would now be thought poetical or at least metaphorical, but were then the simplest expressions of popular intuition. The *nomina* became *numina*.

The Egyptian mythology, as far as I can see, dealt only with those phenomena of nature which are conspicuously the result of fixed law, such as the rising and setting of the sun, moon and stars.[1] The recognition of law and order as existing throughout the universe, underlies the whole system of Egyptian religion. The Egyptian *maāt*, derived, like the Sanskrit *r*ita, from merely sensuous impressions, became the name for moral order and righteousness.

Besides the powers recognized by the mythology, the Egyptians from the very first spoke of the Power by whom the whole physical and moral government of the universe is directed, upon whom each individual depends, and to whom he is responsible.

The moral code which they identified with the law governing the universe, was a pure and noble one. The summary of it as given in the Book of the Dead has often been quoted: "He hath given bread to the hungry, water to the thirsty, clothes to the naked; he

---

[1] See Preface.

hath given a boat to the shipwrecked; he hath made the offerings to the gods, and paid the due rites to the departed."

The rites are paid to the departed, because death is but the beginning of a new life, and that life will never end.

A sense of the Eternal and Infinite, Holy and Good, governing the world, and upon which we are dependent, of Right and Wrong, of Holiness and Virtue, of Immortality and Retribution—such are the elements of Egyptian religion. But where are these grand elements of a religion found in their simple purity?

Mythology, we know, is the disease which springs up at a peculiar stage of human culture, and is in its first stage as harmless as it is inevitable. It ceases to be harmless when its original meaning is forgotten, when, instead of being the simple expression of man's intuition of real facts, it obtains a mastery over his thought, and leads him to conclusions which are not involved in the original premisses. This disease of thought was terribly aggravated, I believe, by the early development of Art, and the forms which it assumed in Egypt. That Power which the Egyptians recognized without any mythological adjunct, to whom no temple was ever raised, "who was not graven in stone," "whose shrine was never found with painted figures," "who had neither ministrants nor offerings," and "whose abode was unknown," must practically have been forgotten by the worshippers at the magnificent temples of Memphis, Heliopolis, Abydos, Thebes or Dendera, where quite other deities received the homage of prayer and praise and sacrifice.

A highly cultured and intelligent people like the Egyptians, it is true, did not simply acquiesce in the polytheistic view of things, and efforts are visible from the very first to cling to the notion of the Unity of God. The "self-existent" or "self-becoming" One, the One, the One of One, "the One without a second," "the Beginner of becoming, from the first," "who made all things, but was not made," are expressions which we meet constantly in the religious texts, and they are applied to this or that god, each in his turn being considered as the supreme God of gods, the Maker and Creator of all things. But the conclusion which seems to have remained was, that all gods were in fact but names of the One who resided in them all. But this God is no other than Nature. Both individuals and entire nations may long continue to hold this view, without drawing the inevitable conclusion, that if there is no other God than this, the world is really without a God. But when the conclusion is once brought home, it is, as we have seen in our own day, most eagerly accepted. But the fate of a religion which involves such a conclusion, and with that conclusion the loss of faith in immortality, and even in the distinction of Right and Wrong, except as far as they are connected with ritual prescriptions, is inevitably sealed.[1]

---

[1] On looking back over these pages, I find that I have quoted (p. 99) from Professor Max Müller an etymology of the Sanskrit Brahman which is at variance with his more mature judgment in Hibbert Lectures, p. 358, note.

At page 20, the name of M. Guyesse is too important to be omitted from the list of French scholars. M. Revillout, the most eminent Coptic scholar now in Europe, is also highly distinguished for his publication and interpretation of demotic records. To the German names I should add those of Pietschmann, Erman and Meyer.

And I do not think it out of place here to say, that as the thanks of scholars are due to private persons like Mr. Sharpe and the late Mr. Bonomi, for the publication of accurate Egyptian texts, no small amount of gratitude should be felt towards booksellers like Messrs. Hinrichs, of Leipzig, for the publication of so many inestimable works by Brugsch, Dümichen and Mariette, which, however indispensable to the student, have necessarily but a limited sale, and cannot be immediately remunerative.

INDEX.

AĀHHOTEP, Queen, 66.
Abdallatif, on ruins of Memphis, 25.
Abydos, tablet of, 38, 66.
Achmu urctu, the stars which set, 108.
Akerblad, 12, 16.
Alexandria, 246.
Amenemhāt, Instructions of, 75.
Amenti, 130.
Amesi, ithyphallic form of Horus, 199.
Amon, god of Thebes, 83, 224.
— hymns to, 224.
— proscription of name, 42, 229.
Ampère, 78, 247.
Anaxandrides, 3.
Anchiu, "the living," designation of the departed, 127.
Angels, 158.
— of death, 159.
Ani, Maxims of, 76, 101, 139, 159.
Anpu, Anubis, the Dusk, child of the Sun and of Sunset, 112, 114, 237.
— "he has swallowed his own father," 112.
Ansted, 51.
Antiphanes, 3.
Antuf, Song of, 60.
Antuf-āa, 46.
Apap, the dragon, Darkness, 109.
Apis, 35, 84, 237, 238.
Apollonios of Tyana, 7.
Ass, supposed worship of, by Christians and Jews, 5.

BA, steel, 131.
Ba signifies "ram" and "soul," 239.
Baillet, 20.
Bechten, possessed princess of, 154.
Bergmann, 19.
Biot, 48.
Birch, 10, 14, 19, 21, 45, 54, 177, 210.
Bohlen, P. von, on India, 29.
Book of the Dead described, 172.
— of the Lamentations of Isis and Nephthys, 203.
— of glorifying Osiris, 205.
— of the Breaths of Life, 207.
Brahman, 99, 253.
Drücker, 9.
Brugsch, 19, 101, 121, 128, 178, 208, 211, 233, 239.
Buddhism, 105.
Bulaq Museum, 61, 66, 151.
Bull, symbol of kings and gods, 236.
Bunsen, 197.

CALENDARS, 48, 81, 157.
Canon, hieratic, of Turin, 37.
Castes, 78.
Cat, symbol of Light, 114, 237.
Celibacy, 142.
Celsus, 8.
Chabas, 19, 21, 49, 72, 73, 76, 101, 141, 154, 157, 164, 210, 218.
Champollion, 14.
Champollion-Figeac, 16.

Cher-heb, a priestly official, 132.
"Children of inertness," 199.
China, 124.
Chonsu, the Moon, 155, 179.
Chu, glorified one, the dead, 132.
Chut en Aten, 42, 229.
Clement of Alexandria, 1.
Cook, Canon, 20.
Cow signifies the Sky, the Dawn and other powers, 236.
Curtius, 95, 96, 120.

DARKNESS, mythological forms of:
— Apap, 109.
— Anpu, 112.
— Set, 115.
— Māka, 115.
— Crocodile, 108.
Dawn, names of the:
— Isis, 111.
— Hathor, 87, 159.
— Renenet, 160.
— Neith, 179.
"Death-absolute," 242.
Decimal notation, 81.
Deities, 83.
Dendera, Zodiac of, 29.
Destiny, 159.
Devéria, 20, 209.
Diodoros, 5, 127.
Dreams, 155.
Dual form of all words designating space traversed by the sun, 195.
Dümichen, 19, 24, 49, 68, 117, 128, 164.

EARTH, the father of gods, 111.
— his wife, the Sky, 111.
Ebers, 19, 211.
Egg of Rā, 190.
— Seb, 111.
Eight elementary gods, 199, 232.
Eisenlohr, 19.
El, God, power, 98.
Em hotep = in pace, 131.
Enneads, 83.
Erman, 253.
Ethnology of Egypt, 53.
Everlasting life, 127.

Evil eye, 158.
Eye, name of the sun, 187.

FABLES of Æsop are found in Egyptian, 77.
Fergusson on the architecture of Egypt, 124, 147.
Firmament of steel, 131.
Fravashis, 124, 147.

GENEALOGIES, 46.
Genius, 147.
Gensler, 48.
George, St., and the Dragon, 118.
Gibbon, 214.
God, true notion of, 215.
Golden calf, 245.
Golenischeff, 20, 101.
Goodwin, 19, 21, 77, 164, 211.
Goose, 111, 237.
Grébaut, 20, 123, 162, 164, 195.
Guizot, 153.
Guyesse, 199, 253.

HALL of Nut = Heaven, 190.
— Seb = Earth, 190.
— Maāt = the Nether world, 190.
Harem, 79.
Harper, Lay of the, 70.
Hathor, many names of, 87.
— the Dawn, 159.
— the Fates, 159.
— name given to beatified women, 184.
Hatshepsu, Queen (wrongly called Hashop), 41, 162.
Hawk, name of the sun, 236.
Hearne, 142.
Heaven, the mother of gods and wife of Earth.
— the Hall of Nut, 190.
Hen en ānchiu, name of coffin, 128.
Hen ka, a priestly official, 149.
Henotheism, 217.
Henry, Matthew, 50.
Hermes Trismegistos, 116.
Herodotos, 9.
Hincks, 19, 47.
Horns, symbols of sun or moon, 236.
Horrack, 20, 203, 208.

Horus, the sun in his full strength, 112.
— blindness of, 114.
— Eye of, 114.
— "the Youth in Town," 245.
— "the Lad in the Country," 245.
Huc, 196.
Hyksos, 44.
Hymn to Osiris, 218.
— Ptah, 222.
— the Nile, 223.
— Amon, 224, 228, 229.
— Pantheistic, 231, 233.
— to Hathor, 239.

IBIS, 116, 237.
Ideography in modern writing, 171.
Idolatry, 149.
Ἱερὸς, etymology of, 95.
Imago, a ghost, 149.
Inscriptions of Apis tablets, 35.
— Canopus, 21.
— obelisk of Philæ, 16.
— Pasherenptah and his wife, 156.
— Ptolemy, son of Lagos, 140.
— Rosetta, 11.
Isaios, 142.
Isis, the Dawn, daughter of Earth and Sky, sister and wife of Osiris, 112.

JABLONSKI, 9.
Jamblichos, 213.
Joshua, book of, 50.
Juvenal, 4.

KA, 135, 147.
Kamit, the Black land, name of Egypt, 22, 202.
King, the, as god, 161.
Kircher, 10.
Klaproth, 15, 16.

LAMENTATIONS of Isis and Nephthys, 203.
Language of Egypt, 55.
Lauth, 19, 49, 68, 76, 101.
Lefébure, 20, 113, 123, 202.
Legend, 105, 106.
Leonidas, 142.
Lepsius, 18, 20, 88, 172, 197.

Lieblein, 20, 47.
Litanies of Rā, 234.
Lucretius, 240.
Lunar eclipses, 113.
Lustral water, 139.
Lyell, 52, 126 and note.

MAĀT, 71, 119.
Magical literature, 210.
Maine, Sir Henry, 125.
Māka, crocodile god, son of Set, 115.
Manetho, 47.
Manicheism, 145.
Manuscripts, Egyptian, Greek, Latin and Hebrew, 169.
Mariette, 19, 23, 35, 54, 128, 156, 237, 239.
Marriage, 79.
Maspero, 20, 94, 211.
Materialism, 239.
McLennan, 29, 30.
Mena, 33.
Menti, afterwards Amenti, 130.
Mentu, a name of the sun, 88.
Mentuhotep III., 45.
Moira, 160.
Monasticism, 144.
Monogamy, 79.
Monotheism, 89, 230.
Moon, the measurer, 116.
— names of: Tehuti, 116. Chonsu, 155. An, 203.
— Osiris identified with, 112, 203.
Moral code, 71.
Moral doctrines of the Book of the Dead, 194.
Moses not author of Pentateuch, 49.
— contemporary of Rameses II., 50.
Müller, Professor Max, 99, 100, 109, 118, 142, 218, 253.
Mykerinos, 128.
Myth, 106.

NAHRE-SE-CHNUMHOTEP, tomb of, 132, 134.
Names, superstitious repetition of, 193.
Naville, 20, 123, 199, 234.
Neb-ānch, lord of life, name of coffin, 128.

Neith, the Dawn, mother of the Sun, goddess of Sais, 179.
Nemmat, infernal block, 189.
Nephthys, the Sunset, sister of the Sun and of the Dawn, wedded to the Darkness, and mother of the Dusk, 112.
Newman, J. H., on the notion of God, 215.
Nile, hymn to the, 223.
Nile mud, depth of, 51.
Nomes, 81.
Notation, decimal, 81.
Nu, father of the gods, the celestial ocean, 109, 198, 199.
Nuk pu nuk, 244.
Nuntar, nasalized form of nutar, 96.
Nut, goddess, Heaven, 111.
Nutar, its meaning, 93.
Nutar nutra = El Shaddai, 99.
Nutra, 95.
Nutrit, name of town, 98. Eye-ball, 98.

"ONE of One," 90.
Origen, 2, 241.
Osiris, 83, 84, 85, 86, 87, 110, 112.
Owen, Prof., 54.
Oxyrinchus, 214.

PALIN, 10.
Pantheism, 230.
Papyri, age of, 168.
Paradigms, 57.
Pasherenptah, 141, 156, 242.
Pentaur, 59.
Perring, 42.
Persia, 142, 147, 151.
Phallic emblems, imaginary, 194.
Philo, 6.
Philostratos, 7.
Pierret, 20, 205.
Pietschmann, 253.
Pignorius, 11.
Pithom and Rameses, 38.
Pitris, 124.
Pleyte, 19, 210.
Plutarch, 105, 241.
Polygamy, 79.

Polytheism, 85.
Porphyry, 8, 213.
Possession, 154.
Pott on Proper Names, 106.
Power, words of, 192.
Ptah, the Opener, the Artist, 178.
Ptah-hotep, Maxims of, 75, 100, 178.
Pyramid, date of Great, 50.
Pythagorean system not of Egyptian origin, 183, 246.

RĀ, the Sun, 109.
Ram of Mendes, 239.
Rameses, name of, 38.
Rameses II., great inscription at Abydos, 135.
— prayer to Amon, 227.
Reinisch, 9.
Renan, 60.
Renenet, 160.
Revillout, 253.
Rhind papyri, 209.
Robiou, 20.
Rochemonteix, 20.
Romieu, 48.
Rosetta inscriptions, 11.
Rossi, 20, 57.
Rougé, E. de, 19, 21, 40, 48, 57, 89, 94, 99, 101, 119, 172, 195, 197, 198.
Rougé, J. de, 20.
Royal Lists, 27, 37.
— Abydos, 38.
— Karnak, 37.
— Saqāra, 37.

SALVOLINI, 18.
Sata, 182.
Savages, habits of, worthless as evidence of ancient belief, 125.
Sciaparelli, 20.
Szedlo, 20.
Seb, the Earth, husband of the Sky and father of gods, 110.
— a goose so named, 111.
Sebekhotep monuments, 44.
Sebekhotep III., statue of, 45.
Sechet, raging heat of the sun, 179.

Sekenen-Rā, 93.
Self-existence, 217.
Semench-ka-Rā, statue of, 45.
Sepulchral rites, 124.
Set, Darkness, 84, 110, 112, 115.
Seti I., father of Rameses II., his sarcophagus, 201.
Shadow, 150, 152.
Shai, the divider, Fate, 160.
Shu, the Air, 109.
Smer, a priestly official, 32.
Song of King Antuf, 69.
— of the Harper, 70.
— of the Oxen, 130.
Souls, 152.
— of Rā, 164.
Spencer, H., 64, 127, 148, 150.
Spinoza, 234.
Stanley on Apis tombs, 238.
— king's divinity, 165.
— Pyramids, 61.
Stern, 19, 195.
Sun, names of the :
— Rā, 111. Osiris, 107. Horus, 112.
— Ptah, Opener, Artist, 178.
— Chnemu, Builder, 178.
— Tmu, Closer, 178.
— Chepera, Scarabaeus in his bark, 190.
— Sebek, Crocodile, 237.
Suten-hotep-tā, 134.
Symbols, 135.

TANEN, 178.
Tebha = Typhon, 114.
Techu, meaning of, 116.

Tefnut, goddess, the Dew, 109, 250.
Tehuti, Thoth, the Moon, 116, 122.
Tehutimes III., annals of, 28.
Tehutimes IV., dream of, 155.
Temples, 82.
Thoth, 116.
Thunder, roaring of a lion, 250.
— bellowing of a bull, 250.
Timokles, 3.
Tmu, or Atmu, name of the sun, 88, 198.
Tomb, parts of an Egyptian, 128.
Triads, 83.
Tuat, world beneath the earth, 201.

UNBU, son of Nu and Nut, name of Osiris, 111.
Unnefer, name of Osiris, 204.
Uranes, a celestial stream in the Tuat, 201.
Usertsen (wrongly called Usertesen), 43.

Valens, edict against the monks of Egypt, 214.

Wescher, 141.
Wiedemann, 19, 35, 209.
Wilkinson, 67, 129.

Xenophanes of Colophon, 3.

Yama, 110.
Young, 12.

Zoega, 13.
Zoolatry, 1, 235.

PRINTED BY C. GREEN & SON, 178, STRAND.

14, Henrietta Street, Covent Garden, London;
20, South Frederick Street, Edinburgh.

CATALOGUE OF SOME WORKS
PUBLISHED BY
WILLIAMS & NORGATE.

Baur (F. C.) Church History of the First Three Centuries. Translated from the Third German Edition. Edited by the Rev. ALLAN MENZIES. 2 vols. 8vo. 21s.
— Vide Theological Translation Fund Library.

Baur (F. C.) Paul, the Apostle of Jesus Christ, his Life and Work, his Epistles and his Doctrine. A Contribution to the Critical History of Primitive Christianity. Edited by E. ZELLER. Translated by Rev. ALLAN MENZIES. 2 vols. 8vo, cloth. 21s.
— Vide Theological Translation Fund Library.

Beard (Rev. Dr. C.) Lectures on the Reformation of the Sixteenth Century in its Relation to Modern Thought and Knowledge. Hibbert Lectures, 1883. 8vo, cloth. (Cheap Edition, 4s. 6d.) 10s. 6d.

Beard (Rev. Dr. C.) The Universal Christ, and other Sermons. Crown 8vo, cloth. 7s. 6d.

Beard (Rev. Dr. C.) Port Royal, a Contribution to the History of Religion and Literature in France. Cheaper Edition. 2 vols. Crown 8vo. 12s.

Beard (Rev. Dr. J. R.) The Autobiography of Satan. Crown 8vo, cloth. 7s. 6d.

Bithell (Dr. R.) Agnostic Problems. Being an Examination of some Questions of the deepest Interest, as viewed from the Agnostic Standpoint. 8vo, cloth. 6s.

Bleek (F.) Lectures on the Apocalypse. Edited by T. HOSSBACH. Edited by the Rev. Dr. S. DAVIDSON. 8vo, cloth. 10s. 6d.
— Vide Theological Translation Fund Library.

Booth (C.) Life and Labour of the People of the East End of London. Large coloured Map. Second Edition. 600 pp. 8vo, cloth. 10s. 6d.

Christ and the Fathers; or the Reformers of the Roman Empire. Being a Critical Analysis of the Religious Thoughts and Opinion derived from their Lives and Letters, as well as from the Latin and Greek Fathers of the Eastern and Western Empires until the Nicene Council. Crown 8vo, cloth. 7s. 6d.

Cobbe (Miss F. P.) The Hopes of the Human Race, Hereafter and
Here. Essays on the Life after Death. With a Preface having special
reference to Mr. Mill's Essay on Religion. Second Edition. Crown 8vo,
cloth. 5s.

Cobbe (Miss F. P.) Alone to the Alone. Prayers for Theists, by
several Contributors. Third Edition. Crown 8vo, cloth, gilt edges. 5s.

Cobbe (Miss F. P.) Darwinism in Morals, and (13) other Essays
(Religion in Childhood, Unconscious Cerebration, Dreams, the Devil, Auricular
Confession, &c. &c.). 400 pp. 8vo, cloth. (pub. at 10s.) 5s.

Cobbe (Miss F. P.) The Duties of Women. A Course of Lectures
delivered in London and Clifton. Eighth Edition. Crown 8vo, cloth. 3s. 6d.

Cobbe (Miss F. P.) The Peak in Darien, and other Riddles of Life
and Death. Crown 8vo, cloth. 7s. 6d.

Cobbe (Miss F. P.) Broken Lights. An Inquiry into the Present
Condition and Future Prospects of Religious Faith. Third Edition. Crown
8vo, cloth. 5s.

Cobbe (Miss F. P.) Dawning Lights. An Inquiry concerning the
Secular Results of the New Reformation. 8vo, cloth. 5s.

Davids (T. W. Rhys) Lectures on the Origin and Growth of Religion, as illustrated by some Points in the History of Indian Buddhism.
Hibbert Lectures, 1881. 8vo, cloth. 10s. 6d.

Drummond (Dr.) Philo Judæus; or, the Jewish Alexandrian
Philosophy in its Development and Completion. By JAMES DRUMMOND, LL.D.,
Principal of Manchester New College, London. 2 vols. 8vo, cloth. 21s.

Evolution of Christianity, The. By CHARLES GILL. Second Edition,
with Dissertations in answer to Criticism. 8vo, cloth. 12s.

Ewald (Professor H.) Commentary on the Prophets of the Old Testament. Translated by the Rev. J. FRED. SMITH. Vol. I. Yoel, Amos,
Hozea, and Zakharya ix.—xi. Vol. II. Yesayah, Obadya, Micah. Vol. III.
Nahum, Sephanya, Habaqquq, Zakharya xii.—xiv., Yeremiah. Vol. IV.
Hezekiel, Yesaya xl.—lxvi., with Translation. Vol. V. Haggai, Zakharya,
Malaki, Jona, Baruch, Appendix and Index. Complete in 5 vols. 8vo,
cloth. each 10s. 6d.
—— Vide Theological Translation Fund Library.

Ewald (Professor H.) Commentary on the Psalms. (Poetical Books
of the Old Testament. Part I.) Translated by the Rev. E. JOHNSON, M.A.
2 vols. 8vo, cloth. each 10s. 6d.
—— Vide Theological Translation Fund Library.

Ewald (Professor H.) Commentary on the Book of Job. (Poetical Books, Part II.) Translated by the Rev. J. FREDERICK SMITH. 8vo, cloth. 10s. 6d.
—— Vide Theological Translation Fund Library.

Gould (S. Baring) Lost and Hostile Gospels. An Account of the Toledoth Jesher, two Hebrew Gospels circulating in the Middle Ages, and extant Fragments of the Gospels of the First Three Centuries of Petrine and Pauline Origin. By the Rev. S. BARING GOULD. Crown 8vo, cloth. 7s. 6d.

Hanson (Sir Richard) The Apostle Paul and the Preaching of Christianity in the Primitive Church. By Sir RICHARD DAVIS HANSON, Chief Justice of South Australia, Author of "The Jesus of History," "Letters to and from Rome," &c. 8vo, cloth. (pub. at 12s.) 7s. 6d.

Hatch (Rev. Dr.) The Origin and Growth of Religion, as illustrated by the Greek Influence on Christianity. Hibbert Lectures, 1888. 8vo, cloth. 10s. 6d.

Hausrath. History of the New Testament Times. The Time of Jesus. By Dr. A. HAUSRATH, Professor of Theology, Heidelberg. Translated, with the Author's sanction, from the Second German Edition, by the Revds. C. T. POYNTING and P. QUENZER. 2 vols. 8vo, cloth. 21s.
—— Vide Theological Translation Fund Library.

Hibbert Lectures, vide Beard, Davids, Hatch, Kuenen, Müller, Pfleiderer, Renan, Renouf, Reville, Rhys, Sayce.

Jones (Rev. R. Crompton) Hymns of Duty and Faith, selected and arranged by the late Rev. R. CROMPTON JONES. 247 pp. Second Edition. Foolscap 8vo, cloth. 3s. 6d.

Jones (Rev. R. Crompton) Psalms and Canticles, selected and pointed for Chanting. 18mo, cloth. 1s. 6d.
—— Anthems, with Indexes and References to the Music. 18mo, cloth. 1s. 3d.
—— The Chants and Anthems, together in 1 vol. 2s. 6d.
—— A Book of Prayer in 30 Orders of Worship, for Public or Private Devotions. 12mo, cloth. 2s. 6d.
—— The same with the Chants. 18mo, cloth. 3s.

Keim's History of Jesus of Nazara, considered in its connection with the National Life of Israel, and related in detail. Translated from the German by A. RANSOM and the Rev. E. M. GELDART, in 6 vols. 8vo, cloth. each 10s. 6d.
—— Vide Theological Translation Fund Library.

Kuenen (Dr. A.) The Religion of Israel to the Fall of the Jewish State. By Dr. A. KUENEN, Professor of Theology at the University, Leyden. Translated from the Dutch by A. H. MAY. 3 vols. 8vo, cloth. 31s. 6d.
—— Vide Theological Translation Fund Library.

Kuenen (Professor A.) Lectures on National Religions and Universal Religions. Delivered in Oxford and London. By A. KUENEN, LL.D., D.D. Professor of Theology at Leyden. Hibbert Lectures, 1882. 10s. 6d

Laurie (Professor Simon) Metaphysica Nova et Vetusta : a Return to Dualism. Second Edition, extended and enlarged. Crown 8vo, cloth. 6s

Lubbock (Sir John, F.R.S.) Pre-historic Times, as illustrated by Ancient Remains and the Manners and Customs of Modern Savages. With Wood-cut Illustrations and Plates. Fifth Edition. 8vo, cloth. 18s

Macan (Reg. W.) The Resurrection of Jesus Christ. An Essay in Three Chapters. Published for the Hibbert Trustees. 8vo, cloth. 5s

Mackay (R. W.) Sketch of the Rise and Progress of Christianity 8vo, cloth. (pub. at 10s. 6d.) 6s

Martineau (Rev. Dr. James) Religion as affected by Modern Materialism ; and, Modern Materialism : its Attitude towards Theology. A Critique and Defence. 8vo. 2s. 6d
—— The Relation between Ethics and Religion. 8vo. 1s
—— Ideal Substitutes for God considered. 8vo. 1s

Mind: a Quarterly Review of Psychology and Philosophy. Contributions by Mr. Herbert Spencer, Professor Bain, Mr. Henry Sidgwick, Mr. Shadworth H. Hodgson, Professor Flint, Mr. James Sully, the Rev. John Venn, the Editor (Professor Croom Robertson), and others. Vols. I. to XIV. 1876 to 1889, each 12s.; cloth, 13s. 6d. 12s. per annum, post free

Müller (Professor Max) Lectures on the Origin and Growth of Religion, as illustrated by the Religions of India. Hibbert Lectures, 1878 8vo, cloth. 10s. 6d

Oldenberg (Prof. H.) Buddha : his Life, his Doctrine, his Order. Translated by WILLIAM HOEY, M.A., D.Lit., Member of the Royal Asiatic Society, Asiatic Society of Bengal, &c., of her Majesty's Bengal Civil Service. Cloth, gilt. 18s

Pfleiderer (O.) Philosophy of Religion on the Basis of its History. Translated by the Rev. ALAN MENZIES, and the Rev. ALEX. STEWART, of Dundee. Complete in 4 vols. 8vo. each 10s. 6d
—— Vide Theological Translation Fund Library.

Pfleiderer (O.) Paulinism. An Essay towards the History of the Theology of Primitive Christianity. Translated by E. PETERS, Esq. 2 vols 8vo, cloth. 21s
—— Vide Theological Translation Fund Library.

Poole (Reg. Lane) Illustrations of the History of Medieval Thought in the Departments of Theology and Ecclesiastical Politics. 8vo, cloth. 10s. 6d

Prescott (Rev. Thos.) Christianity made Science ; or a Life Thoughts on Religion and Morals. 8vo, cloth. 6

Protestant Commentary, A Short, on the New Testament, with General and Special Introductions. From the German of Hilgenfeld, Holtzmann, Lang, Pfleiderer, Lipsius, and others. Translated by the Rev. F. H. Jones. 3 vols. 8vo, cloth. each 10s. 6d.
—— Vide Theological Translation Fund Library.

Renan (E.) On the Influence of the Institutions, Thought and Culture of Rome on Christianity, and the Development of the Catholic Church. Translated by the Rev. C. Beard. Hibbert Lectures, 1880. 8vo, cloth. (Cheap Edition, 2s. 6d.) 10s. 6d.

Renouf (P. Le Page) Lectures on the Origin and Growth of Religion, as illustrated by the Religion of Ancient Egypt. Hibbert Lectures, 1879. 8vo, cloth. 10s. 6d.

Reville (Prof. Albert) Prolegomena of the History of Religions. By Albert Reville, D.D., Professor in the Collége de France, and Hibbert Lecturer, 1884. Translated from the French. With an Introduction by Professor F. Max Müller. 8vo, cloth. 10s. 6d.
—— Vide Theological Translation Fund Library.

Reville (Prof. Albert) Lectures on the Origin and Growth of Religion, as illustrated by the Native Religions of Mexico and Peru. Translated by the Rev. P. H. Wicksteed, M.A. Hibbert Lectures, 1884. 8vo, cl. 10s. 6d.

Reville (Rev. Dr. A.) The Song of Songs, commonly called the Song of Solomon, or the Canticle. Crown 8vo, cloth. 1s. 6d.

Rhys (Prof. J.) On the Origin and Growth of Religion, as illustrated by Celtic Heathendom. Hibbert Lectures, 1886. 8vo, cloth. 10s. 6d.

Sadler (Rev. Dr.) Prayers for Christian Worship. Crown 8vo, cloth. 3s. 6d.

Sadler (Rev. Dr.) Closet Prayers, Original and Compiled. 18mo, cloth. 1s. 6d.

Samuelson (Jas.) Views of the Deity, Traditional and Scientific; a Contribution to the Study of Theological Science. By James Samuelson, Esq., of the Middle Temple, Barrister-at-law, Founder and former Editor of the Quarterly Journal of Science. Crown 8vo, cloth. 4s. 6d.

Savage (Rev. M. J.) Beliefs about the Bible. By the Rev. M. J. Savage, of the Unity Church, Boston, Mass., Author of "Belief in God," "Beliefs about Man," &c. &c. 8vo, cloth. 7s. 6d.

Sayce (Prof. A. H.) On the Religion of Ancient Assyria and Babylonia. Hibbert Lectures, 1887. 8vo, cloth. 10s. 6d.

Schrader (Prof. E.) The Cuneiform Inscriptions and the Old Testament. Translated from the second Enlarged Edition, with Additions by the Author, and an Introduction by the Rev. Owen C. Whitehouse, M.A. 2 vols. With a Map. 8vo, cloth. each 10s. 6d.
—— Vide Theological Translation Fund Library.

Schurman (J. G.) Kantian Ethics and the Ethics of Evolution. A Critical Study, by J. GOULD SCHURMAN, M.A. D.Sc., Professor of Logic and Metaphysics in Acadia College, Nova Scotia. Published by the Hibbert Trustees. 8vo, cloth. 5s

Schurman (J. G.) The Ethical Import of Darwinism. Crown 8vo cloth. 5s

Sharpe (S.) History of the Hebrew Nation and its Literature, with an Appendix on the Hebrew Chronology. Fourth Edition. 487 pp. 8vo cloth. 7s. 6d

Sharpe (S.) Bible. The Holy Bible, translated by SAMUEL SHARPE being a Revision of the Authorized English Version. Fourth Edition of the Old Testament; Eighth Edition of the New Testament. 8vo, roan. 4s. 6d

Sharpe (S.) The New Testament. Translated from Griesbach's Text. 14th Thousand, fcap. 8vo, cloth. 1s. 6d

Smith (Rev. J. Fred.) Studies in Religion under German Masters Essays on Herder, Goethe, Lessing, Franck, and Lang. By the Rev. J. FREDERICK SMITH, of Mansfield. Crown 8vo, cloth. 5s

Spencer (Herbert) Works. The Doctrine of Evolution. 8vo, cloth
First Principles. Seventh Thousand. 16s
Principles of Biology. 2 vols. 34s
Principles of Psychology. Fourth Thousand. 2 vols. 36s
Principles of Sociology. Vol. I. Third Thousand. 21s
Ceremonial Institutions. Principles of Sociology. Vol. II. Part I. 7s
Political Institutions. Principles of Sociology. Vol. II. Part II. 12s
Ecclesiastical Institutions. 5s
The Data of Ethics. Principles of Morality. Part I. Fourth Thousand. 8s

Spencer (Herbert) The Study of Sociology. Library Edition (being the Ninth), with a Postscript. 8vo, cloth. 10s. 6d
—— Education. (Cheap Edition, Seventh Thousand, 2s. 6d.) 6s
—— Essays. 3 vols. Third Edition. 24s

Spencer (Herbert) The Man versus the State. 1s.; or on better paper, in cloth, 2s. 6d

Spencer's (Herbert) Theory of Religion and Morality. By SYLVAN DREY. 1s

Spinoza. Four Essays, by Professors J. LAND, KUNO FISCHER, and VAN VLOTEN, and ERNEST RENAN. Edited, with an Introduction, by Professor W. KNIGHT, of St. Andrews. 8vo, cloth. 5s

Stokes (G. J.) The Objectivity of Truth. By GEORGE J. STOKES B.A., Senior Moderator and Gold Medallist, Trinity College, Dublin; late Hibbert Travelling Scholar. Published by the Hibbert Trustees. 8vo, cloth. 5s

Strauss (Dr. D. F.) New Life of Jesus, for the People. The Authorized English Edition. 2 vols. 8vo, cloth. 24s

Stuart (Jas.) Principles of Christianity: being an Essay towards a more correct Apprehension of Christian Doctrine, mainly Soteriological. 636 pp. 8vo, cloth. 12s. 6d.

Taine (H.) English Positivism. A Study of John Stuart Mill. Translated by T. D. HAYE. Second Edition. Crown 8vo, cloth. 3s.

Tayler (Rev. J. J.) An Attempt to ascertain the Character of the Fourth Gospel, especially in its Relation to the First Three. New Edition, 8vo, cloth. 5s.

Ten Services of Public Prayer, taken in Substance from the "Common Prayer for Christian Worship," with a few additional Prayers for particular Days.
  Ten Services alone, crown 8vo, cloth, 2s. 6d.; with Special Collects. 3s.
  Ten Services alone, 32mo, 1s.; with Special Collects. 1s. 6d.
  Psalms and Canticles. (To accompany the same.) Crown 8vo, 1s. 6d.
  With Anthems. 2s.

Thoughts for Every Day in the Year. Selected from the Writings of Spiritually-minded Persons. By the Author of "Visiting my Relations." Printed within red lines. Crown 8vo, cloth. 2s. 6d.

Theological Translation Fund. A Series of Translations, by which the best results of recent Theological investigations on the Continent, conducted without reference to doctrinal considerations, and with the sole purpose of arriving at truth, will be placed within reach of English readers. A literature which is represented by such works as those of Ewald, F. C. Baur, Zeller, Roth, Keim, Nöldeke, &c., in Germany, and by those of Kuenen, Scholten and others in Holland.

8 *Volumes published* (1873 to 1888) *for* £13. 4s. *(separately,* 10s. 6d. *per vol.).*
Baur's Church History of the First Three Centuries. 2 vols.
Baur's Paul, his Life and Work. 2 vols.
Bleek, on the Apocalypse.
Ewald. Prophets of the Old Testament. 5 vols.
Ewald's Commentary on the Psalms. 2 vols.
Ewald. Book of Job.
Hausrath's History of the New Testament Times. 2 vols.
Keim's History of Jesus of Nazara. 6 vols.
Kuenen. The Religion of Israel. 3 vols.
Pfleiderer's Paulinism. 2 vols.
Pfleiderer's Philosophy of Religion. 4 vols.
Protestant Commentary, a Short, on the New Testament. 3 vols.
Reville's Prolegomena of the History of Religions.
Schrader's The Cuneiform Inscriptions and the Old Testament. 2 vols.
Zeller, on the Acts of the Apostles. 2 vols.

A selection of six or more volumes from the list may be had at the Subscribers price, or 7s. per volume.

Wallis (H. W.) The Cosmology of the Rigveda: an Essay. 8vo, cloth. 5s.

What I have taught my Children. By a Member of the Theistic Church. 12mo, cloth. 2s. 6d.

Williams (Dr. Rowland) The Hebrew Prophets. Translated afresh and illustrated for English Readers. 2 vols. 8vo, cloth. 22s. 6d.

Zeller (Dr. E.) The Contents and Origin of the Acts of the Apostles, critically investigated. Preceded by Dr. Fr. Overbeck's Introduction to the Acts of the Apostles from De Wette's Handbook. Translated by Joseph Dare. 2 vols. 8vo, cloth. 21s.
—— Vide Theological Translation Fund Library.

PAMPHLETS.

Athanasian Creed. Two Prize Essays. By C. Peabody and C. S. Kenny. 1s.
Butler's Analogy: A Lay Argument. By a Lancashire Manufacturer. 1s.
Jesus of Nazareth and his Contemporaries. 1s.
Journey to Emmaus. By a Modern Traveller. 2s.
Marriage of Cana, as read by a Layman. 6d.
Martineau (Rev. Dr. James) New Affinities of Faith; a Plea for free Christian Union. 12mo. 1s.
Must God Annihilate the Wicked? A Reply to Dr. Jos. Parker. 1s.
Reasonable Faith, A, the Want of our Age. 1s.
Tayler (Rev. J. J.) Christianity: What is it? and What has it done? 1s.
Who was Jesus Christ? 8vo, sewed. 6d.

WILLIAMS AND NORGATE,
14, Henrietta Street, Covent Garden, London;
And 20, South Frederick Street, Edinburgh.

www.ingramcontent.com/pod-product-compliance
Lightning Source LLC
Chambersburg PA
CBHW032055220426
43664CB00008B/1010